Lecture Notes
in Business Information Processing

456

Balbir S. Barn · Kurt Sandkuhl (Eds.)

The Practice of Enterprise Modeling

15th IFIP WG 8.1 Working Conference, PoEM 2022
London, UK, November 23–25, 2022
Proceedings

 Springer

Editors
Balbir S. Barn 🆔
Middlesex University
London, UK

Kurt Sandkuhl 🆔
Rostock University
Rostock, Germany

ISSN 1865-1348 ISSN 1865-1356 (electronic)
Lecture Notes in Business Information Processing
ISBN 978-3-031-21487-5 ISBN 978-3-031-21488-2 (eBook)
https://doi.org/10.1007/978-3-031-21488-2

This Springer imprint is published by the registered company Springer Nature Switzerland AG
The registered company address is: Gewerbestrasse 11, 6330 Cham, Switzerland

Preface

The 15th IFIP WG 8.1 Working Conference on the Practice of Enterprise Modelling (PoEM 2022) had the aim of improving the understanding of the practice of Enterprise Modelling (EM) by offering a forum for sharing experiences and knowledge between the academic community and practitioners from industry and the public sector.

This year, the theme of the conference was 'Enterprise Modeling and Model-based Development and Engineering'. The theme reflects the importance of enterprise modeling methods, techniques, and tools in the development of complex solutions and systems, for example in the context of digital transformation, implementation of artificial intelligence, the Internet of Things, big data solutions, or information and software systems. The diversity of stakeholders and variety of modeling techniques and perspectives to be integrated requires agile ways of working and techniques for efficiently dealing with unexpected changes. The field of enterprise modeling should seek to support these challenges by providing methods and tools, as well as investigating and reporting on the current state of research and state of practice.

PoEM 2022 took place from November 23 to 25. The conference was organized by Middlesex University London and arranged on the Hendon campus by the Faculty of Science and Technology.

Following tradition, PoEM 2022 was open for submissions in three categories: 1) research papers describing original research contributions in enterprise modeling; 2) practitioner/experience papers presenting problems, challenges, or experience related to any aspect of enterprise modeling encountered in practice; and 3) short papers presenting work in progress and emerging enterprise modeling challenges.

This year, the main conference track attracted 45 submissions with authors from 19 countries. Each submission was single-blind reviewed by at least four members of the Program Committee. As a result, 15 high-quality papers were selected for publication in this volume (i.e., a 33% acceptance rate) and for presentation at the conference. They cover different aspects of the conference's main subjects and were grouped by the following topics: Models in Information System Development, Modeling Enterprise Architectures, Modeling Capabilities and Ecosystems, DSML and Meta-Modeling, and Participatory Modeling.

The conference program also included three keynotes with a mix of both academic and practitioner viewpoints. Alan W. Brown, Professor of Digital Economy at Exeter University, UK, addressed lessons from models and modeling that can be applied in this era of rapid digital transformation. Richard Veryard, writer and experienced practitioner, provided a historical and reflective perspective on enterprise modeling. Mick Dudley, Chief Technology Officer at a leading UK food services business, discussed how to build, nurture, and grow both enterprise models and teams through a culture of innovation.

In addition to the main conference, PoEM 2022 featured two workshops: the 3rd Workshop on Blockchain and Enterprise Systems (BES 2022), organized by Petra Maria Asprion, Alessandro Marcelletti, Andrea Morichetta, and Bettina Schneider, and the 1st International Workshop on Digital Twin Engineering, organized by Souvik Barat, Ruth

Breu, Vinay Kulkarni, and Philipp Zech. Also, the PoEM Forum was organized by Tony Clark and Steffen Zschaler and two tutorials were offered: "Hands-on Artefact-Centric Business Process Modelling with MERODE" by Monique Snoeck and "Enterprise modeling of digital business ecosystems - business cases, solutions and methodology gaps" by Janis Grabis, Janis Stirna, and Jelena Zdravkovic.

We would like to thank everyone who contributed to the PoEM 2022 working conference, the workshops, the PoEM Forum, and the tutorials. We thank the authors for contributing and presenting their research, we appreciate the invaluable contribution of the members of the Program Committee and the external reviewers, we thank the keynote speakers for their inspiring talks, and we are grateful to the Springer team for providing excellent support regarding the proceedings production. We also thank IFIP WG 8.1 for allowing this conference series to evolve under its auspices. Last but not least, we thank all members of the local organization team from Middlesex University London.

October 2022   Balbir S. Barn
                                                                    Kurt Sandkuhl

Organization

PoEM 2022 was organized and hosted at Middlesex University London, UK, during November 23–25, 2022.

Program Chairs

Balbir S. Barn — Middlesex University London, UK
Kurt Sandkuhl — University of Rostock, Germany

Workshop Chairs

Souvik Barat — Tata Consultancy Services Research, India
Dominik Bork — TU Wien, Austria

Forum Chairs

Tony Clark — Aston University, UK
Steffen Zschaler — King's College London, UK

Local Organization Chair

Nicola Skinner — Middlesex University London, UK

Steering Committee

Anne Persson — University of Skövde, Sweden
Janis Stirna — Stockholm University, Sweden
Kurt Sandkuhl — University of Rostock, Germany

Program Committee

Raian Ali — Hamad Bin Khalifa University, Qatar
Joao Paulo Almeida — Federal University of Espirito Santo, Brazil
Souvik Barat — Tata Consultancy Services Research, India
Balbir S. Barn — Middlesex University London, UK
Judith Barrios Albornoz — University of Los Andes, Venezuela
Dominik Bork — TU Wien, Austria
Robert Andrei Buchmann — Babeș-Bolyai University of Cluj Napoca, Romania

Janis Stirna	Stockholm University, Sweden
Darijus Strasunskas	HEMIT, Norway
Stefan Strecker	University of Hagen, Germany
Yves Wautelet	Katholieke Universiteit Leuven, Belgium
Hans Weigand	Tilburg University, Netherlands
Robert Woitsch	BOC Asset Management, Austria
Jelena Zdravkovic	Stockholm University, Sweden
Steffen Zschaler	King's College London, UK

Additional Reviewers

Morena Barboni	University of Camerino, Italy
Nedo Bartels	Fraunhofer IESE, Germany
Sven Christ	University of Hagen, Germany
Isaac Da Silva Torres	Open Universiteit, Netherlands
Arianna Fedeli	University of Camerino, Italy
Fadime Kaya	Open Universiteit, Netherlands
Henning Dirk Richter	University of Rostock, Germany

Contents

DSML and Meta-modeling

Participatory Modeling

Models in Information System Development

Investigating The Effectiveness of Model-Based Testing on Testing Skill Acquisition

Felix Cammaerts$^{(\boxtimes)}$ ⓘ, Charlotte Verbruggen ⓘ, and Monique Snoeck ⓘ

Research Center for Information System Engineering, Leuven, KU, Belgium
{felix.cammaerts,charlotte.verbruggen,monique.snoeck}@kuleuven.be

Abstract. Software does not only need to be developed but also needs to get tested. Testing of software reduces the development and maintenance costs and increases software quality. Unfortunately, few software development courses focus on good testing practices. Some prior work has nevertheless researched possible ways of teaching software testing techniques to students. Unfortunately, all these approaches are code-oriented approaches, implying that a strong technical background is needed to effectively use them. They are also mostly focused on improving students' knowledge on basic testing techniques. In contrast, TesCaV, a software tool used for teaching testing skills to university students, focuses on teaching testing to novice users with limited technical skills by providing a model-based testing (MBT) approach. MBT is a black-box testing technique in which the tests are automatically generated from a software model. This automatic generation allows for easy maintenance of the test suite when the software changes. These tests can be automatically generated by using a.o. Finite State Machines (FSMs), Markov Chains and Logic Programming. TesCaV is mainly based on Finite State Machines. The effect of using TesCaV on testing coverage is quantitatively analysed in this research. The preliminary results of TesCaV show that it is a promising tool for the teaching of MBT.

Keywords: Model-based testing · Testing skill acquisition · TesCaV

1 Introduction

The cost of poor software quality for 2020 in the US alone has been estimated at $2.08 trillion [10]. The quality of software can be improved by adequate testing of the software. Software testing does not only improve the quality of software by avoiding bugs, but also reduces the financial loss that would occur from having developers focus on solving these bugs instead of focusing on the features for the next release.

An important cause of the large amount of time spent on solving bugs rather than developing new features is due to the lack of attention spent on software

© IFIP International Federation for Information Processing 2022
Published by Springer Nature Switzerland AG 2022
B. S. Barn and K. Sandkuhl (Eds.): PoEM 2022, LNBIP 456, pp. 3–17, 2022.
https://doi.org/10.1007/978-3-031-21488-2_1

testing in software courses. It has been reported that senior-level computer science students fail to provide adequate tests for even a small computer program [2]. This is because in software engineering classes more time is spent on topics that are considered more glamorous than testing. Some of these topics include requirements analysis and system design and implementation. Spending the majority of the time on covering these other topics means little time remains for the topic of software testing [5].

One possible solution is the usage of a software testing tool. Such a tool would allow the teaching staff to still focus on the other topics while, in a less time consuming way, also introducing their students to testing techniques. An example of such a tool is TesCaV, which has been built as a module in the MERODE code generator. MERODE is an approach for creating conceptual models based on UML class diagrams and finite state machines [22]. These conceptual models are platform independent models, which entails that no low-level details of the system need to be known, making it easier for novice users to understand [19]. The MERODE code generator helps non-technical students to create executable code from the MERODE models. After the executable code has been generated for a model, students are able to test whether the generated application supports the requirements. The TesCaV module can be used by these students to visualize which test cases a student has not yet covered during the experimentation with the generated code [12].

TesCaV is based on model-based testing and has already been proven to be perceived as helpful by students [12]. However, no prior research has been conducted to ascertain the actual increase in testing quality when using TesCaV. This research will evaluate the effect of using TesCaV on the code coverage of novice users. Henceforth, this paper will focus on the following research question: *Does providing novice users with TesCaV create a (lasting) positive effect for the test coverage achieved by these novice users?*

The remainder of this paper is structured as follows: in Sect. 2, related work about MBT and teaching of software testing is discussed. In Sect. 3, the experimental setup of this research is explained. In Sect. 4, the results of the experiment are analyzed and critically reviewed. In Sect. 5, the limitations and validity of the research are discussed. In Sect. 6, the conclusion of this research is given. Lastly, in Sect. 7, further research possibilities are explored.

2   Related Work

2.1   Teaching of Software Testing

A lot of testing techniques exist, and these can be subdivided into two categories: black-box testing and white-box testing [17]. In black-box testing, tests are designed making an abstraction of the source code, henceforth only the input and output of the software are considered [8]. Contrary to that, in white-box testing, the tests are written with knowledge of the internal implementation of the software [9].

In [1], students were provided with a tutorial and assignment on black-box and white-box testing. For the black-box testing assignment, the students were giving a specification of what the software is supposed to do and were asked to derive test cases from this specification. For the white-box testing assignment, students were given the program code of several algorithms and were asked to derive test cases from those implementations. Students reported that it was difficult to work with an ambiguous specification when doing black-box testing. For both the black-box and white-box testing assignments, the students reportedly increased their number of reasonable test cases: from two to three tests to at least twenty to thirty tests, which is a fair amount for a program of the size used in the research. There are two factors that contributed to this result. Firstly, students achieve a higher amount of satisfaction finding bugs in somebody else's code, while receiving a psychological setback from finding bugs in their own code. Secondly, the assignment requires that each possible outcome of compound booleans was tested.

Web-CAT is a web-based application built for students to learn how to write good code and test cases based on a specification [7]. This is based on the Test-Driven Development approach, in which the test cases for a software system are written prior to the implementation of the software system. The students are provided a specification of a program and are requested to write source code for the specification and test cases for their own source code. Once students submit their written tests, the tests are run on the code. The students are then provided feedback about incorrect and missing tests. Students are allowed to re-upload their code and test cases unlimited times. This feedback allows students to understand the importance of Test-Driven Development, as writing new test cases for each new implementation is the only way of getting feedback.

In [14], a Question-Driven Teaching Method was applied: students are given an exploratory test case with some guiding questions for them to analyze the test case. The Question-Driven Teaching Method yields a question list from the students which the teacher can use to introduce the rational solution to the testing strategy. Research has proven that the Question-Driven Teaching Method yields improved test quality in real applications [14].

Code Defenders is a framework developed to teach students how to do proper software testing based on mutation testing [3]. Mutation testing is a white-box testing technique that creates small syntactic deviations of the original program under test, with the assumption that developers write almost correct programs. These variations are called mutants and are also tested by the test cases. If a mutant does not pass a test case it is killed, while a mutant that does pass all test cases remains alive and can be used for the creation of new mutants. A mutation score can then be calculated as the amount of live mutants compared to the total amount of mutants. This mutation score gives an indication of how well the tests have tested the program under test. In the Code Defenders game students are either attackers or defenders. The defenders are tasked with writing test cases so that each mutation would be killed. The attackers are tasked with writing mutations so that they survive the test cases. Defenders gain points by killing mutations, while attackers gain points by having surviving mutations.

So, even though some research has already been done on teaching software testing, most of these approaches are code-oriented approaches, requiring the students to have a technical background to use them effectively. As they are also mostly focused on black-box and white-box testing approaches, they focus on improving students' existing knowledge of these approaches, rather than teaching novice users how to get started with adequate testing. All of these techniques require the students to manually find all possible test cases and then execute them. This means that students might unknowingly execute equivalent test cases multiple times and might not be aware of when a program has been fully tested.

2.2 Model-Based Testing

Model-based testing (MBT) is a black-boxing testing technique that can be used to automatically generate test cases from a given software model [6]. It partially solves the issue of manual testing, by automatically generating test cases from a given software model. This means that instead of requiring students to manually generate test cases, this task can be automated. MBT consists of several steps, as defined by [24]:

1. Creating a test model: the requirements of the system or the design models are used to specify a test model.
2. Generating abstract test cases: a series of abstract test cases are defined based on a criterion such as transition coverage.
3. Concretizing the abstract test cases: the abstract test cases are transformed into executable testing scripts.
4. Executing the generated test cases.
5. Analyzing the results: after running the test cases the results must be interpreted and possible faults in the code need to be fixed.

A modelling language such as UML is used as input for the automatic generation [13]. Concretizing from the abstract to the executable test cases can either be done manually or automatically. In [13], a testing approach that automatically creates executable test cases from the abstract test cases was introduced. This new testing approach allowed for a significant reduction in the testing time. Nine testing criteria, based on [15], were used to generate the abstract test cases.

TCGen is a software tool developed by [16], which allows for the automatic generation of abstract test cases from UML conceptual models. These abstract test cases are generated based on a set of testing criteria. TCGen has been shown to yield better results concerning efficiency and code coverage compared to the manual generation of abstract test cases.

2.3 MERODE Code Generator and TesCaV

When using MBT still a lot of technical knowledge is needed to understand how the test cases can be automatically generated. TesCaV makes use of MBT to help a novice user to visualize their test coverage. It generates test cases and provides feedback about the manual testing the user has done by comparing it with these generated tests. In the case of TesCaV, the models used for MBT are models created according to the MERODE-method. The MERODE approach in itself only results in a conceptual model, however, making use of the MERODE code generator, a fully functional Java application can be generated from the model. Henceforth, the MERODE code generator is a Model-Driven Development tool. With this generated Java application, a user can perform several tests using the (default) user interface [20]. The generated application is augmented with feedback referring to the models used for generating the application. Prior research has already shown that this approach of feedback-enriched code generation is effective in increasing novice users' understanding of a conceptual model, resulting in better quality of the models [21]. However, this experiment also revealed students' limited testing skills, as witnessed from their use of a too limited number of test cases to assess the correct modelling of a requirement.

Although a multitude of model-based testing tools exist, they all automatically generate test cases and execute them, making it difficult to use them to teach novice users how to perform adequate testing [11]. To the best of our knowledge, TesCaV is the only model-based testing tool that can be used to teach novice users how to perform adequate testing. TesCaV does this by not automatically executing the generated test cases but instead using the automatically generated test cases to provide the user feedback about the covered and non-covered test cases as achieved by the manual testing the user has conducted. This feedback is provided by visualizing which test cases the user has successfully tested and which ones the user has not yet executed. TesCaV provides the user feedback about the transition and class attribute criteria, which are part of the structural coverage criterion [12]. This feedback-enabled system means that TesCaV can be used to teach novice users how test cases are generated and how MBT should be conducted. TesCaV uses the test cases generated by TCGen, which are a subset of the testing criteria used in [13] and [16].

3   Research Method

The research method used in this paper is based on the research method used in [18] and [21]. The effectiveness of using TesCaV is empirically evaluated by the use of two experimental studies: a pilot study and a replication study. The participants of each of these studies were given models to test. The effectiveness of the usage of TesCaV was measured by comparing the effectiveness of tests between participants who used TesCaV and participants who did not. A pre-experimental survey was conducted to ascertain the personal characteristics of the participants in terms of prior knowledge on testing.

3.1   Hypotheses

The usage of TesCaV is expected to improve the effectiveness of tests a student is able to conduct on the model in terms of coverage. Hence, the first hypothesis becomes:

Hypothesis 1 (H1). *TesCaV improves the effectiveness of the test cases, in terms of coverage, conducted by a student.*

After having used TesCaV, a student is expected to be able to conduct more effective tests, even when being presented to a new case, without using TesCaV. This leads to the second hypothesis:

Hypothesis 2 (H2). *TesCaV creates a lasting improved effectiveness of the tests conducted by students on new models, even when not using TesCaV anymore.*

It is possible that personal characteristics, such as prior knowledge to testing and programming experience, also have an impact on the effectiveness of TesCaV [4]. Therefore, the last hypothesis is:

Hypothesis 3 (H3). *Personal characteristics, such as age, gender and prior knowledge on testing, do not influence the effectiveness of TesCaV.*

3.2   Experimental Design

Design. For this research two experimental studies were conducted. The first experimental study was a pilot study, which was conducted with four participants and the second experimental study was a replication study, which was conducted with 50 students. For each experiment a factorial two group design was followed [23]. This means that the experiments were each conducted with two groups in two stages. The order of the stages is different for both groups. The usage of the two groups allows to discover possible learning effects due to doing the first stage prior to the second stage. It also allows to understand possible influences from the group composition on the experimental result.

Figure 1 shows the experimental design used for both the pilot and replicated study. For each study the participants are split into two groups, named Group 1 and Group 2. All participants are given a pre-experimental survey. Participants of Group 1 are given time to conduct tests on Case 1 without the usage of TesCaV. After completing the testing for Case 1, Group 1 moves on to test Case 2 with the usage of TesCaV. This allows to determine the effect on testing effectiveness when using TesCaV. Group 2 also starts by testing Case 1, however they do use TesCaV. For Case 2, Group 2 does not use TesCaV. This allows to ascertain to what extent learnings are transferred from testing Case 1 with the use of TesCaV to testing Case 2 without the use of TesCaV. The experiment does not include any training on TesCaV prior to solving the first case.

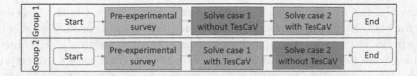

Fig. 1. Experimental setup for the pilot and replication study.

Cases. The participants are provided with case descriptions. For each case description, a corresponding model is provided. The case descriptions provided to the participants are called the Orchid and the Bus case[1].

Pilot Study. A pilot study was conducted to find any possible issues with the experimental design and the cases used, which can still be adjusted prior to the replication study. For this study only four participants were recruited, making it impossible to analyse the results of this pilot study quantitatively. No major issues were detected. Nonetheless, the feedback from the pilot study was used to clarify the instructions provided in the replication study.

Replication Study. For the replication study students from the Architecture and Modelling of Management Information Systems course at the university of Leuven were recruited. In this course, the MERODE approach is taught, and students can use the code generation tool to test their solutions of the exercises. Students were also previously given classes on class diagrams and FSMs. This ensures that participants have adequate knowledge of the MERODE approach. The students have heterogeneous backgrounds and different levels of technical backgrounds. A total of 50 participants were recruited.

Variables. For H1, the dependent variable is the effectiveness of the tests conducted by the students. This can be measured by measuring the test coverage of the students when solving a case without TesCaV and when solving a case with TesCaV. In this case, the test coverage is measured via the test criteria used in TesCaV, namely: class attribute (CA), association-end multiplicity (AEM), all-loop-free-paths (ALFP), all-transitions (AT), all-states (AS) and all-one-loop-paths (AOLP) [12]. CA and AEM are class diagram criteria, while the others are transition-based criteria. Class diagram criteria are covered by instantiating objects of the class diagram, and taking into account the attributes of a class or the multiplicities of the associations between classes. Transition-based criteria are covered by executing transition of FSMs of classes. Some of these criteria require a sequence of transitions to be executed. The independent variable here is the usage of TesCaV. The same dependent and independent variables are

---

[1] The case descriptions, generated applications and solutions can be found at http://merode.econ.kuleuven.ac.be/cases/index.asp as "Rent An Orchid" and "Bus Scheduling" respectively.

used for H2. For within-groups comparisons a Wilcoxon signed-rank test is used, while for between groups comparisons a Kruskal-Wallis test is used. This is in line with a previous experiment using the same experimental design [21]. Extraneous variables were also measured during this experiment. This allows understanding whether personal characteristics such as prior knowledge on testing have an influence on the effect of using TesCaV, which can be used for H3.

Pre-experimental Survey. At the start of the experiment each participant is given a pre-experimental survey to assess their personal characteristics in terms of prior knowledge on testing, age and gender. The questions are based on [18] and [21].

3.3   Evaluation

To evaluate the effectiveness of tests (H1) conducted by each participant in the two test cases, the usage logs of the MERODE application were used. This log contains information about the user actions related to invoking creating, modifying and ending operations of the classes in the model of the cases. For each test criterion there is a maximum of test cases that can be covered. Henceforth, the actual amount of covered test cases can be compared to this maximum amount. To measure the lasting effect of using TesCaV on test effectiveness (H2), the results of the two groups can be compared. In particular, the results of Group 1 for Case 1 can be compared to the results of Group 2 for Case 2 (this is for both groups the case in which TesCaV is not used): we expect that Group 2 will perform better for having had a training with TesCaV first. Both H1 and H2 are evaluated using between-groups and within-groups comparisons. For hypothesis 3 regression analysis can be used on the results of the pre-experimental survey to compare in both groups the gain in test effectiveness obtained by using TesCaV. The significance threshold for p-values for this experiment is taken at the industry standard of 0.05.

4   Results

To verify that both groups of the experiment are equivalent, the pre-experimental survey results have been checked for normality, using a Shapiro-Wilk test. An encoding has been used for the possible responses to the ordinal questions. Only prior knowledge in Group 1, computer self-efficacy in Group 2 and age in both groups have a p-value smaller than 0.05, and are henceforth not normally distributed. Thus, an additional Kruskal-Wallis test has been done for these questions. A p-value of 0.317 (>0.05) for prior knowledge, a p-value of 0.290 (>0.05) for computer self-efficacy and a p-value of 0.541 (>0.05) for age were found. This means that, despite these questions not having normally distributed responses in both groups, the groups can still be considered equivalent. For all the other questions an insignificant p-value was obtained, and henceforth, groups can be considered statistically equivalent.

4.1   Personal Characteristic of the Participants

A total of 50 participants were recruited. However, only 39 handed in a valid submission (i.e. both a valid questionnaire submission and event log submission). Out of these 39 participants, 19 participants belonged to Group 1 and 20 participants belonged to Group 2. Further, 61.5% of the participants were male and the other 38.5% were female, and 95% of the participants were less than 25 years old at the time of the experiment. Lastly, 65% of the participants mentioned having no to little prior knowledge on testing via previous education.

4.2   Test Case Coverage Scores

The test case coverage score for each participant is calculated per case. The test case coverage score is calculated as the number of test cases covered by the participants compared to the total number of test cases, using a weighted average per criterion. An average test case coverage score of 74.55% was achieved in the cases where TesCaV was used, while in the cases with no use of TesCaV only 64.27% coverage was reached.

Figure 2 depicts a comparison of the test coverage scores per group and case. Both Group 1 and Group 2 had a higher test coverage score when solving the case with TesCaV. However, Group 2 has a bigger difference in test case coverage when comparing the cases with each other. For Case 1 a significant difference favouring the group using TesCaV can be found. Across the two cases, a significant decrease in test coverage score is found for Group 2 after they can not use TesCaV anymore. There is also no significant difference between Group 1 Case 1 (no TesCaV) and Group 1 Case 2 (TesCaV) and no significant difference between Group 1 Case 1 (no TesCaV) and Group 2 Case 2 (no TesCaV).

It is also possible to further analyze these results for each test criterion separately (Table 1). Significant differences, favouring TesCaV, for the first case are found for the ALFP, AT, AS and AOLP criteria. This means that only the CA and AEM criteria did not yield a significant difference. These two criteria are the only two class diagram criteria, while the others are transition-based criteria. For Group 1 a significant increase has been found when starting to use TesCaV in the scores of the ALFP, AS and AOLP criteria. These are all the transition-based criteria except AT. No significant differences for the second case have been found when comparing the groups to each other.

Time Analysis. The time the participants of the groups spent on each case was also measured (Fig. 2). The average time for participating in the entire experiment is 79.22 min. An average time of 39.18 min has been spent on solving Case 1, while only an average time of 32.45 min was spent on solving Case 2. The Wilcoxon signed-rank test shows that this is a significant difference ($p = 0.014$). Most notably, Group 2 spent significantly less ($p = 0.014$) time on Case 2 (no TesCaV).

Table 1. Comparison of test case coverage per criterion. Significant differences are indicated in **bold**.

	Crit.	Group	Case 1				Case 2				Wil. sign.-rank	
			Min	Max	Med.	Stdev.	Min	Max	Med.	Stdev.	C1 v. C2	
Class diagram	CA	Group 1	0.800	1.000	1.000	0.063	0.200	1.000	1.000	0.187	0.705	
		Group 2	0.800	1.000	1.000	0.062	0.800	1.000	1.000	0.045	0.317	
	K.W.	G1 v. G2	0.957				0.504				0.553†	0.915††
	AEM	Group 1	0.250	1.000	0.750	0.197	0.000	1.000	0.750	0.314	0.100	
		Group 2	0.500	1.00	0.750	0.179	0.250	1.000	0.500	0.291	**0.005**	
	K.W.	G1 v. G2	0.070				0.664				**0.006**†	**0.021**††
Transition-based	ALFP	Group 1	0.000	0.833	0.333	0.239	0.000	1.000	0.333	0.333	**0.012**	
		Group 2	0.000	1.000	0.833	0.294	0.000	1.000	0.167	0.296	**0.000**	
	K.W.	G1 v. G2	**0.000**				0.102				**0.000**†	**0.034**††
	AT	Group 1	0.455	0.909	0.727	0.136	0.040	1.000	0.800	0.249	0.145	
		Group 2	0.636	0.955	0.909	0.110	0.400	1.000	0.680	0.163	**0.000**	
	K.W.	G1 v. G2	**0.000**				0.265				**0.002**†	0.113††
	AS	Group 1	0.611	0.944	0.778	0.092	0.105	1.000	0.895	0.223	**0.045**	
		Group 2	0.722	1.000	1.000	0.106	0.579	1.000	0.789	0.127	**0.003**	
	K.W.	G1 v. G2	**0.000**				0.310				**0.026**†	0.119††
	AOLP	Group 1	0.000	0.333	0.000	0.112	0.000	0.500	0.000	0.161	**0.028**	
		Group 2	0.000	0.833	0.417	0.273	0.000	0.625	0.000	0.208	**0.003**	
	K.W.	G1 v. G2	**0.001**				0.317				**0.005**†	**0.017**††

† Comparing both cases in which TesCaV could not be used (Group 1 Case 1 and Group 2 Case 2).
†† Comparing both cases in which TesCaV could be used (Group 1 Case 2 and Group 2 Case 1).

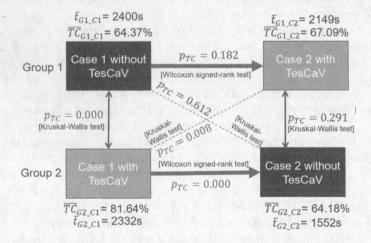

Fig. 2. Comparison of the weighted test case coverage results (TC) and time spent (t) between Group 1 and 2 and Case 1 and 2. Significant differences are indicated in green, insignificant differences in red. (Color figure online)

Effect of Personal Characteristics on Test Scores. For analysing the responses in terms of the computer self-efficacy of the participants, an encoding has been used for the possible responses to the questions. With these encoded scores, it was possible to look for possible correlations between these scores and the test scores using the Pearson correlation coefficient. For gender an ANOVA test has been done instead. All of the Pearson correlation coefficients (Table 2) are within [-0.6, 0.6] and the p-values for the ANOVA test of gender are all insignificant, thus no correlation has been detected.

Table 2. Effect of personal characteristics on test scores, using the Pearson correlation coefficient. (ANOVA for gender)

Metric	Prior knowledge on testing	Computer self-efficacy	Gender (ANOVA)	Age
Test coverage score without TesCaV	0.089	0.011	0.663	−0.105
Test coverage score with TesCaV	0.151	0.268	0.551	−0.335
Test coverage score improvement	0.103	0.303	0.761	−0.303

5 Discussion

5.1 Contributions

When comparing the results for Case 1, the group that could use TesCaV obtained a significantly higher weighted test score than the group who could not. This is in line with our expectations, and can be seen as confirming H1. However, when looking at each of the test criteria separately, only the transition-based criteria are significantly better. This could indicate that novice users, merely by being shown a class diagram, already obtain a good grasp of how the class diagram criteria (CA and AEM) should be tested and that no significant gain can be obtained via the usage of TesCaV. When comparing the performance for both cases for Group 2 (Case 1 with, and Case 2 without TesCaV), the group performs, as expected better in Case 1. Also per test criterion, we see a significant better performance when using TesCaV for all transition-based criteria, and for AEM. This again confirms H1. When comparing the performance for both cases for Group 1 (Case 1 without, and Case 2 with TesCaV), the small difference in the weighted test score is not significant. Looking at the individual test criteria, the difference is significant for ALFP, AS and AOLP but seems only of reasonable size for AS. This provides but weak additional support for H1. When comparing the performance of both groups for Case 2, strangely, the test scores between the groups are (likewise) not significantly different.

Under the assumption that TesCaV would have a lasting effect (H2), we would expect Group 2 to perform better in Case 2 compared to Group 1 in Case 1. However, their weighted test score is identical and no significant difference was found. This could be because of a possible fatigue effect occurring for Group 2 during Case 2. Several results hint at this fatigue effect. Firstly, Group 2 has spent significantly less time on Case 2 than on Case 1 and compared to Group 1 Case 2. Secondly, Group 2 has obtained significantly less test coverage for the ALFP, AT and AEM test criteria when comparing their results to Group 1 Case 1, this is for both groups the case where they could not use TesCaV. Lastly, Group 2 has a significant decrease in the scores after not using TesCaV anymore for all class diagram criteria and the AEM criterion. However, no significant difference between the weighted average test scores between Group 1 Case 1 and Group 2 Case 2 has been found, showing that the fatigue effect is minimal.

Due to this possible fatigue effect, it is better to evaluate H1 only on the first case. Due to the fact that Group 2 did significantly better on the first case than Group 1 on all transition-based criteria, H1 can be validated partially, namely for those transition-based criteria. Transition-based criteria require several states in an FSM to be visited, sometimes even in a particular order, while class diagram criteria only require objects to be instantiated. This means that class diagram criteria for an object will already be partially covered by the time it becomes possible to test transition-based criteria. Henceforth, it can be said that TesCaV improves the coverage of non-trivial test cases. Due to there not being a significant difference between Group 1 Case 1 (no TesCaV) and Group 2 Case 2 (no TesCaV), again possibly due to the fatigue effect, it is not possible to prove H2 at this point in time. No correlation between the personal characteristic of the participants and the test scores have been found, thus validating H3.

5.2 Internal Validity

In this experiment two different cases were used. Despite both cases being similar, it is hard to prove that these two cases were of exactly the same difficulty and henceforth that the test scores can be compared just like that. This could be measured by introducing a third group that solves both cases either with or without the tool. However, it is not possible to introduce such a group in the context of a course, because this would create unequal learning opportunities in education. The issue of finding two different cases of equal difficulty, but also avoiding too much similarity so that a learning effect could be avoided, was partially addressed by using a case which has been used for many years in the Architecture and Modelling of Management Information Systems course. This case is the Orchid case (Case 1). This case was robust and known to be a good exercise in terms of all students having a similar understanding of the requirements, as feedback has already been gathered by different students in previous iterations of the course. To have a second case, the Bus case was introduced, which was based on the Orchid case. However, the Bus case does not have exactly the same structure as the Orchid case, as certain changes where necessitated to make the model of the Bus case match with a realistic case description. Moreover, its use by a large group of students revealed small understandability problems by a limited number of students. This may have affected the way they tested the generated application. The experiment also did not give the participants a lot of time to actually gain a learning effect from the provided tool. This is because both cases of the experiment had to be solved within two hours. It would be better to run the experiment over the duration of a semester.

5.3 External Validity

For the external validity of the research a pilot study was conducted. However, only four participants were recruited, due to timing constraints. This means it was not possible to do a statistical analysis on their responses. Nonetheless, their responses were still useful for finding any mistakes and ambiguities in the provided experimental design. To further ensure the external validity of this research, the sampling method should be taken into consideration. In the conducted experiment, students all followed the same course during the same year and on the same campus. Ideally, students from different teachers and different campuses can be recruited into another replication experiment.

6   Conclusion

This research has evaluated the effectiveness of TesCaV, a tool that provides users with feedback about the testing they have done on an application generated from a given software model. TesCaV is mainly focused on helping novice users conduct adequate testing. The improvement of test effectiveness when using TesCaV was measured using a two-group factorial experimental design. The participants were each given two cases, in which they could use TesCaV in only one case. This allowed to measure the test coverage scores. In terms of transition-based criteria TesCaV helps improve the testing effectiveness conducted by novice users. This experiment was not yet able to conclude whether TesCaV creates a lasting positive effect on the testing effectiveness. Analysing the personal characteristics of the participants also showed that no difference in learning effect was present based on different personal characteristics.

7   Further Research

The most obvious way further research can be conducted on this subject, is by conducting a second replication experiment to check the external validity. This second replication experiment can then also focus on measuring any possible lasting effect after having used TesCaV. In terms of further improvements to TesCaV itself, more test cases as defined by TCGen can be implemented [13,16], henceforth, providing the users with more feedback on the testing they have done. At this point TesCaV provides static visualizations, in which the user is presented with one enhanced image based on the model (i.e. a class diagram or FSM), further research could investigate which visualizations work best for which criteria and could also aim at visualizing the coverage of disallowed transitions.

TesCaV aims at visualizing the manual test coverage done by users. However, some improvements can still be made. Firstly, there is a discrepancy between the actual coverage and the reported coverage. This is due to the fact that firing one transition from a source state to a target state would mark all methods that fire that transition as covered by the test case. Secondly, in an FSM, transitions which are disallowed in a certain state are not modelled explicitly. They are only modelled implicitly by the fact that those transitions are not present in those states. This is in line with how statecharts are used in UML, but this means that it is not possible to visually indicate that these transitions have not been tested. An alternative representation can be found in Fig. 3, which represents a state transition table. In such a state transition table, the transitions which are disallowed in a state are indicated with a ϵ, while the transitions that are allowed in a certain state are indicated by placing the target state in the table. ϵ can be considered as an error state. In the state transition table it would be possible to indicate for each cell whether or not a test has been done, thus making it possible to also visualize whether the disallowed transitions have been tested [22, p. 160].

To gain a better understanding of the obtained results in this experiment, other experimental setups can be used. These experimental setups can focus on understanding students' needs when learning testing and whether TesCaV addresses these. This could be done by for instance conducting interviews with the participants.

method	From state						
	-	1	2	3	4	5	6(F)
acquire	1	ε	ε	ε	ε	ε	ε
classify	ε	2	ε	ε	ε	ε	ε
borrow	ε	ε	3	ε	ε	ε	ε
renew	ε	ε	ε	3	ε	ε	ε
return	ε	ε	ε	2	ε	ε	ε
lose	ε	ε	ε	4	ε	ε	ε
declassify	ε	ε	5	ε	5	ε	ε
end_of_copy	ε	ε	ε	ε	ε	6	ε

Fig. 3. Example of a state transition table as provided in [22, p. 160].

References

1. Carrington, D.: Teaching software testing. In: Proceedings of the 2nd Australasian Conference on Computer Science Education, pp. 59–64 (1997)
2. Carver, J.C., Kraft, N.A.: Evaluating the testing ability of senior-level computer science students. In: 2011 24th IEEE-CS Conference on Software Engineering Education and Training (CSEE&T), pp. 169–178. IEEE (2011)
3. Clegg, B.S., Rojas, J.M., Fraser, G.: Teaching software testing concepts using a mutation testing game. In: 2017 IEEE/ACM 39th International Conference on Software Engineering: Software Engineering Education and Training Track (ICSE-SEET), pp. 33–36. IEEE (2017)
4. Compeau, D.R., Higgins, C.A.: Computer self-efficacy: development of a measure and initial test. MIS Q. 189–211 (1995)
5. Cowling, T.: Stages in teaching software testing. In: 2012 34th International Conference on Software Engineering (ICSE), pp. 1185–1194. IEEE (2012)
6. Dalal, S.R., et al.: Model-based testing in practice. In: Proceedings of the 21st International Conference on Software Engineering, pp. 285–294 (1999)
7. Edwards, S.H.: Teaching software testing: automatic grading meets test-first coding. In: Companion of the 18th Annual ACM SIGPLAN Conference on Object-oriented Programming, Systems, Languages, and Applications, pp. 318–319 (2003)

8. Jovanović, I.: Software testing methods and techniques. IPSI BgD Trans. Internet Res. **30** (2006)
9. Khan, M.E., Khan, F.: A comparative study of white box, black box and grey box testing techniques. Int. J. Adv. Comput. Sci. Appl. **3**(6) (2012)
10. Krasner, H.: The cost of poor software quality in the US: a 2020 report. Proc. Consortium Inf. Softw, QualityTM (CISQTM) (2021)
11. Li, W., Le Gall, F., Spaseski, N.: A survey on model-based testing tools for test case generation. In: Itsykson, V., Scedrov, A., Zakharov, V. (eds.) TMPA 2017. CCIS, vol. 779, pp. 77–89. Springer, Cham (2018). https://doi.org/10.1007/978-3-319-71734-0_7
12. Marín, B., Alarcón, S., Giachetti, G., Snoeck, M.: TesCaV: an approach for learning model-based testing and coverage in practice. In: Dalpiaz, F., Zdravkovic, J., Loucopoulos, P. (eds.) RCIS 2020. LNBIP, vol. 385, pp. 302–317. Springer, Cham (2020). https://doi.org/10.1007/978-3-030-50316-1_18
13. Marín, B., Gallardo, C., Quiroga, D., Giachetti, G., Serral, E.: Testing of model-driven development applications. Softw. Qual. J. **25**(2), 407–435 (2017)
14. Martinez, A.: Use of JiTT in a graduate software testing course: an experience report. In: 2018 IEEE/ACM 40th International Conference on Software Engineering: Software Engineering Education and Training (ICSE-SEET), pp. 108–115. IEEE (2018)
15. OMG: OMG Unified Modeling Language (OMG UML), Superstructure, Version 2.4. 1. Object Management Group (2011)
16. Pérez, C., Marín, B.: Automatic generation of test cases from UML models. CLEI Electron. J. **21**(1) (2018)
17. Sawant, A.A., Bari, P.H., Chawan, P.: Software testing techniques and strategies. Int. J. Eng. Res. Appl. (IJERA) **2**(3), 980–986 (2012)
18. Sedrakyan, G., Poelmans, S., Snoeck, M.: Assessing the influence of feedback-inclusive rapid prototyping on understanding the semantics of parallel UML statecharts by novice modellers. Inf. Softw. Technol. **82**, 159–172 (2017)
19. Sedrakyan, G., Snoeck, M.: A PIM-to-Code requirements engineering framework. In: Modelsward 2013–1st International Conference on Model-driven Engineering and Software Development-Proceedings, pp. 163–169. SciTePress (2013)
20. Sedrakyan, G., Snoeck, M.: Lightweight semantic prototyper for conceptual modeling. In: Indulska, M., Purao, S. (eds.) ER 2014. LNCS, vol. 8823, pp. 298–302. Springer, Cham (2014). https://doi.org/10.1007/978-3-319-12256-4_32
21. Sedrakyan, G., Snoeck, M., Poelmans, S.: Assessing the effectiveness of feedback enabled simulation in teaching conceptual modeling. Comput. Educ. **78**, 367–382 (2014)
22. Snoeck, M.: Enterprise information systems engineering. MERODE Approach (2014)
23. Trochim, W.M., Donnelly, J.P.: Research methods knowledge base, vol. 2. Atomic Dog Pub. (2001)
24. Utting, M., Legeard, B.: Practical Model-based Testing: a Tools Approach. Elsevier (2010)

Generating Low-Code Applications from Enterprise Ontology

Marien R. Krouwel[1,2]([✉]) [iD], Martin Op 't Land[1,3] [iD],
and Henderik A. Proper[4,5] [iD]

[1] Capgemini Netherlands, PO Box 2575, 3500, GN Utrecht, The Netherlands
{Marien.Krouwel,Martin.OptLand}@capgemini.com
[2] Maastricht University, Maastricht, The Netherlands
[3] Antwerp Management School, Boogkeers 5, 2000 Antwerp, Belgium
[4] Luxembourg Institute of Science and Technology, Esch-sur-Alzette, Luxembourg
e.proper@acm.org
[5] TU Wien, Vienna, Austria

Abstract. Due to factors such as hyper-competition, increasing expectations from customers, regulatory changes, and technological advancements, the conditions in which enterprises need to thrive become increasingly turbulent. As a result, enterprise agility, or flexibility, becomes an increasingly important determinant for enterprise success.

Since Information System (IS) development often is a limiting factor in achieving enterprise flexibility, enterprise flexibility and (automated) IS flexibility cannot be viewed separately and choices that regard flexibility should not be left to developers. By taking a Model-based Engineering (MBE) approach, starting from ontological models of the enterprise and explicit organization design decisions, we bridge the gap from organizational flexibility to (automated) IS flexibility, in such a way that IT is no longer the limiting factor for enterprise flexibility.

Low-code technology is a growing market trend that builds on MBE concepts. In this paper, we report on an mapping for (the automation of) the creation of a Mendix low-code application from the ontological model of an enterprise, while also accommodating the required organizational implementation flexibility. Even though the algorithm has been tested successfully on multiple cases, supporting all possible organizational flexibility seems to be an $\mathcal{NP}$-hard problem, and more research is required to check the feasibility and usability of this approach.

Keywords: Enterprise ontology · DEMO · MBE · Low code · Mendix

1 Introduction

Due to factors such as hyper-competition [7], increasing expectations from customers, regulatory changes, and technological advancements, the conditions in which enterprises need to thrive become increasingly turbulent. As a result,

---

The original version of this chapter was revised: minor error in the author name tag was corrected. The correction to this chapter is available at
https://doi.org/10.1007/978-3-031-21488-2_16

© IFIP International Federation for Information Processing 2022, corrected publication 2023
Published by Springer Nature Switzerland AG 2022
B. S. Barn and K. Sandkuhl (Eds.): PoEM 2022, LNBIP 456, pp. 18–32, 2022.
https://doi.org/10.1007/978-3-031-21488-2_2

the ability to change with an ever decreasing time-to-market, often referred to as 'agility' [32], becomes an important determinant for the success of enterprises [34] – with enterprise we mean every goal-oriented cooperative or network of actors [13], including government agencies, commercial companies, etc. The notion of 'agile enterprise' is also referred to as the 'run-time adaptive enterprise' [25] or the 'flexible enterprise' [41]. One can, actually, identify different flavors of flexibility that can be considered as cornerstones in creating a flexible enterprise, including strategic flexibility, organizational flexibility, financial flexibility, marketing flexibility, manufacturing flexibility and (automated) Information System (IS) flexibility [41, Fig. 1.4].

Since an IS supports (the implementation of) an organization, the organization and its IS are in fact intrinsically intertwined [13, p. 251]. As a consequence, organizational flexibility and (automated[1]) IS flexibility can not be viewed separately. Organization design decisions are often hard-coded into ISs [2] – something the authors recognize in their current practice quite frequently[2]. This essentially leaves it up to developers to make the right choices to ensure the IS supports the required organizational flexibility. Therefore it is necessary to make the organization design decisions explicit and to make transparent how they are implemented in Information Systems.

The field of enterprise engineering connects the organizational and IS perspective. DEMO (Design and Engineering Methodology for Organizations) is a leading method within the discipline of enterprise engineering [12], with strong methodological and theoretical roots [13, 35]. At the same time, there is an increasing uptake of DEMO in practice, illustrated by the active community and certification institute[3] as well as the reported cases concerning the use of DEMO [2, 13, 29] and integration with other mainstream enterprise modeling approaches such as ArchiMate [14, 21] and BPMN [6, 16, 28].

DEMO distinguishes between *Enterprise Ontology* and *Enterprise Implementation*. Enterprise Ontology concerns the 'essence' of an organization in terms of products and services delivered. Enterprise Implementation pertains to the organizational structure(s) and (socio-technical) means, including the division of work between human actors and IT solutions, as well as their assignment(s) to the organizational structures. Enterprise Implementation can be expressed in a set of values (choices) in relation to a set of Organization Implementation Variables (OIVs) [22], such as functionary type and organizational unit. Though changes to an Enterprise's ontology do occur, most of the time changes pertain to its Enterprise Implementation [11]. As mentioned above, the authors have observed in practice how organization design decisions – values for some OIVs – are often hard-coded into ISs, essentially leaving it up to developers to determine the involved OIVs and associated design decisions.

---

[1] In the remainder of this paper, whenever we refer to IS, we do so in the sense of being an automated Information System using Information Technology (IT).

[2] Two of the authors are practitioners, with an average of 25 years of experience in the field of enterprise (architecture) modeling and (model-based) IS development.

[3] https://ee-institute.org

According to Brambilla e.a. [3], Model-based Engineering (MBE)[4] is a model-based approach for the creation of (automated) ISs that promises to bridge the gap between requirements of an organization and technical implementation of the IS. Claimed advantages over traditional software development approaches include a) common and better understanding of the IS, b) increased productivity of the development team due to (partial) automation of the development process, and c) reducing the number of defects. In order to be able to execute/transform a model, the model must be comprehensive – describing all business requirements – and consistent – free from contradictions – and must have its semantics fully specified. MBE can involve combinations of code generation from and interpretation of models.

As ontological enterprise models claim to be coherent, comprehensive, consistent and concise [13, p. 14], it seems a good starting point for an MBE approach. Practice already showed that DEMO's ontological models have proven to be a solid starting point for model-based IS design [15,19,29] and code generation [20,23,24] in particular. However, to the best of our knowledge, there is no complete mapping from the full DEMO metamodel to any software implementation model. Also, existing research seems to neglect the organization implementation aspects (i.e. the OIVs), still resulting in the need for developers to deal with these aspects themselves, thereby not making the mapping from implementation decision to software transparent. For instance, Van Kervel [20] reports on a software engine able to generate working operational software, taking the ontological enterprise model of a domain as input. However, in that approach all choices in terms of organizational implementation remain implicit and end up being hard-coded by choices in the software engine.

A potential explanation for the latter issue is the fact that creating code to support a mapping of the complete metamodel of a modeling method such as DEMO is a highly complex and time consuming task. This is also why we, in principle, suggest using a model-based code generation strategy, as real-time interpreters can become even more complex. At the same time, such an approach makes it harder to make (controlled) customizations and extensions that are often needed in practice. This is where we suggest to turn to low-code technology.

The idea of low-code technology is to add an(other) abstraction layer on top of (high) code such as Java and .Net. Low-code technology applies techniques from MBE, while still allowing for (controlled) customizations and extensions [5]. While low-code technology improves enterprise flexibility, compared to traditional code [39], practical experience shows that these platforms mainly offer IS technical implementation flexibility – for instance changing the database management platform from e.g. MySQL to Postgres, or moving from one front-end framework to another – and some flexibility on the IS (functional) requirements level – for instance changing a specific process flow or screen lay-out. At the same time, however, changes in the organization, such as the organizational

---

[4] For this article we consider Model-driven Software Engineering (MDSE), Model-driven Development (MDD), Model-based Development (MBD) and Model-Driven Enterprise Systems Engineering (MDESE) as being specializations of MBE.

structures or its portfolio products and services, still can take quite some time to implement.

Goal and Approach. In the research reported on in this paper, we hypothesize that by taking an MBE approach towards low-code, starting from enterprise ontology, one can improve enterprise flexibility even more, at least to the point that IT is not the limiting factor anymore. More specifically, this paper reports on the design of an (automated) mapping to create a Mendix application model from Enterprise Ontology and OIVs. We choose Mendix as low-code platform because it provides good documentation about its metamodel and offers an SDK (model API) to create Mendix applications using TypeScript. Next to that, the authors are experienced in using the Mendix platform in real-world situations.

In line with this, the overall goal of the research reported on in this paper is to create an automatic translation ('mapping') from the ontological enterprise model (cf. DEMO Specification Language (DEMO-SL) [9]) to a Mendix application (cf. the Mendix metamodel[5]) in order to be able to generate low-code applications from ontological (enterprise) models. As this mapping is a designed artifact, we follow the Design Science methodology [40]. In terms of design science, the main focus of this paper is on the design cycle; i.e. the construction of the mapping. The mapping has been evaluated multiple times involving different DEMO models, ranging from academic cases such as EU-Rent [31,33] to real-world cases including Social Housing [24,25]. While the mapping has evolved and improved over time, this paper presents the final version of the mapping.

The remainder of this paper is structured as follows. In Sect. 2 we outline the theoretical background on Enterprise Ontology, Enterprise Implementation, MBE and low-code technology. In Sect. 3 we discuss the mapping, while Sect. 4 provides a summary of the evaluations conducted so-far. We finish with conclusions and a discussion of the limitations in Sect. 5.

2   Theoretical Background

The discipline of Enterprise Engineering encompasses Enterprise Ontology, Enterprise Architecture, Enterprise Design and Enterprise Governance [13]. Building upon the Language/Action Perspective [43], based on Speech Act Theory [1,38] and Theory of Communicative Action [18], it sets communication as the primal notion for the design of enterprises and its Information Systems.

As mentioned in the introduction, DEMO is a leading method within the discipline of Enterprise Engineering, that has been applied at several enterprises. Reported benefits of DEMO include: *a*) ensuring completeness and helping to find omissions and ambiguous situations [13;29], *b*) providing a solid, consistent and integrated set of (aspect) models (see below) [13], *c*) creating a shared understanding [29], *d*) providing a stable base to discuss required flexibility [2],

---

[5] https://docs.mendix.com/apidocs-mxsdk/mxsdk/understanding-the-metamodel/

e) offering a good Return On Modeling Effort [13], and *f)* offering a good basis to define IS requirements and design or generate such systems [13].

This section will briefly introduce the most important aspects of Enterprise Ontology and Enterprise Implementation, as well as the concepts of MBE and low-code technology for the IT implementation of Enterprises.

2.1 Enterprise Ontology

An ontology is defined as a conceptual specification describing knowledge about some domain [17]. More specifically, Enterprise Ontology describes both the dynamics and statics of an enterprise, seen as a network of actors that enter into and comply with commitments [13]. Such commitments are raised by actors in acts, the atomic units of action, and follow the Complete Transaction Pattern (CTP). The CTP consists of 19 *general step kinds* and deals with the basic flow – request, promise, execute, declare and accept – as well as discussion states – decline, reject – and cancellations (or revocations). The idea is that actors constantly check whether there are acts they have to deal with or respond to. The total set of acts for an actor to deal with is called the actor's *agenda*.

By abstracting actors to actor roles the model becomes independent of the people involved in the operation. Commitments regarding a specific product kind are abstracted to transaction kinds, all having one actor role as executor and one or more actor roles as initiator. An Enterprise Ontology is expressed in a set of aspect models that is comprehensive, coherent, consistent, and concise [13]. The reader is referred to [9] for the complete DEMO metamodel.

Ontological Aspect Models. The ontological model of an organization consists of an integrated whole of four aspect models [13]. The *Cooperation Model (CM)* models the *construction* of the enterprise; it consists of transaction kinds, associated (initiating and executing) actor roles, fact banks, access links between actor roles and fact banks, and wait links between transaction kinds and actor roles. The *Process Model (PM)* models the *processes* (dynamics) that take place as the effect of acts by actors, by detailing the coordination between actor roles; it makes explicit the causal and wait links between acts from the CTP. The *Fact Model (FM)* is the semantic model of *products* (statics) of the enterprise; it defines (elementary or derived) fact types (entity types with their related product kinds, property types, attribute types and value types), existence laws and occurrence laws. The *Action Model (AM)* is the model of the *operation* of the enterprise, guiding actors in performing their acts; guidelines consist of an *event part* detailing the act to respond to, an *assess part* detailing the conditions to check and a *response part* stating how to respond. Note that these guidelines look like rules, but offer the actors the possibility to – responsibly – deviate.

2.2 Enterprise Implementation

In order for an organization to be operational, it has to be implemented with appropriate technology [13]. When a product or service is decided upon, and the collaboration network needed for its delivery has been revealed in the ontological (enterprise) model, still many degrees of freedom exist before an organization can become operational [13, p. 349]. Implementation design starts from the (enterprise) ontology of a system and ends with a fully detailed specification of the implementation, within the design space constrained by Enterprise Architecture [10]. The lowest level and most detailed model of an organization describes all implementation design decisions, including organizational structure(s), the decision to automate certain tasks, as well as the assignment of parties, people as well as IT and other means to the organizational structures [22].

The notion of OIV expresses a category of design choice(s) for organizational implementation [22]. It is a variable in the sense that its value can be different for different implementation alternatives. Some examples of the ∼25 of such OIVs [22] include:

- deciding upon *functionary types* and which actor roles or acts they should fulfill – e.g., the functionary type 'cook' that fulfills both the actor roles 'baker' and 'stock controller'; or the functionary type 'deliverer' who is authorized for the acts promise and declare of the (transaction kind) transport and also for the act of accept for the customer payment;
- deciding on *order of working* – e.g., should delivery only be done after receiving payment (as common in retail) or is it (also) possible to pay afterwards (more common in B2B); and
- deciding on *work locations* & *organizational units*, e.g., which branches exist, and what functionary types do exist there.

Implementations of organization, and therefore the value of OIVs, will change far more often than the products/services they help deliver. E.g., actor roles as 'sales' and 'baker' are stable notions in a pizzeria, just as the act 'accept payment'; what might change often is the authority of a functionary type – answering questions such as 'shall we combine the actor roles of sales and baker in one functionary type in the first months of opening our new pizzeria branch?' or 'shall we take the responsibility for accepting payments away from our functionary type deliverer, now payment accepting is executed automatically by a web agent under the (outsourced) responsibility of a payment service provider?'.

For a flexible enterprise it is a priority that frequently occurring changes, typically implementation choices, are not on its critical path; therefore ideally it should be possible to make such changes with no or only little impact in IS. However, organizationally variability is so large that conscious choices have to be made what organizational changes should be supported by the IS to what extent. Even the simplistic assumption of each of the 25 OIVs being able to independently change with 3 values each already creates $3^{25} \approx 8.5 * 10^{11}$ different organizational implementations for each transaction kind – a problem for automation, but even more so for human overview. OIVs make it possible to make explicit the organization design decisions that need to get a place in IS. It also provides the possibility to make an explicit requirement that the values should be (easily) changeable in the IS.

2.3   Model-Based Engineering and Low-Code Technology

Model-based Engineering is an approach to application development where models are transformed to (high) code by means of code generation or model interpretation [3]. While there are differences between code generation and model interpretation in terms of easiness to understand, debugging possibilities, performance of the execution environment, and compile and deploy time, from a usage perspective these difference do not really matter; both need a mapping from higher order (business domain) model to lower order software model, and they can even be combined [4].

The term low code was introduced by Forrester in 2014 [36]. Low-code development platforms enable quick creation of software with minimum efforts compared to traditional procedural computer programming [42] – also known as 'high code', such as Java and .Net. It builds upon existing concepts including MBE, code generation and visual programming [8]. Claimed benefits of low code include [26,37,39] *a*) less hand-coding, faster development, and, as a result, cost reduction in both development and maintenance and a shorter time-to-market, *b*) complexity reduction by using prebuilt components, *c*) the ability for nontechnical people to create applications, thus opening up the possible population for application development as well as improving business and IT collaboration while increasing IT productivity, and *d*) enabling digital transformation and increasing IT and business agility.

Low-code platforms, including Mendix, rely on 3 basic concepts: *data* (in Mendix: Entity, Enumerations, Attribute and Association), *logic* (also called action or (micro)service; in Mendix: Microflow) and *interface* (Application Programming Interface (API) and screen; in Mendix: Page, containing data views and/or Buttons), as well as their interrelations and (Access) Rules for User Roles enabling users with certain roles to use these parts of the application. Due to page limitations, the reader is referred to the footnote (see footnote 5) for the complete Mendix metamodel.

3   Mapping

The mapping is based on DEMO-SL [9] and we included all concepts relevant for IT implementation. As the current version of DEMO-SL only describes the metamodel of Enterprise Ontology, we added the concept of Organization Implementation Variable. The resulting mapping can be found in Table 1. Some of the design decisions regarding the mapping include:

D.1 Transaction kinds are not mapped. Instead, Product kinds or Event types are mapped to an Entity in order to be able to capture the state of a transaction.

D.2 For aggregate transaction kinds (ATKs) it is usually not needed to capture the coordination acts around these facts, so no mapping is needed. The production facts in the ATK are present in the FM and thus mapped to a Mendix unit, see also D.4.

D.3 As the page for showing the agenda for an actor is very generic function-ality, we choose not to generate it but built it in Mendix as a reusable component. The logic to support the state machine representing the Com-plete Transaction Pattern is also built as a generic module. Note that the details of this module are not part of this paper.

D.4 For external entity types in the FM, the decision has to be made whether the data is stored within the generated application, or used from another source, typically through an API. For the latter, in Mendix an external entity can be created, but it requires the API to be available in Mendix Data Hub. For now we decided to not use that possibility, especially as this does not seem possible (yet) through the Mendix SDK. Instead, we will create some basic CRUD (Create, Read, Update, and Delete) pages to modify and view the data. It is fairly easy in the generated application to change this later.

D.5 We have not seen enough DEMO models to provide a mapping for the generalization and specialization concepts.

D.6 Attribute types can have different kinds of Value Types. If the scale sort of a Value type is categorical, the Value Type can either be mapped to an Enumeration or to an Entity. The Attribute Type using the Value Type will then either be an EnumerationTypeAttribute or an Association. If the scale sort of the Value Type is of some other type (day, money, etc.) the Attribute Type will be mapped to some AttributeType (DateTime, Decimal, etc.).

D.7 *Transaction.Proposition* is an Entity that is part of the generic module handling the CTP. By extending it, we can use the generic state machine, but also relate it to the specific entity or entities the Event type is about.

D.8 Derived fact kinds need to be calculated. Currently we suggest to create a microflow in order to do that. Its (mathematical) definition needs to be implemented in the microflow, preferably this mapping is also provided but we consider this too detailed for the scope of this paper. A decision that goes along with this is that from a performance perspective one would like to decide whether this calculation is performed on read or on save. The low-code approach we take makes it easy to make such a decision in the platform, as it currently seems to difficult to insert that aspect into the mapping.

D.9 For the handling of Action rules, we decided to implement this as an Action Button for the user role that has to deal with the agendum (type), a Page to see all the relevant information to decide on a response, as well as one or more Action Buttons for the different choices. In this way we respect the autonomy of the actor(s) involved, and only automate the parts for retrieving all the information. The detailing of the assess-part is similar to that of a derived fact kind and a similar reasoning as D.8 holds.

D.10 OIVs are considered to be adaptable at run-time, and are therefore mapped to an Entity. The different values of such an OIV can have impact on authorization, redirecting and handling of an act, and much more. This is considered to be part of the logic and state machine and supports our choice for low code as target platform because we consider it is easier to build it into the state machine than into the translator. A more elaborate mapping can therefore not be provided, this mapping at makes it possible to change the (values of the) OIVs in the running application. In Subsect. 2.2 we already showed that the possible number of configurations grows exponentially with the number of OIVs and we therefore think incorporating OIVs into the logic might turn out to be a $\mathcal{NP}$-hard problem.

Table 1. Mapping from DEMO metamodel (concept) to Mendix metamodel (unit)

DEMO concept (aspect model)	Example	Mendix unit
Elementary transaction kind (CM)	TK01	n/a, see D.1
Aggregate transaction kind (CM)	MTK01	n/a, see D.2
Actor role (both elementary and aggregate) (CM)	AR01	User Role, see D.3
Executor link (CM)	AR01-TK01	Action button and (Microflow) Access rule
Initiator link (CM)	CAR01-TK01	Action button and (Microflow) Access rule
Access link (CM)	CA01-MTK01	Entity access rule
Product kind (CM)	[registration] is started	n/a, see Event type
Transaction general step kind (PM)	TK01/rq	Page
Non-derived entity type (FM)	Registration	Entity and Pages, see D.4
Aggregation entity type (FM)	{Registration X Year}	Entity with Associations to its aggregates
Specialization entity type (FM)	Started Registration	n/a, see D.5
Generalization entity type (FM)		n/a, see D.5
Property type (FM)	member	Association
Attribute type (FM)	start date	Attribute or Association, see D.6
Value type (FM)	day, money	Enumeration or Entity, see D.6
Event type (FM)	[registration] is started	Entity having *Transaction. Proposition* as generalization, with Association(s) to its Variable(s), see D.7
Derived fact kind (FM)	age	Microflow, see D.8
Action rule-event part (AM)		Action Button and (Microflow) Access Rule, see D.9
Action rule-assess part (AM)		Microflow and Page, see D.9
Action rule-response part (AM)		Action Button, Microflow and (Microflow) Access Rule, see D.9
Organization Implementation Variable	Functionary type	Entity, see D.10

4 Implementation and Evaluation

As part of the design cycle of Design Science, we have evaluated the mapping on several cases, ranging from academic cases such as EU-Rent [31,33] to real-world cases including Social Housing [24,25]. At first, this mapping was performed manually, while later we created a TypeScript[6] implementation of the mapping[7], that has been evaluated, improved and extended to deal with additional concepts and cases by executing it with different DEMO models as input. Newer cases did not result in major redesigns of the mapping.

While there is an XML-based exchange model for DEMO available [30], we decided to use a more compact JSON format to represent the DEMO metamodel including the concept of OIV, while leaving out parts that are for representation only, such as diagrams and tables. As an illustration, building upon the Social Housing case described in [25], Fig. 1 shows the input (JSON) files for the automated translator, while Fig. 2 shows the project folder and domain (data) model of the generated Mendix application[8].

By introducing the concept of Organization Implementation Variable into the MBE process or code generation, we were able to make transparent the mapping from organizational design decision to software implementation, thereby not

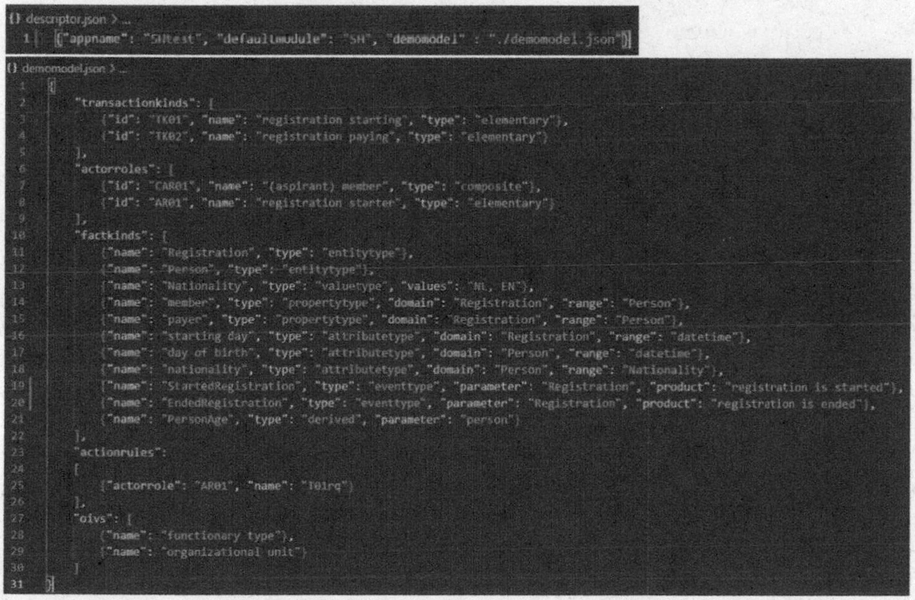

```
{} descriptor.json > ...
{"appname": "SHtest", "defaultmodule": "SH", "demomodel" : "./demomodel.json"}
```

```
{} demomodel.json > ...
{
    "transactionkinds": [
        {"id": "TK01", "name": "registration starting", "type": "elementary"},
        {"id": "TK02", "name": "registration paying", "type": "elementary"}
    ],
    "actorroles": [
        {"id": "CAR01", "name": "(aspirant) member", "type": "composite"},
        {"id": "AR01", "name": "registration starter", "type": "elementary"}
    ],
    "factkinds": [
        {"name": "Registration", "type": "entitytype"},
        {"name": "Person", "type": "entitytype"},
        {"name": "Nationality", "type": "valuetype", "values": "NL, EN"},
        {"name": "member", "type": "propertytype", "domain": "Registration", "range": "Person"},
        {"name": "payer", "type": "propertytype", "domain": "Registration", "range": "Person"},
        {"name": "starting day", "type": "attributetype", "domain": "Registration", "range": "datetime"},
        {"name": "day of birth", "type": "attributetype", "domain": "Person", "range": "datetime"},
        {"name": "nationality", "type": "attributetype", "domain": "Person", "range": "Nationality"},
        {"name": "StartedRegistration", "type": "eventtype", "parameter": "Registration", "product": "registration is started"},
        {"name": "EndedRegistration", "type": "eventtype", "parameter": "Registration", "product": "registration is ended"},
        {"name": "PersonAge", "type": "derived", "parameter": "person"}
    ],
    "actionrules":
    [
        {"actorrole": "AR01", "name": "T01rq"}
    ],
    "oivs": [
        {"name": "functionary type"},
        {"name": "organizational unit"}
    ]
}
```

Fig. 1. Descriptor file and DEMO model in JSON format for Social Housing

[6] TypeScript is the language to access the Mendix SDK, see https://docs.mendix.com/apidocs-mxsdk/mxsdk/

[7] Source code is available at https://github.com/mkrouwel/demo2mendix

[8] More details on the case as well as screen shots can be found in [25].

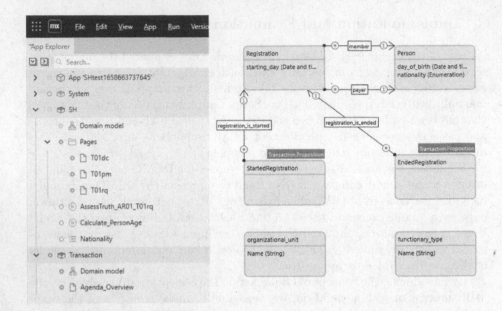

Fig. 2. Project outline and domain model of the generated Mendix application for Social Housing

leaving it up to developers to make the right choice. As the Enterprise Implementation is implemented as a configurable unit in terms of OIVs, it is easy to change the Enterprise Implementation for a given Enterprise Ontology, thereby improving the enterprise flexibility, as was shown in earlier research [25].

5   Conclusions and Discussion

Given the choice for Mendix as low-code target platform, we defined a complete mapping from the DEMO metamodel, including organization implementation, to the Mendix metamodel. We implemented this mapping in TypeScript, using the Mendix SDK, in order to generate a readily deployable low code application from the ontological model of an enterprise, including the support for OIVs. In doing so, we created a reusable component in Mendix to support the CTP as well as for showing relevant agenda to the actors that have to deal with them.

One advantage of the proposed approach follows from the use of an ontological enterprise model as the starting point. Since these models are coherent, comprehensive, consistent and concise, the generated software is of high quality and only contains the necessary constructs to support the enterprise end users.

It also adds flexibility as parts of the IS are simply (re)generated when new transaction kinds arise. By adding OIVs to the MBE approach, it becomes possible to change (some) design decisions at run-time, therefore allowing for even more flexibility and agility for the enterprise.

Another advantage of this approach seems to be that the generated code can easily be adapted through the low-code visual paradigm. This allows for changes in the UI, to make use of APIs, or to implement the execution of the action rules or calculations in a more efficient way. A warning should be given that changes in the generated code can become a source of hidden design decisions.

Reflecting on our MBE approach, by making explicit the required organizational flexibility and giving it a specific place in the generated code, we have successfully connected organizational flexibility and IS flexibility, thereby at least improving enterprise flexibility. As the code can easily be regenerated, changing the IS is not the limiting factor anymore in changing the enterprises service or product portfolio or its implementation.

Limitations and Future Research Recommendations

As the details of the generic component supporting the CTP do not fit into this paper, it has to be described and published separately.

In creating the mapping, we noticed the DEMO metamodel in DEMO-SL is not specified from an operational point of view but from a diagramming perspective. In the (manual) conversion to JSON, we also had to add aspects that were relevant for generating software, such as the application and module name. It seems necessary to better detail the generic metamodel, containing only the true DEMO concepts and separating the core of DEMO from the purpose-specific information such as visualization or code generation.

For the implementation of an external entity type, such as person, in the FM, one typically chooses to use an existing source (through an API) or to create an own database table to store the relevant data (incl. Create, Read, Update, and Delete (CRUD) pages). The current version of the mapping does not yet allow for this differentiation, partly as a result of lack of support through the SDK. A future version of the translator should incorporate this. Note that by the nature of low-code, it is always possible to change the output model to incorporate the usage of existing APIs.

Mendix has launched native workflow capability in the platform. As the majority of the mapping and its implementation was set up before that time, it doesn't use this feature. It could be interesting to look into these possibilities and see how it can support the CTP. As this component is created as a generic component, it is easy to rebuild without impacting the code generator.

The implementation of OIVs in Mendix, or maybe even software in general, is not straightforward. The impact of certain choices on the state machine and logic is not completely detailed yet. This will differ per OIV and can only be detailed per individual OIV. It can even be that when combining different OIVs, the problem becomes to complex to solve. It is not clear whether all OIVs can be implemented completely independent of others, as suggested by Normalized Systems theory [27]. We will need more evaluations with more cases involving more OIVs to fully understand the complexity of this problem. Supporting all possible organization design decisions could even be an $\mathcal{NP}$-hard problem. Further research is required to check the feasibility and limitations of this approach.

The mapping we made is specific towards the Mendix platform. Although other low-code platforms rely on similar concepts, the question arises whether the mapping can be abstracted to facilitate other low-code platforms, or even high code. Further research is needed to get a perspective on the feasibility and usability of such an abstraction.

It's hard to compare our MBE approach to ones that use a different kind of input, such as BPMN or UML. It could be interesting to research ways to compare the advantages and disadvantages of different approaches towards MBE.

References

1. Austin, J.L.: How to do Things with Words. Oxford University Press, William James Lectures (1962)
2. Bockhooven, S.v., Op 't Land, M.: Organization implementation fundamentals: a case study validation in the youthcare sector. In: Complementary Proceedings of the Workshops TEE, CoBI, and XOC-BPM at IEEE-COBI 2015. CEUR Workshop Proceedings, vol. 1408. Lisbon, Portugal (2015). http://ceur-ws.org/Vol-1408/paper3-tee.pdf
3. Brambilla, M., Cabot, J., Wimmer, M.: Model-Driven Software Engineering in Practice. Morgan & Claypool Publishers (2012). https://doi.org/10.2200/S00441ED1V01Y201208SWE001
4. Cabot, J.: Executable models vs code-generation vs model interpretation. Online, August 2010. https://modeling-languages.com/executable-models-vs-code-generation-vs-model-interpretation-2/. Accessed 17 May 2022
5. Cabot, J.: Positioning of the low-code movement within the field of model-driven engineering. In: Proceedings of the 23rd ACM/IEEE International Conference on Model Driven Engineering Languages and Systems: Companion Proceedings. Association for Computing Machinery, New York (2020). https://doi.org/10.1145/3417990.3420210
6. Caetano, A., Assis, A., Tribolet, J.: Using DEMO to analyse the consistency of business process models. Adv. Enterpr. Inf. Syst. II, 133–146. CRC Press (2012). https://doi.org/10.1201/b12295-17
7. D'aveni, R.A., Gunther, R.: Hypercompetition. Free Press (1994)
8. Di Ruscio, D., Kolovos, D., de Lara, J., Pierantonio, A., Tisi, M., Wimmer, M.: Low-code development and model-driven engineering: Two sides of the same coin? Softw. Syst. Model. **21**(2), 437–446 (2022). https://doi.org/10.1007/s10270-021-00970-2
9. Dietz, J.: The DEMO Specification Language v4.7. Tech. rep., Enterprise Engineering Institute (2022). https://ee-institute.org/download/demo-specification-language-4-7-1/
10. Dietz, J.L.G.: Architecture - Building strategy into design. Netherlands Architecture Forum, Academic Service - SDU, The Hague, The Netherlands (2008)
11. Dietz, J.L.G., Hoogervorst, J.A.P.: Enterprise ontology and enterprise architecture - how to let them evolve into effective complementary notions. GEAO J. Enterpr. Architect. **2007**, 1 (2007)
12. Dietz, J.L.G., et al.: The discipline of enterprise engineering. Int. J. Organ. Des. Eng. **3**(1), 86–114 (2013). https://doi.org/10.1504/IJODE.2013.053669

13. Dietz, J.L.G., Mulder, J.B.F.: Enterprise Ontology – A Human-Centric Approach to Understanding the Essence of Organisation. The Enterprise Engineering Series, Springer, Cham (2020). https://doi.org/10.1007/978-3-030-38854-6
14. Ettema, R., Dietz, J.L.G.: ArchiMate and DEMO - Mates to date? In: Albani, A., Barjis, J., Dietz, J.L.G., Aalst, W., Mylopoulos, J., Rosemann, M., Shaw, M.J., Szyperski, C. (eds.) Advances in Enterprise Engineering III, Lecture Notes in Business Information Processing, vol. 34, pp. 172–186. Springer, Berlin Heidelberg (2009). https://doi.org/10.1007/978-3-642-01915-9_13
15. Falbo, R., Guizzardi, G., Duarte, K., Natali, A.: Developing software for and with reuse: an ontological approach. In: ACIS International Conference on Computer Science, Software Engineering, Information Technology, e-Business, and Applications, pp. 311–316. International Association for Computer and Information Science (ACIS) (2002)
16. Gray, T., Bork, D., De Vries, M.: A new DEMO modelling tool that facilitates model transformations. In: Nurcan, S., Reinhartz-Berger, I., Soffer, P., Zdravkovic, J. (eds.) BPMDS/EMMSAD -2020. LNBIP, vol. 387, pp. 359–374. Springer, Cham (2020). https://doi.org/10.1007/978-3-030-49418-6_25
17. Guizzardi, G.: Ontological foundations for structural conceptual models. Ph.D. thesis, University of Twente (Oct 2005)
18. Habermas, J.: The Theory of Communicative Action. Polity Press, Cambridge (1986)
19. de Jong, J.: A Method for Enterprise Ontology based Design of for Enterprise Information Systems. Ph.D. thesis, TU Delft (2013)
20. van Kervel, S.: Ontology driven Enterprise Information Systems Engineering. Ph.D. thesis, TU Delft (2012)
21. de Kinderen, S., Gaaloul, K., Proper, H.A.E.: On transforming DEMO models to archiMate. In: Bider, I., Halpin, T., Krogstie, J., Nurcan, S., Proper, E., Schmidt, R., Soffer, P., Wrycza, S. (eds.) BPMDS/EMMSAD -2012. LNBIP, vol. 113, pp. 270–284. Springer, Heidelberg (2012). https://doi.org/10.1007/978-3-642-31072-0_19
22. Krouwel, M.R., Op 't Land, M., Offerman, T.: Formalizing organization implementation. In: Aveiro, D., Pergl, R., Gouveia, D. (eds.) EEWC 2016. LNBIP, vol. 252, pp. 3–18. Springer, Cham (2016). https://doi.org/10.1007/978-3-319-39567-8_1
23. Krouwel, M.R., Op 't Land, M.: Combining DEMO and normalized systems for developing agile enterprise information systems. In: Albani, A., Dietz, J.L.G., Verelst, J. (eds.) EEWC 2011. LNBIP, vol. 79, pp. 31–45. Springer, Heidelberg (2011). https://doi.org/10.1007/978-3-642-21058-7_3
24. Krouwel, M.R., Op 't L.M: Business driven micro service design - an enterprise ontology based approach to API specifications. In: Aveiro, D., Proper, H., Guerreiro, S., de Vries, M. (eds.) Advances in Enterprise Engineering XV, vol. 441. Springer (2021). https://doi.org/10.1007/978-3-031-11520-2_7
25. Op 't Land, M., Krouwel, M.R., Gort, S.: Testing the concept of the *RUN-Time Adaptive* enterprise. In: Aveiro, D., Guizzardi, G., Pergl, R., Proper, H.A. (eds.) EEWC 2020. LNBIP, vol. 411, pp. 228–242. Springer, Cham (2021). https://doi.org/10.1007/978-3-030-74196-9_13
26. Luo, Y., Liang, P., Wang, C., Shahin, M., Zhan, J.: Characteristics and challenges of low-code development: the practitioners' perspective. In: Proceedings of the 15th ACM/IEEE International Symposium on Empirical Software Engineering and Measurement (ESEM), pp. 1–11. CoRR (2021). https://arxiv.org/abs/2107.07482
27. Mannaert, H., Verelst, J.: Normalized systems: re-creating. Inf. Technol. laws Softw. Evol. Koppa, Kermt, Belgium (2009)

28. Mráz, O., Náplava, P., Pergl, R., Skotnica, M.: Converting demo psi transaction pattern into BPMN: a complete method. In: Aveiro, D., Pergl, R., Guizzardi, G., Almeida, J.P., Magalhães, R., Lekkerkerk, H. (eds.) Advances in Enterprise Engineering XI, pp. 85–98. Springer International Publishing, Cham (2017)
29. Mulder, J.B.F.: Rapid Enterprise Design. Ph.D. thesis, Delft University of Technology (2006)
30. Mulder, M.: Enabling the automatic verification and exchange of DEMO models. Ph.D. thesis, Radboud University Nijmegen (2022). https://repository.ubn.ru.nl/handle/2066/247698
31. Object Management Group: Business Motivation Model. Tech. Rep. Version 1.3, Object Management Group (2015). http://www.omg.org/spec/BMM/1.3/PDF/
32. Oosterhout, M.P.A.v.: Business Agility and Information Technology in Service Organizations. Ph.D. thesis, Erasmus University Rotterdam (2010)
33. Op 't Land, M., Krouwel, M.R.: Exploring organizational implementation fundamentals. In: H.A. Proper, D.A., Gaaloul, K. (eds.) Advances in Enterprise Engineering VII. Lecture Notes in Business Information Processing, vol. 146, pp. 28–42. Springer-Verlag, Berlin Heidelberg (2013). https://doi.org/10.1007/978-3-642-38117-1_3
34. Overby, E., Bharadwaj, A., Sambamurthy, V.: Enterprise agility and the enabling role of information technology. Eur. J. Inf. Syst. **15**, 120–131 (2006). https://doi.org/10.1057/palgrave.ejis.3000600
35. Reijswoud, V.E.V., Mulder, J.B.F., Dietz, J.L.G.: Communicative action based business process and information modelling with DEMO. Inf. Syst. J. **9**(2), 117–138 (1999)
36. Richardson, C., Rymer, J.: New Development Platforms Emerge For Customer-Facing Applications. Tech. rep, Forrester (2014)
37. Sanchis, R., García-Perales, Fraile, F., Poler: low-code as enabler of digital transformation in manufacturing industry. Appl. Sci. **10**, 12 (2019). https://doi.org/10.3390/app10010012
38. Searle, J.R.: Speech Acts: An Essay in the Philosophy of Language. Cambridge University Press, Cambridge, London (1969)
39. Sijtstra, J.: Quantifying low-code development platforms effectiveness in the Dutch public sector. mathesis, Leiden University (2022). https://theses.liacs.nl/2221
40. Simon, H.A.: The Sciences of the Artificial, 3rd edn. MIT Press, Cambridge, MA, USA (1996)
41. Sushil, Stohr, E.A. (eds.): The flexible enterprise. In: Flexible Systems Management, Springer India, pp. 333–345 (2014). https://doi.org/10.1007/978-81-322-1560-8
42. Waszkowski, R.: Low-code platform for automating business processes in manufacturing. IFAC-PapersOnLine **52**(10), 376–381 (2019). https://doi.org/10.1016/j.ifacol.2019.10.060, 13th IFAC Workshop on Intelligent Manufacturing Systems IMS 2019
43. Weigand, H.: Two decades of language/action perspective. Natl. Lang. Eng. **49**, 45–46 (2006)

Supporting the Individuation, Analysis and Gamification of Software Components for Acceptance Requirements Fulfilment

Federico Calabrese[1], Luca Piras[2], and Paolo Giorgini[1(✉)]

[1] Department of Information Engineering and Computer Science,
University of Trento, Trento, Italy
`federico.calabrese@alumni.unitn.it`, `paolo.giorgini@unitn.it`
[2] Department of Computer Science, Middlesex University, London, United Kingdom
`L.Piras@mdx.ac.uk`

Abstract. In the last few years, Gamification has proved effective for motivating users in using software systems. Gamification Engineering has been proposed as a systematic way to gamify systems. Goal-Oriented Requirements Engineering (GORE) techniques have been emerging for supporting the gamification of a system from the initial stages. However, the gamification of a system itself proved not effective, unless requirements engineers design the gamification solution being driven by characterising users, the context, and considering factors and strategies coming from Social Sciences (e.g., Psychology, Sociology, Human Behaviour, Organisational Behaviour). GORE Gamification Engineering techniques have been enhanced for supporting such concepts, referred to as Acceptance Requirements, and the Agon Framework, with its systematic Acceptance Requirements Analysis Based on Gamification, has been proven effective in different EU Projects. However, according to engineers we interviewed in our projects, some GORE gamification activities remain difficult and require further support. In this paper, our contributions are: **(i)** individuating such activities and providing lessons learned, **(ii)** considering a crucial activity, i.e. individuation of software components to gamify and how to gamify them, and proposing a solution for this. Our solution is called *Supporting the individuation, analysis, and GAMification* (SiaGAM) algorithm. To evaluate SiaGAM, we considered the gamification results of 5 EU projects, compared them with the results of applying SiaGAM, and we found that SiaGAM is effective in supporting the engineer in individuating software functions to gamify.

Keywords: Requirements engineering · Acceptance requirements · Gamification · Goal models · Goal modeling analysis · Software engineering

1 Introduction

Gamification is becoming a crucial element to consider when designing software systems to engage the user and to stimulate them to use the system [1, 12, 18].

© IFIP International Federation for Information Processing 2022
Published by Springer Nature Switzerland AG 2022
B. S. Barn and K. Sandkuhl (Eds.): PoEM 2022, LNBIP 456, pp. 33–48, 2022.
https://doi.org/10.1007/978-3-031-21488-2_3

Gamification has been defined by Deterding et al. as "the use of game design elements in non-game contexts" [6]. Non-game contexts are environments whose purpose is not to have fun but to induce a certain behaviour in the user [7]. This behaviour allows to fulfill the goals of the environment. A potential way to encourage the user to embrace such behaviour is to use game design elements [6]. This means that it is possible to decorate system functions with game elements, thus making software more attractive, interesting, and engaging for the user [5,25].

Accordingly, in the Software Engineering area, the important term and concept of "Gamification Engineering" has been proposed recently and, as far as we know, the first related definition comes from Piras et al. "Gamification Engineering is the Software Engineering of Gamification" [17,22]. Gamification Engineering includes new languages, engines, models, frameworks, and tools [9,17–19,21–23,25] for making the gamification of software systems more systematic and supported. In relation to Requirements Engineering, Goal-Oriented Requirements Engineering (GORE) techniques emerged for supporting the gamification of a system from the initial stages. However, the gamification of a system itself has proved not effective unless requirements engineers design the gamification solution being driven by user characterisation and considering factors and strategies coming from Social Sciences (e.g., Psychology, Sociology, Human Behaviour, Organisational Behaviour) [5,7,16–19,25]. Consequently, GORE Gamification Engineering techniques have been enhanced to support such concepts, referred to as Acceptance Requirements. In parallel, the Agon Framework, with its systematic Acceptance Requirements Analysis Based on Gamification, proved effective in different EU Research Projects [11,17–19,23].

In this context, according to the perspective of requirements analysts, the current GORE gamification engineering techniques are considered useful [11,17–19,23]. However, requirements analysts also identified that some GORE gamification activities, although useful, remain difficult and require further support or improvement [18]. Accordingly, we derived the following Research Questions (RQs), which we address in this paper:

RQ1. What are the current gamification supporting phases that can be improved or automated to better support the analyst in the gamification of software systems?

RQ2. How can we support the analyst in the analysis and individuation of software functionalities to gamify in a guided/supported/automated way?

To answer **RQ1**, we identified within our projects [11,17–19,23] the activities that are still complex and difficult to carry on, and thus require support or improvement. We obtained such insights by observing analysts directly using GORE gamification engineering techniques, and by interviewing them via questionnaires.

RQ2 concerns the investigation on how to further support analysts regarding problematic activities found through **RQ1**. The most problematic activity, indicated by analysts as requiring more support [18], concerns the identification of the *subset* of software components to gamify. This is a crucial aspect because the gamification of the *entire* software system can be expensive and could not give the expected outcome [5, 25]. Thus, to minimise organisations' effort and costs related to gamification design activities, it is necessary to identify what *subset* of system functionalities it is better to gamify [5, 25]. In this paper, the solution we devised to **RQ2** is an algorithm that we call: *Supporting the individuation, analysis, and GAMification* (SiaGAM) of software components. SiaGAM guides and supports the analyst in a semi-automated way by: **(i)** representing the software to be gamified as a goal model; **(ii)** characterising software functionalities in relation to different qualities; **(iii)** guiding during functionalities annotation, using the algorithm in a semi-automated way, to identify the set of functionalities to consider to gamify according to criteria identified.

To evaluate SiaGAM, we considered the gamification results obtained in 5 case studies from EU projects [11, 17–19, 23]. We focused on the subsets of functionalities that had to be gamified, and had been selected manually by the researchers. We then applied SiaGAM to the same goal models and obtained subsets of functionalities to consider to be gamified. Finally, we compared our results with the previous ones, and we found that SiaGAM is effective in supporting the analyst in identifying software functionalities to gamify, as it can derive the same set of functionalities. It is important to note that the results of the projects had been obtained manually: analysts highlighted this aspect as the one needing further support [18]. An essential advantage of SiaGAM is that it offers analogous results in a guiding, supporting, and semi-automated way.

The rest of the paper is organised as follows: Sect. 2 **RQ1**, discussing lessons learned identifying which gamification activities require more support and how to provide it. Section 2 also provides the basis and motivation for The rest of the paper is organised, explaining the context in which our algorithm and approach are applied. Section 3 addresses **RQ2** describing our algorithm and approach. Section 4 addresses **RQ2** by describing our case study and the evaluation of SiaGAM. Section 5 discusses related work, while Sect. 6 concludes this work.

2   Motivation and Lessons Learned

In this section we address **RQ1**. Specifically, in 2.1 we outline the Agon Framework and its systematic Acceptance Requirements Analysis based on Gamification, focusing on the phases relevant to our RQs. In 2.2, we summarise research projects where Agon has been applied successfully, and address **RQ1** by discussing Lessons Learned (LL) we derived from such real-world experiences.

2.1   Agon Framework

Agon [17, 18, 21–23] is a framework for performing systematic Acceptance Requirements analysis on software systems based on modeling, analysis and strategies to fulfil such requirements using Gamification operationalisations. Agon allows to analyse and gamify any kind of software, as demonstrated in many domains [17, 18, 21–23]. For instance, it has been applied successfully to

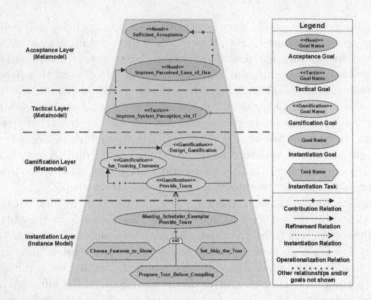

Fig. 1. Simplified example of agon multi-layer meta-model [17,23], descriptions of the example available at [17,21,22], and the Agon full models available at [20]

a real case study within the PACAS EU Project [17,23] to analyse Acceptance Requirements and gamify the PACAS platform in the context of architectural change management for ATM (Air Traffic Management) systems.

Agon is composed of a multi-layer meta-model (Fig. 1), based on Goal Modeling, extending the NFR framework [4,13,15]. It has been designed with the next models [17,23]: **(i)** Acceptance Meta-Model (AM) capturing user needs, which the analyst can consider to determine aspects able to stimulate the target user, to accept and use a software system; **(ii)** Tactical Meta-Model (TM), which allows the analyst to identify tactical goals, as refinements for needs selected in AM [21]; **(iii)** Gamification Meta-Model (GM), which provides the analyst with ready-to-use, game design solutions operationalising tactical goals and (in turn) needs selected in the higher-level models (AM and TM) [21]; **(iv)** Instance Model (IM), produced by the analyst via a goal modeling language. This instantiates GM by defining tasks, relations and lower-level gamification goals. The final purpose of IM is to decorate software functions by instantiating and configuring ready-to-use game-based elements (suggested by Agon and chosen also taking into account the specific software domain) to stimulate the target user [17,18,21,23].

The next 2 subsections briefly illustrate the first 2 phases of the Agon process, to which we applied SiaGAM to further support the analyst addressing **RQ2**. The third subsection summarises the other phases of the Agon process, which are relevant for discussing our lessons learned (**RQ1**).

Phase 1: Base System Requirements Modelling (BSRM). This is the first activity analysts performs with the Agon process. The aim is to analyse the software to gamify, for creating a Goal Model representing the system and its functionalities [17,18]. Those will be potential functionalities to gamify through analysis of acceptance requirements, tactics and game design strategies [17,18, 23].

Phase 2: Acceptance Requirements Elicitation Analysis (AREA). In this phase the BSRM goal model is analysed for identifying the *subset* of functions to gamify. This is performed manually by the analyst and Agon just provides recommendations. Specifically, the identification should aim at selecting functions of the software that meet the following conditions: *"(a)cannot be fulfilled automatically by IT procedures; (b) needs human contribution; (c) has to stimulate and engage the user to carry out the activity (e.g., the activity is boring, complex, repetitive, etc.); (d) contributes positively to the achievement of critical purposes of the system and depends on human contribution to be fulfilled."* [17,18].

Next Phases of the Agon Process. The other phases relevant to our lessons learned (**RQ1**) are [17,18]: Phase 3, Context Characterization; Phase 4, Context-Based Analysis of Acceptance Requirements; Phase 5, Acceptance Requirements Refinement; Phase 6, Context-Based Operationalization via Gamification; Phase 7, Domain-Dependent Instantiation of Incentive Mechanisms.

2.2   Activities and Lessons Learned.

The Agon Framework, with its systematic Acceptance Requirements Analysis Based on Gamification, proved effective in different EU Research Projects [11,17–19,23]. Specifically, according to the perspective of requirements analysts, the current GORE gamification engineering techniques, included in Agon and its process, have been recognised as useful [11,17–19,23]. The case studies we consider refer to the following 5 research projects[1] [11,17–19,23] **(i)** in the context of the VisiOn EU project (See footnote 1) [18], a complex platform for Public Administration (PA) has been delivered to support citizens in improving their awareness on privacy aspects of their personal data and to support them and organisations in the management of personal data. In this case study, a core tool of this platform, STS-Tool, has been gamified to engage analysts in complex modeling-related scenarios for the analysis of privacy and security requirements [2,17,18]; **(ii)** within the PACAS EU project (See footnote 1) [17,23], a participatory system that supports collaborative decision-making and related to Air Traffic Management (ATM) has been delivered and gamified [17,23]. In this

---

[1] VisiOn, PACAS, SUPERSEDE, SUM and MA4C Case Studies available at: https://pirasluca.wordpress.com/home/acceptance/case-studies/.

case, it was important to motivate heterogeneous professionals to collaborate to improve complex ATM procedures. The aim was to support the analysis and design of strategies and to improve the interest, engagement and pro-activeness of the professionals involved [17,23]; **(iii)** within the SUPERSEDE EU project (See footnote 1) [17,19], the focus was the gamification of a system to motivate analysts to contribute pro-actively to *Collaborative Requirements Prioritization* activities [17,19]; **(iv)** the SUM project (See footnote 1) [11,17] gamified a system providing a solution to encourage citizens to use *Sustainable urban Mobility* [11,17]; **(v)** the MA4C project (See footnote 1) [11,17] gamified a system to promote *Mobility Assistance for Children* to progressively support the child in autonomous growth to avoid manifesting different problems as adults [11,17].

In total, we involved 32 participants as requirements analysts (5 junior in a preliminary phase, then 21 junior and 4 senior) within case studies, using semi-structured interviews, questionnaires and evaluation reports (full details available at [17]). Even though requirements analysts found these activities useful, they declared that some of them remained difficult and require further support or improvement [18]. To identify the activities needing further development, we observed the analysts while using GORE techniques and we interviewed them using questionnaires. This allowed us to address **RQ1**, and in the next subsections we will show the activities found and provide the lessons learned.

Analysis on Large Models and Concepts Interpretation. Among the difficulties, analysts found problematic to interpret AM, the Goal Model provided by Agon representing acceptance solutions (Fig. 1). Junior analysts have been the most affected, having less knowledge and experience related to goal models, and Social Sciences concepts, while senior analysts faced fewer difficulties [17,18]. In this context, a glossary[2] of the concepts, and explanations from us, helped with the interpretation. Similarly, further explanations were needed to mitigate analysis issues regarding the Agon models structure. Furthermore, when the analysis moved towards the Gamification Model (Fig. 1), which is an even larger model, they started experiencing difficulties again. In this case, the issue was not related to the interpretation of gamification concepts (also thanks to the glossary), but more related to the dimension of the model. Again, the problem was more evident in junior than in senior analysts [17,18].

In summary, analysts recognised the models and the overall systematic process as useful; however, the approach still needs improvements. To mitigate the interpretation problem, the glossary and explanations helped. For the size of goal models, analysts suggested abstraction layers on goal models, or concepts separated in different perspectives, and proposed at different times. Regarding abstractions layers, analysts would like graphical visualisations able to show simplified models, or alternative summarised graphical solutions. For the perspectives, we could consider categorising parts of the models, and devising strategies for proposing solutions and concepts at different stages, making users to focus

---

[2] Agon Glossary:https://pirasluca.wordpress.com/home/acceptance/glossary/.

on a separate aspect at a time. However, such strategies should also consider situations where separate parts are involved and contribute to the same solution.

Instantiation of Gamification Solutions. The last phase "Domain-Dependent Instantiation of Incentive Mechanisms" [17] requires a huge effort from the analyst. Indeed, since GM is already a large model, its instantiation (Fig. 1) can result in a even larger model, and it is up to the analyst to instantiate it. At the moment, this is a manual activity supported by a graphical editor. A potential solution for further supporting the analyst can be to enhance the editor with further functionalities suggesting typical instantiations of high-level gamification solutions, according to the domain, as low-level patterns. Another solution could be to enhance this phase with automatic code generation, or skeleton code, based on the analyst's instantiation. In this way, the instantiation work could be merged with the development phase. Moreover, the process can be iteratively refined.

Individuation of Software Components to Gamify. This lesson learned is related to the first two phases, discussed above (BSRM and AREA phases), of the systematic Acceptance Requirements Analysis Based on Gamification of the Agon Framework. These are crucial phases where the analyst needs to select the *subset* of system functionalities to gamify. Agon provides high-level guidelines for this, but no further support. In the research projects considered [11,17–19,23], analysts have generally recognised Agon and its process as useful and have been able to properly identify the functionalities to gamify, designing effective gamification solutions. However, they highlighted the need for further guided and automated support concerning these crucial phases. Agon indicates specifically for this part that the analyst should identify the functions that need to be gamified through the analysis of BSRM. To support the identification, Agon provides guidelines to select software functions satisfying certain conditions (see "Phase 2", Sect. 2.1). In this paper, to address RQ2, we focus on such critical phases (BSRM and AREA). Based on the feedback of the analysts and by following the high-level guidelines of Agon, we have designed the SiaGAM algorithm. SiaGAM guides the analyst (semi-automatically) in characterising system functionalities, identifying qualities, and applying annotations for identifying functions to gamify.

3   SiaGAM Algorithm and Process

This section addresses **RQ2** by describing the algorithm we implemented within Agon, to further support the analyst in relation to *Supporting the individuation, analysis, and GAMification* (SiaGAM) of software components. Agon is an Acceptance Requirements and Gamification framework for gamifying software systems by fulfilling User Acceptance. In this context, SiaGAM and our approach improve a crucial part of the Agon process and tool: SiaGAM provides semi-automatic support to BSRM and AREA phases of Agon (addressing

the last lesson learned, discussed above). BSRM and AREA are early phases of
the Agon process. These are crucial for building an effective gamification solution. Redesigning such phases as semi-automatic can provide further support to
analysts, both reducing their effort and minimising errors occurrence. To make
such phases semi-automatic (**RQ2**), we devised modifications of BSRM and a
redesign of AREA to make it more goal modeling oriented. The idea was to
change the process by guiding the analyst to characterise and annotate a goal
model of the system (BSRM enhancement) with factors that SiaGAM can consider for providing solutions as a filtered goal model based on choices made by
the analyst (redesign of AREA). The process can be reiterated to produce further refinements of the solution. We designed the SiaGAM process in 2 phases,
i.e. *Annotation Model* and *Algorithm Execution*. These are illustrated in the
following.

Annotation Model. This phase extends BSRM, and the outcome expected is
an annotated goal model. The analyst designs the goal model by representing
the system to gamify, and follows guidelines allowing to assign annotations to
concepts of the model. This step is fundamental since the analyst, who has a
deep knowledge of the software, can find and annotate the most relevant system functions. Annotations are expressed using human language (making the
assignment of annotations easier) and indicated/supported by SiaGAM (these
are extensible). Thus, annotations support the analyst in the system functions
characterisation. Below, we outline annotations and related guidelines to consider for using our approach by applying annotations properly.

B: indicates `Boring`. This includes unattractive, tedious, monotonous or repetitive system functions. These are usually interesting from the gamification
perspective because they could require users to be motivated to use them.

HC: indicates `High Complexity`. These functions could demand high knowledge, skills, or require engaging or collaborating with other people, which
could increase the difficulty. They could require also significant effort by
the user. These functions are the most complex of the software and could
require considerable stimuli to allow adequate user engagement.

LC: indicates `Low Complexity`. These functions could require a limited amount
of time to be completed, or indicate no need to collaborate with other people, or can be simple actions (e.g., clicking a confirmation button). This
annotation identifies simple tasks that could require little attention, but
that could still need to be gamified to motivate the user to complete them.

A: indicates `Automatic`. This annotation is assigned to a system function that
does not require any effort/intervention by the user.

M: indicates `Manual`. This includes activities fully performed manually by the
user (the goal model represents both "Socio" and "Technical" activities)
or semi-automatically (i.e. where more than 50% is performed manually).

Accordingly, we specify an Annotations Set (AS) composed by {B, HC, LC,
A, M}. Furthermore, we designed SiaGAM to be flexible enough to enable the

analyst to extend AS, by adding new annotations, in case other characteristics of particular software domains/contexts need to be considered. Another concept we included in our approach is called Gamification Impact Probability (GIP). This represents the probability of a function to receive a positive impact if gamified, i.e. the higher the GIP, the more likely the related function will be considered for gamification. However, the GIP that SiaGAM considers is calculated on a path, which we call GIPPath. The range considered is: $0 \leq GIPPath \leq 1$. From our experience in gamifying software successfully in different EU projects [11,17–19,23], and according to the feedback we received by requirements analysts involved, we determined the default SiaGAM GIP values as: B = 0.5; HC = 1; LC = 0.25; A = 0; M = 0.8. Such values, as well as AS, are configurable based on specific domain/context characteristics, needs, constraints.

Another annotation is Current Engagement Probability (CEP). This represents the current probability of user engagement recorded by a particular function. CEP is summed to GIPPath during its calculation and is expressed negatively to decrease GIPPath: decreasing GIPPath indicates decreasing the need of gamifying functions of that path. CEP is useful in case the organisation has already measured the user engagement per function. If this information is not available, CEP value will be 0 and will not affect the GIPPath calculation.

A significant aspect of SiaGAM is its flexibility. In fact, the analyst can specify if to consider the full AS, or subsets of it, via an expression, which is passed to SiaGAM. This can be reiterated with different subsets, by specifying different annotations until the analyst is satisfied with the analysis results. Hereafter, we call the subset chosen by the analyst as Analyst Annotation Set (AAS).

Figure 2 shows a simplified example of SiaGAM applied, within the VisiOn EU Project, for the gamification of STS-Tool [3,18].

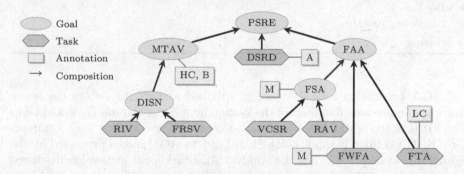

Fig. 2. Annotated goal model: applying SiaGAM for gamifying STS-Tool [3,18]

The example shows how we improved the first phase of Agon process (BSRM): now the analyst is guided and supported semi-automatically in applying the annotations to the BSRM model during the definition of the Goal Model by following the guidelines and aspects of SiaGAM discussed above. To achieve this, an Annotation Goal Model (AGM) [3] is produced, which includes characteristics of both the original BSRM and AREA models. In this phase, analysts can use the default configuration of SiaGAM (determined from our experience in successfully gamifying software in different ·EU projects [11,17–19,23], and according to feedback received from analysts involved), reducing their effort, or configure it. For instance, Fig. 2 shows that the analyst decided to annotate MTAV, i.e. "Model The Authorization View" goal [3,18], as High Complex and Boring (HC and B annotations respectively) to be fulfilled.

Algorithm Execution. This phase regards the support provided to the analyst by SiaGAM through the semi-automation of AREA. SiaGAM analyses AGM and supports the analyst in identifying the most interesting paths related to the functions where to apply gamification. Specifically, SiaGAM analyses AGM with an adapted pre-order visit, considering annotations of the functionalities for calculating GIPPath, and providing a final model with functionalities that, according to annotations and criteria specified, are considered candidates to be gamified. The next Figure shows the pseudo-code of the SiaGAM algorithm.

Algorithm 1: SiaGAM(GoalModel g, Expression aasExp, Float minGIPPath)

```
1  if (g.root isNull) then
2  │   return g;
3  else if (g.root.annotations isEmpty) then
4  │   while ((GoalModel child = nextChild(g)) != null) do
5  │   └   SiaGAM(child, aasExp, minGIPPath);
6  │   delete(g.root);
7  else if (evaluate(g.root, g.root.annotations, aasExp, minGIPPath)) then
8  │   printModel(g.root, g.root.annotations, g.root.GIPPath);
9  else
10 └   delete(g.root);
11 return g;
```

SiaGAM works on a Goal Model g, specified as g=(C,R), where the set of concepts C represents functions of the system by using goals, sub-goals and tasks (Fig. 2). R is the set of relations used to connect the concepts (e.g., composition). SiaGAM takes in input a GoalModel g (the AGM model processed by the algorithm), aasExp (i.e. AAS, the Analyst Annotation Set expression discussed before), and minGIPPath (the minimum GIPPath value a function should have to be selected as a candidate function to gamify). Thus, aasExp variable represents AAS, the satisfactory annotations the algorithm must verify. AAS can be specified by the analyst and defined through aasExp. In this way, the analyst can perform different simulations based on different expressions, with the possibility to perform an accurate, iterative analysis by considering distinct aspects each time. For instance, according to the example in Fig. 2, we can·express the aim of knowing which are the candidate functions satisfying minGIPPath ≥ 0.8, and AAS = {M, HC, B} specified through aasExp. To achieve this, SiaGAM checks the root node (Fig. 2): if the result is `null`, the algorithm stops; otherwise, the annotations set of the current functionality (represented as a goal) must be checked to see if it is empty. If the value is `True`, i.e. current element is not annotated, the algorithm is recursively called for each of `g` children (from the left child to the latest to the right side). Once on a node with annotations, the `evaluate` function checks if there is a match among annotations of the current node and `aasExp`, it updates `GIPPath` of the node accordingly, and checks if `minGIPPath` is satisfied for the node. If `evaluate` returns `True`, the node is automatically kept, otherwise it is deleted. This process is executed in AGM, and, at the end, the process returns the filtered AGM with the functionalities to gamify according to criteria specified.

SiaGAM Example and Results. The example illustrated in Fig. 2, is an extract, simplified, example from the VisiOn EU Project [3,18], aiming at identifying candidate functions to gamify for the STS-Tool, a tool used by analysts for modeling privacy and security requirements via different views [3,18]. In the example we execute SiaGAM with `g`, representing the Goal Model of STS-Tool functions (Fig. 2), `minGIPPath` ≥ 0.8, and `aasExp` = {M, HC, B}. SiaGAM starts from the PSRE (i.e. performing "Privacy and Security Requirements Engineering" via the STS-Tool) root goal, and, not being annotated, SiaGAM recursively continues with the first, left, child: MTAV. MTAV is the "Model The Authorization View" goal, and it is annotated with High Complex (`HC`) and Boring (B). Thus, the `evaluate` function is called, it finds a match among such annotations and `aasExp` ones, and `minGIPPath` is satisfied, therefore MTAV is kept becoming candidate function to be gamified. Then, SiaGAM recursively visit the other children of `PSRE`. `DSRD`, being annotated as Automatic function, is deleted. Continuing the recursion, `FSA` and `FWFA`, become candidate functions due to their annotation (i.e. Manual), and `FTA` is discarded being annotated with Low Complexity (`LC`). With this process, based on the filtered AGM processed by SiaGAM, it is also possible to obtain a formula extracted by the AGM. For instance, the following one has been obtained after the application of SiaGAM for the gamification of STS-Tool (Fig. 2) [3,18] (VisiOn EU Project).

$$Acceptance~[\{MTAV,~FSA,~FWFA\},~Users] \geq 80\%$$

This formula represents an acceptance requirement, indicating that to achieve (at least 80%) acceptance of our system by users, we need to consider gamifying functions obtained using SiaGAM, i.e. {*MTAV, FSA, FWFA*} (Fig. 2) [3,18].

4 Case Study and Evaluation

We evaluated SiaGAM by considering the successful results obtained from 5 case studies within EU projects [11,17–19,23]. Analysts had manually selected various subsets of functions to gamify. We started by reusing the original Goal Model of the system (from each case study [11,17–19,23]) as designed in the original

BSRM phase. Models did not show decisions about what functions to gamify, which were made in the original AREA phase. We used such models as input for our enhanced BSRM phase (*Annotation Model*, Sect. 3) and proceeded creating a new AGM. The aim was to compare the 2 resulting models, by checking if SiaGAM is able to support the analyst in finding a subset of functions to gamify similar to the one of the original case study. We used the default configuration of SiaGAM described in Sect. 3. Our case study, including both original results and our results for each of them, is available at [3]. The results of our analysis, as shown in [3] and summarised in Table 1, are based on the comparison of the Original Solution (**OS**) and the new solution, called SiaGAM Solution (**SGS**).

The 5 case studies from EU Research Projects we considered[3] [11,17–19,23] are indicated below (more details in Sect. 2.2) and in Table 1 with the results of our evaluation: **(i)** VisiOn Case Study on *"Gamification for Privacy Requirements Modelling"* (See footnote 3) [18]; **(ii)** PACAS Case Study on *"Gamification for Participatory Architectural Change Management in ATM Systems"* (See footnote 3) [17,23]; **(iii)** SUPERSEDE Case Study on *"Gamification for Collaborative Requirements Prioritization, the DMGame Case"* (See footnote 3) [17,19]; **(iv)** SUM Case Study on *"Sustainable Urban Mobility (SUM)"* (See footnote 3) [11,17]; **(v)** MA4C Case Study on *"Mobility Assistance for Children (MA4C)"* (See footnote 3) [11,17]. The results of our analysis show that SiaGAM is an effective tool for supporting the analysts in this crucial phase: in fact, SiaGAM had been able to derive sets very close to those obtained manually (Table 1). As the main issue found by the analysts was the manual aspect of the subset definition, it is evident that SiaGAM offers valuable help with its semi-automatic guide. According to Ghezzi [8], being our problem undecidable, we aimed at evaluating if SiaGAM is a sound and complete algorithm by calculating its precision and recall [8] in the cases considered. In fact, according to Ghezzi [8], our results "Oracles" stem from the results of the EU Projects considered, and we calculated false positives, false negatives and true positives in relation to the application of SiaGAM and its results. We defined such parameters as follows: **(i)** a *True Positive* (TP) is obtained when SiaGAM selects a task that was selected in the OS case study as well; **(ii)** a *False Positive* (FP) is obtained when SiaGAM selects a task that was not selected in the OS case study; **(iii)** a *False Negative* (FN) is obtained when SiaGAM discards a task that was selected in the OS case study. In Table 1 we show such values calculated per case study.

In Table 1 we indicate also precision and recall calculated as [8]: Precision $= \frac{TP}{(TP+FP)}$ and Recall $= \frac{TP}{(TP+FN)}$. If precision is equal to 1, the algorithm is sound; if recall is equal to 1, the algorithm is complete [8]. According to Table 1, most cases show precision and recall equal to 1. However, we can see that for the PACAS case study, the precision is slightly less than 1. This is because SiaGAM selects one functionality that was not considered in the OS. Conversely, the recall parameter shows a lower value only in the SUM case study: in this case, SiaGAM selects a function that was not considered in the OS.

---

[3] VisiOn, PACAS, SUPERSEDE, SUM and MA4C original Case Studies available at: https://pirasluca.wordpress.com/home/acceptance/case-studies/.

Table 1. Case studies with functions identified ("OS Func.") considered as Oracles [8], functions identified with SiaGAM ("SGS Func.") and related False Positives (FP), False Negatives (FN), True Positives, Precision and Recall.

Case studies	OS Func.	SGS Func.	FP	FN	TP	Precision	Recall
VisiOn[6] [18]	7	7	0	0	7	1	1
PACAS (See footnote 3) [17,23]	5	6	1	0	5	0.83	1
SUPERSEDE (See footnote 3) [17,19]	2	2	0	0	2	1	1
SUM (See footnote 3) [11,17]	4	4	0	1	3	1	0.75
MA4C (See footnote 3) [11,17]	3	3	0	0	3	1	1

Overall, the results of the application of SiaGAM show that, according to most of the cases considered (Table 1), the algorithm and our approach can support *semi-automatically* the identification of the same acceptance requirements and system functionalities to gamify, which had been identified by previous, successful, *manual* analyses (See footnote 3) [11,17–19,23]. Finally, it is important to compare our approach, proposed in this paper, with previous approaches. The main differences are summarised as follow: **(i)** with our approach, the analyst is guided and supported during BSRM in analysing the goal model, representing the system and its functions, characterising them with relevant annotations (suggested and supported by SiaGAM), which can help identifying functions to gamify. Previously, in this phase there was only the "pure" creation of the goal model; **(ii)** with previous approaches, AREA offered only high-level guidelines for identifying functions to gamify and specifying acceptance requirements, which meant the effort was entirely manual. Now, during AREA, the execution of SiaGAM provides the analyst with semi-automatic, flexible and extensible support for identifying functions to gamify; **(iii)** SiaGAM generates the AGM goal model, within the new AREA phase, together with the generation of formal definition of acceptance requirements obtained, including the subset of functions to gamify.

5   Related Work

Available contributions regarding Goal Modeling are various. The work by Jureta et al. [10] proposes a Goal Argumentation Method (GAM) and is composed of three roles. It defines the guidelines of the argumentation and justifications of the choices, while through the reasoning of a goal model it is possible to detect problematic argumentation and check if the information is contained in both the argumentation itself and the model elements. The main difference with our work is that SiaGAM provides guidelines and supporting annotations, which are specific for characterising systems concerning the identification of components to gamify, with the specific purpose of making a system more engaging. Moreover, our approach is extensible and can be applied to different goal modeling contexts and domains. Furthermore, our approach allows the analyst to iteratively use our algorithm to consider different parts of the system to be gamified. The framework PRACTIONIST proposed by Morreale et al. [14] aims at supporting programmers for the definition of Belief-Desire-Intention (BDI) agents: it captures the purpose of the software from the system goals and creates a Goal Model; then, relations between goals are analysed to determine if goals can be achieved. SiaGAM is not exclusively agent-oriented, it is oriented towards software characterisation from the analyst perspective. User characterisation also plays an essential role for the identification of functions to gamify. Furthermore, SiaGAM analyses goals differently working with the definition of a probability value in the Annotation Model and a list of annotations characterising the software and its usage.

The RationalGRL framework by Van Zee et al. [24] is structured in 4 separate phases: an argumentation phase, which elicits requirements through the definition of arguments; a translation phase, where arguments are translated into a Goal Model; a goal modelling phase, in which stakeholders evaluate the model; a final update phase for translating the model into GRL models, for comparison with argumentation elements. Our approach differs under various aspects. Firstly, we do not generate the goal model from argumentation. Instead, we support the creation of a goal model of the system with a graphical editor, and support analysis and annotations of the model for functionalities characterisation. Furthermore, we also support the analyst with semi-automated analysis provided by SiaGAM.

6   Conclusion

Gamification has clearly proved an effective technique for motivating users to use software systems. Systematic Goal-Oriented Requirements Engineering (GORE) activities have been proposed for supporting engineers to gamify software systems, and have been recognised as effective and useful by requirements analysts in different EU Research Projects. However, analysts have also indicated difficulty in performing some of such activities, highlighting the need for further support.

In this paper we identified such activities, provided related lessons learned, and proposed a solution for further supporting analysts in relation to one of these activities: the identification of software components to gamify. This is a crucial aspect as the gamification of a full software system can be expensive and could give unexpected results. Therefore, to reduce efforts and costs for organisations, the exact identification of functionalities to be gamified is necessary. The solution we devised in this paper is the algorithm SiaGAM (*Supporting the individuation, analysis, and GAMification* of software components), which guides and supports the analyst semi-automatically concerning the next crucial aspects: **(i)** representation of the software to gamify as a Goal Model; **(ii)** characterisation of software functions with the support of representative and decisive qualities; **(iii)** analysis and suggestion of candidate system functions to gamify, based on decisive criteria identified; **(iv)** extensible and iterative approach in terms of qualities considered and criteria defined; **(v)** generation of Acceptance Requirements with functionalities selected to be gamified. To evaluate SiaGAM, we applied it to 5 case studies from EU projects, where requirements analysts had successfully identified system functions to gamify *manually*. Then we compared their results with the ones we obtained using SiaGAM. We found that SiaGAM is effective in supporting the analyst in *semi-automatically* identifying software functions to gamify, as the functions to gamify derived by SiaGAM were in most cases analogous to the ones selected *manually* by the analysts.

As future work, due to the flexibility and configurability of SiaGAM, we will consider using it to support the identification of software components for other GORE purposes. For instance, for the identification of set of functionalities that are candidates to be secured, or to be made GDPR compliant. We will also perform more advanced evaluation, by involving analysts, for considering also further aspects (e.g., ease of use, annotations set adequacy). Furthermore, thanks to the other contribution of this paper (activities and lessons learned), we will consider providing further support to analysts by improving the other GORE gamification activities which were found useful but requiring further support.

References

1. Bassanelli, S., Vasta, N., Bucchiarone, A., Marconi, A.: Gamification for behavior change: a scientometric review. Elsevier Acta Psychol. J. (2022)
2. Calabrese, F.: Gamification with the Agon framework: a case study on privacy requirements modeling. Bachelor thesis, University of Trento, Italy (2018)
3. Calabrese, F., Piras, L., Giorgini, P.: Models and dataset related to Case Study and Evaluation, respectively. https://data.mendeley.com/datasets/6s4c87c494/4 and https://data.mendeley.com/datasets/rczj54927m/1
4. Chung, L., Nixon, B., Yu, E., Mylopoulos, J.: Non-Functional Requirements in Software Engineering. Springer, New York (2012)
5. Deterding, S.: The lens of intrinsic skill atoms: a method for gameful design. Hum.-Comput. Interact. J. **30**(3–4), 294–335 (2015)
6. Deterding, S., Dixon, D., Khaled, R., Nacke, L.: From game design elements to gamefulness: defining gamification. In: Proceedings of the 15th International Academic MindTrek Conference: Envisioning Future Media Environments, pp. 9–15. ACM (2011)
7. Fernández, D., Legaki, N., Hamari, J.: Avatar identities and climate change action in video games: analysis of mitigation and adaptation practices. In: CHI Conference on Human Factors in Computing Systems, pp. 1–18 (2022)
8. Ghezzi, C.: Correction. In: Being a Researcher, pp. C1–C1. Springer, Cham (2021). https://doi.org/10.1007/978-3-030-45157-8_7
9. Herzig, P., Ameling, M., Schill, A.: A generic platform for enterprise gamification. In: 2012 Joint Working IEEE/IFIP Conference on Software Architecture and European Conference on Software Architecture, pp. 219–233. IEEE (2012)
10. Jureta, I.J., Faulkner, S., Schobbens, P.: Clear justification of modeling decisions for goal-oriented requirements engineering. Requirements Eng. **13**(2), 87–115 (2008)

11. Kazhamiakin, R., et al.: Using gamification to incentivize sustainable urban mobility. In: 2015 IEEE First International Smart Cities Conference (ISC2), pp. 1–6. IEEE, New York (2015)

12. Koivisto, J., Hamari, J.: The rise of motivational information systems: a review of gamification research. Int. J. Inf. Manag. **45**, 191–210 (2019)

13. Li, F.L., et al.: Non-functional requirements as qualities, with a spice of ontology. In: International Requirements Engineering Conference (RE), pp. 293–302. IEEE, New York (2014)

14. Morreale, V., Bonura, S., Francaviglia, G., Centineo, F., Cossentino, M., Gaglio, S.: Goal-oriented development of BDI agents: the Practionist approach. In: International Conference on Intelligent Agent Technology, pp. 66–72. IEEE, New York (2006)

15. Mylopoulos, J., Chung, L., Nixon, B.: Representing and using nonfunctional requirements: a process-oriented approach. Trans. Softw. Eng. **18**(6), 483–497 (1992)

16. Peng, C., Xi, N., Hong, Z., Hamari, J.: Acceptance of wearable technology: a meta-analysis. In: Hawaii International Conference on System Sciences (HICSS). (2022)

17. Piras, L.: Agon: a Gamification-Based Framework for Acceptance Requirements. Ph.D. thesis, University of Trento, Italy (2018)

18. Piras, L., Calabrese, F., Giorgini, P.: Applying acceptance requirements to requirements modeling tools via gamification: a case study on privacy and security. In: Grabis, J., Bork, D. (eds.) PoEM 2020. LNBIP, vol. 400, pp. 366–376. Springer, Cham (2020). https://doi.org/10.1007/978-3-030-63479-7_25

19. Piras, L., Dellagiacoma, D., Perini, A., Susi, A., Giorgini, P., Mylopoulos, J.: Design thinking and acceptance requirements for designing gamified software. In: International Conference on Research Challenges in Information Science (RCIS), pp. 1–12. IEEE (2019)

20. Piras, L., Giorgini, P., Mylopoulos, J.: Models, dataset, case studies, prototype and glossary of Agon (an Acceptance Requirements Framework). https://pirasluca.wordpress.com/home/acceptance/ and https://data.mendeley.com/datasets/56w858dr9j/1

21. Piras, L., Giorgini, P., Mylopoulos, J.: Acceptance requirements and their gamification solutions. In: International Requirements Engineering Conference (RE), pp. 365-370. IEEE (2016)

22. Piras, L., Paja, E., Cuel, R., Ponte, D., Giorgini, P., Mylopoulos, J.: Gamification solutions for software acceptance: a comparative study of requirements engineering and organizational behavior techniques. In: IEEE International Conference on Research Challenges in Information Science (RCIS), pp. 255–265. IEEE (2017)

23. Piras, L., Paja, E., Giorgini, P., Mylopoulos, J.: Goal models for acceptance requirements analysis and gamification design. In: Mayr, H.C., Guizzardi, G., Ma, H., Pastor, O. (eds.) ER 2017. LNCS, vol. 10650, pp. 223–230. Springer, Cham (2017). https://doi.org/10.1007/978-3-319-69904-2_18

24. van Zee, M., Marosin, D., Bex, F., Ghanavati, S.: RationalGRL: a framework for rationalizing goal models using argument diagrams. In: Comyn-Wattiau, I., Tanaka, K., Song, I.-Y., Yamamoto, S., Saeki, M. (eds.) ER 2016. LNCS, vol. 9974, pp. 553–560. Springer, Cham (2016). https://doi.org/10.1007/978-3-319-46397-1_43

25. Zichermann, G., Cunningham, C.: Gamification by Design: Implementing Game Mechanics in Web and Mobile Apps. O'Reilly Media, Inc. (2011)

Modeling Enterprise Architectures

Historization of Enterprise Architecture Models via Enterprise Architecture Knowledge Graphs

Robin Bråtfors[1], Simon Hacks[2](✉), and Dominik Bork[3]

[1] KTH Royal Institute of Technology, Stockholm, Sweden
bratfors@kth.se
[2] University of Southern Denmark, Odense, Denmark
shacks@mmmi.sdu.dk
[3] TU Wien, Business Informatics Group, Vienna, Austria
dominik.bork@tuwien.ac.at

Abstract. Enterprise Architecture (EA) is the discipline that aims to provide a holistic view of the enterprise by explicating business and IT alignment from the perspectives of high-level corporate strategy down to daily operations and network infrastructures. EAs are consequently complex as they compose and integrate many aspects on different architecture layers. A recent proposal to cope with this complexity and to make EAs amenable to automated and intuitive visual analysis is the transformation of EA models into EA Knowledge Graphs. A remaining limitation of these approaches is that they perceive the EA to be static, i.e., they represent and analyze EAs at a single point in time. In the paper at hand, we introduce a historization concept, a prototypical implementation, and a performance analysis for how EAs can be represented and processed to enable the analysis of their evolution.

Keywords: Enterprise architecture · Historical analysis · Knowledge graph

1 Introduction

IT and Communication Technology (ICT) is a crucial part of most modern organizations, and many resources are invested to make them more efficient. However, to achieve the full benefits of those investments, the business strategy and the ICT of the organization need to be aligned, which can be achieved by means of Enterprise Architecture (EA) [1]. EA is a discipline that aims to give a comprehensive view on the architecture of an organization, i.e., the structure, processes, and infrastructure of the organization [2]. An EA provides a holistic view of the enterprise and lays out the insight to balance different requirements and turn theoretical corporate strategy into real daily operations.

© IFIP International Federation for Information Processing 2022
Published by Springer Nature Switzerland AG 2022
B. S. Barn and K. Sandkuhl (Eds.): PoEM 2022, LNBIP 456, pp. 51–65, 2022.
https://doi.org/10.1007/978-3-031-21488-2_4

There is no agreement on an exact definition of EA, the literature shows varying definitions [3]. This uncertainty can add challenges when it comes to the quality assessment of EA, as different definitions naturally have different metrics for what is good and what is bad. Providing a standardized way to measure the quality of EA would therefore help with improving that quality and clarify the definition of EA. EA debt is a concept introduced by Hacks et al. [4], which depicts how much the current state of an EA deviates from a hypothetical ideal state. The extent of that deviation naturally indicates the quality of the EA.

But to accurately ascertain that deviation one needs to be able to measure the EA debt. A way to do that was proposed by Salentin and Hacks [5] with the concept of EA smells. These smells are derived from the concept of code smells and, in similar fashion, highlight specific flaws within an EA. Providing additional ways to detect these smells would help with measuring EA debt, which in turn would help with discerning the quality of EA.

Analyzing EA models as graphs is one out of four main categories of EA analysis proposed by Barbosa [6]. The graph's nodes and edges represent the components and relationships of an EA, respectively, and this sort of graph representation enables more ways to assess the quality of the EAs through graph-based analysis methods and algorithms. Graph-based analysis does not need to be overtly complicated to achieve some effect. Just the transformation of EAs into graph structure grants some visual analysis capabilities that a stakeholder can manually utilize [7,8]. That is not to say that graph-based analysis cannot be more complex or automatized. For example, further analysis of graphs can be implemented with the use of filter and search methods [9].

Smajevic et al. [10] created the CM2KG platform [11] that is capable of transforming conceptual models into Knowledge Graphs which enable graph-based analysis of EA models [10,12]. It transforms EA models into graphs, which enable automatic analysis to detect flaws and points of improvement within the EAs. Further work on the CM2KG platform allowed it to automatically detect EA smells in transformed EA models [12] and to realize a plugin to the widely used open EA modeling platform Archi [13,14]. The transformation of EA models to graphs (e.g., using the CM2KG platform) enables the realization of a generic solution in the sense that model quality measures, like EA smells, can be defined on the generic level of graph structures. The generic metrics can then be evaluated on any EA representation, including ArchiMate. As the field of EA is packed with different modeling languages and frameworks, a generic and modeling language agnostic solution is favorable. This is also the value of the approach compared to the analysis functionality offered by EA tools which are always bound to the specific EA modeling language at hand.

While the previous works, particularly the CM2KG platform, show the feasibility of transforming EA models into graph structures and using these EA graphs for analysis, they also come with severe limitations. Most importantly for the scope of our work, they considered only one state of the EA (i.e., the graph) [8,9,15]. In other words, the changes resulting in an evolution of an EA are neither considered not amenable to analysis. Even professional tools often just provide solely basic capabilities to analyze/query the evolution of EA and then are bound to their proprietary model. Thus, the identification of EA smells, that can be identified by comparing different states of the EA, is not possible. For example, to identify a *Big Bang*, a strategy where large changes to a system are made at once instead of in several smaller steps, can be just identified by analyzing the delta between different states of an EA. Adding historization to graphs can provide the needed information by enabling an evolutionary perspective on EA analysis. Such a perspective allows for historical analysis and gives enterprise architects automated and programmatic insight into the evolution of an EA. To be able to analyze the evolution of EA models, we deduce the following two research questions:

RQ1: What is an appropriate means to represent EA models for historical analysis?

RQ2: How performant is the historical analysis of even large EA Knowledge Graphs?

The rest of this work is structured as follows: Background and related works are discussed in Sect. 2. Section 3 proposes a concept for the historization of EA graphs. An implementation of a platform for historical EA graphs is introduced in Sect. 4. Performance and efficacy of the platform are evaluated in Sect. 5. Eventually, we close this paper with a discussion of contributions and limitations in Sect. 6 and concluding remarks in Sect. 7.

2   Background and Related Work

2.1   EA Debts and Smells

In software development, Technical Debt was introduced by Cunningham [16] as a metaphor for the potential cost caused by refactoring code that is not quite right when it is created. The metaphor is inspired by financial debt, where the debt is the future work that has to be done to improve the code.

Technical Debt allows organizations to handle quality issues related to their application landscape, but it does not extend to other domains of an organization. Hacks et al. [4] proposed to combine the Technical Debt metaphor with EA into what they coined EA debt. EA debt aims to provide a more holistic view of the organization by not only measuring the quality of software but also measuring the quality of all the other domains and thus exposing faults within the enterprise. They demonstrated the use of EA debt by giving examples of how it can highlight problems that would be costly to solve at the moment but need to be solved at some point, such as dependency issues [4]. The EA debt can make management aware of the problem so that it can be solved as soon as the dependency is met, instead of potentially forgetting about it.

Schmid [17] presents some shortcomings of Technical Debt, e.g., that the debt needs to be considered with respect to future evolution, since the development might be impacted by the current implementation and structure. Another shortcoming is the fact that a certain debt might not have an actual impact on the development, this potential debt is just structural issues and needs to be differentiated from effective debt that actually impacts the development.

Thus, a goal of EA debt is to provide relevant factors for estimating the architecture's quality to increase awareness and communication about its improvement [5]. However, to accomplish that, EA debt would need to be measured. Salentin and Hacks [5] have proposed to transfer the concept of Code Smells [18] to the EA domain in what they call EA smells. Accordingly, Technical Debt can be seen as a subset of EA debt [4] and thus many EA smells are just direct translations from already existing Code Smells [5]. EA smells can be considered a metric to measure the amount EA debt in an EA [5], representing the symptoms of EA debt and thus increasing awareness of potential deficits in an EA. We can differentiate two basic categories of EA smells regarding their input. The first and biggest category are EA smells, that analyze an EA based on a single state such as *Bloated Service* or *Cyclic Dependency*. The second category demands information about the evolution of an EA to be able to analyze if the EA is flawed. Those EA smells are for example *Big Bang* or *Data-Driven Migration*. For the latter class of EA smells, we are missing means to effectively identify them yet. To close this gap, this work proposes an underlying graph structure that will enable the identification of such EA smells.

2.2   Graph-Based Analysis of EA Models

Graph-based analysis is one of four main categories of EA analysis proposed by Barbosa et al. in [6]. In this approach the architectures are represented as graphs where EA components and relations are transformed into nodes and edges, respectively. Once transformed, such a graph enables the application of many existing graph-based algorithms and metrics [10].

Panas et al. [8] introduced an architecture that dealt purely with the visualization of a model using a graph-based approach. While its visualization does provide some clarity, the user has to process most of the information by their own, which does not scale well for large and complex models. Chan et al. [9] presented a visual graph-based tool to analyze an enterprise, but this tool allows for more interactive exploration of the data. The user can use the tool to navigate, filter, and search the graph to process complex graph structures. Naranjo et al. [15] implemented another visual analysis tool, called PRIMROSe. They wanted to utilize visualization on the basis that the human visual system is a naturally great analysis tool, with the caveat that the complexity of EA models requires additional aid to properly inspect and find information about them.

The common trend through these works is that none of them looked at the history of graphs. Implementing a historization of the graphs on top of the benefits of graph-based analysis would increase the value for enterprise architects. All discussed works are further constrained to a specific kind of data input, which could be improved. Creating a generic solution that allows for several kinds of EA models to be used and analyzed increases its value.

First steps toward graph-based analysis of conceptual models were proposed in [10,11] with the CM2KG platform, which has been recently specialized for the model-based construction of EA Knowledge Graphs (EAKG) [13] and integrated as a plugin to the Archi platform [14]. Their solution transforms EA models into EAKGs to enable the execution of graph analysis metrics like betweenness and centrality. The usage of KGs also allows for automatic, efficient detection of EA smells even in large EA graphs with the help of semantic KG queries [12]. What was lacking in the original proposal of CM2KG, and what is the focus of this work, is the representation of the evolution of EAs and how this evolution can be represented in an EAKG and made accessible to historical analysis. We plan to incorporate that feature also in the newly developed EAKG toolkit [14].

2.3   Graph Historization

Nuha [19] evaluated two different approaches to store the historical data of graph databases: a *delta-based* approach and a *snapshot-based* approach. A combination of the two approaches was then implemented to utilize the strengths of each approach. This combination only created a snapshot whenever the difference between versions got too large and the reconstruction time of a version took too long. The evaluation of the solutions was performance-based and covered the execution time of storing new data, the checkout time of reconstructing and retrieving a past version, and the storage cost.

Other graph versioning solutions also utilized the delta-based approach [20, 21]. Castellort and Laurent [22] aimed to separate the versioned data from the operational data of graphs by storing the versioned data in a *revision graph*. Every node and relation in the *data graph* is represented by a node in the revision graph called revision element. These revision elements are a part of linked lists that represent the history of each data graph element at certain points in time. Any transaction will create a new revision and any data graph element that is modified during that transaction will get a new revision element in their linked list. Conversely, unmodified data graph elements keep their last revision element.

3   Toward Historization for EA Models

The purpose of this work is to conceptualize the transformation of EA models into a KG that preserves and represents the historical information found in EA models over time (cf. RQ1). With such a conceptualization, we aim to develop an IT artifact that enables users to view and interact with the historical graph through visual analysis and queries in a performant manner (cf. RQ2). Such an artifact will thus provide practitioners in the field of EA a generic solution to track, store, and analyze their EA models over a period of time by means of EA smells. The artifact might also create avenues for new research in the field that could further improve architects' ability to enhance their EAs. Accordingly, we have identified the following objectives. Any implementation of the historization would need to:

O1 ... be *performing* well for realistic model sizes. If a system is not responsive enough users might opt to stop using it. Research shows that users maximally tolerate a loading time between 2 and 3 s [23, 24]. Consequently, our solution should not exceed a querying time of 2 s.

O2 ... be *generic* in the sense that it is independent from any particular EA modeling language. We therefore aim to conceptualize a graph format that can store the historical data of an EA independently of the concrete EA modeling language.

O3 ... *integrate* into the existing CM2KG platform to benefit from its existing capabilities such as import from different conceptual models, transformation into graph structures, and graph-based analysis [10, 12].

O4 ... provide users with an *intuitive* way to represent, interact, and query historical states of an EA model.

3.1 Graph Structure

To realize Objective 2, we rely on a GraphML representation of the EA model which has been used by the CM2KG platform since its conception [10]. This design decision also eases the integration of the historization with CM2KG (Objective 3). GraphML is standardized and modeling language-agnostic. Since the graph transformation of the tool converts the EA models into GraphML, there was already a large incentive to stick with that format.

The most important extensions from the original structure are related to the question, how to represent historical EA versions in the graph, to keep track on the *micro evolution* of a single element of the EA model (e.g., adding, removing, or altering an element). We propose to add properties to every element of the graph (cf. "Additional properties" of a_i, b_j, t_k in Fig. 1). The purpose of these properties is to track the modifications of an EA element (i.e., *when?* and *how?*), which is a necessary information to be able to identify history-based EA smells. Since these properties are not inherent to the EA models themselves, they have to be inserted during the model to graph transformation. The properties are further defined in Sect. 3.3, their implementation is reported in Sect. 4.

3.2 Storage

The design choices when it comes to the storage of the transformed graph are not inherently important to the problem at hand since they do not overly affect the requirements of the design. The only vital part is that the historical data is stored in some way that differentiates each version of the model, since that is of course mandatory for historization.

The two major ways to store graph histories are the *snapshot-based* and the *delta-based* approaches. In this work, a design that implements both approaches is satisfactory by storing the change date and the actual changes (cf. "Additional properties" in Fig. 1) as well as each complete graph representation of the EA model's version and their evolutionary relation (cf. m_i in Fig. 1). This is necessary to keep track on the *macro evolution* of the EA model (i.e., the aggregated set of micro evolutions performed in a single iteration). The only drawback of implementing both is the increased storage space. This was weighed towards the

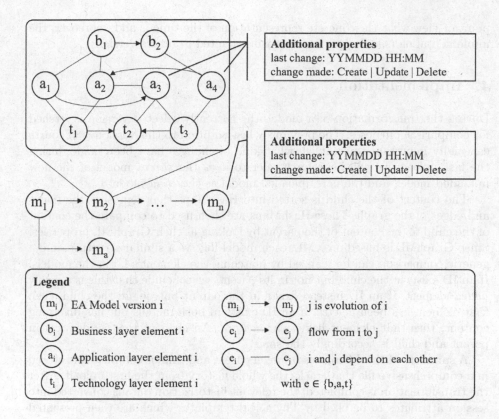

Fig. 1. Conceptual representation of realizing historization for EAKGs

benefit of having fast access to any requested version and the capability to easily show differences between versions of the entire model.

3.3   Historization Properties

To sort and catalog different chronological versions of a model, which is necessary to realize historization and create useful insights for EA smell analysis, those versions need a standardized property to differentiate and contextualize them from each other. The simplest way to implement this is by adding a date property to every element of the model, including the model itself. This property should then be updated each time its respective element gets modified. A property that marks the kind of modification that was performed on the element is also important to be able to efficiently sort and query the history. For simplicity reasons, all modifications to the model are identified and tracked each time the model gets uploaded to our artifact. Of course, a more detailed differentiation between the time of the actual change and the upload of the changes can be made. However, to demonstrate our approach, it is solely important to identify the order of the changes. Consequently, it makes no difference from a conceptual point of view what the concrete representation of the time is and, moreover, the implementation (see Sect. 4) can be easily adapted in future versions.

4 Implementation

During the transformation of a model, the currently selected version is fetched for comparison purposes. The previously last addition to this version is of course especially important to establish what kind of changes have been made during the last upload; we will henceforth refer to it as the *parent* model of the new uploaded model, and the new uploaded model as the *child* model.

The content of the child is sorted into HashMaps that represent the nodes and edges of the graph. These HashMaps are then used to compare the content of the child to the content of the parent by looking at their GraphML properties. Since GraphML is based on XML, each model follows a similar structure, and a generic comparison can be realized by matching the element's ID in the models. If an ID exists in the child but not in its parent, we conclude that this is a newly *added* element. If an ID instead exists in the parent but not in the child, then that element has been *deleted*. If an ID exists in both models but has diverging content, then that element has been *modified*. An element that is identical in parent and child is accordingly the *same*.

A summary of the differences between parent and child is compiled and stored in a comprehensive file that tracks the whole history from the first upload. After the transformation is completed, the relevant historization data is converted into session attributes to be used by Thymeleaf templates which are then presented to the user to interact with.

Interface. The interface of the artifact consists of four areas: *history menu*, *history visualization*, *graph content*, and *querying*.

The *history menu* shows basic information about the history as a whole such as the number of branches, the total number of versions, and the date of the last update to the history. It also offers the option to upload a new version of the model as a new branch or as a continuation of an existing branch. The new graph gets added as a child to the currently selected graph. There are also options to visually compare the currently selected graph to either its parent, the first graph of its branch, or the last graph of its branch (cf. Fig. 2a).

The *history visualization* area shows a visual representation of the history, enabling the user to view and interact with the model history. Each node represents a version of the model and in the baseline view they all have a color to indicate if they belong to the same branch. When hovering over a node, a tooltip appears and provides some information about the version in question, such as the differences to its parent and when it was uploaded. There are some buttons to ease the navigation through large histories. When clicking the buttons, the view instantly adapts to either the first graph, the last graph, or the currently selected graph. A graph can be selected by clicking on its node. The user can also view any version of the history by entering its ID in the search bar.

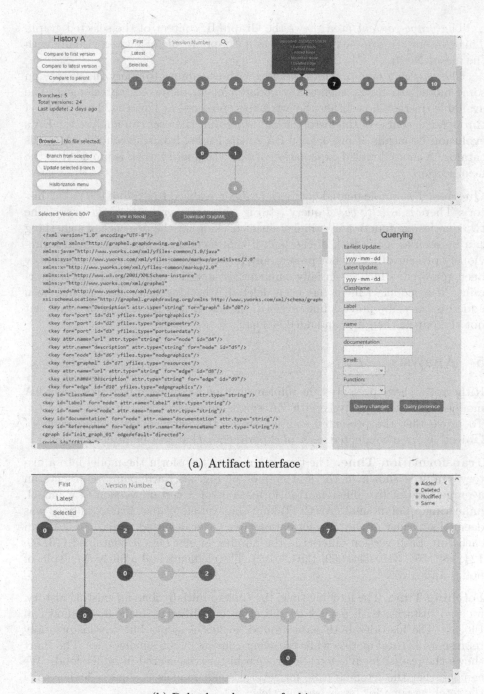

(a) Artifact interface

(b) Delta-based query of a history

Fig. 2. Screenshots of the developed artifact

The *graph content* area shows the GraphML content of the selected graph. This content can also be downloaded as a GraphML file or viewed visually with the aid of Neo4j.

The *querying area* provides the user with the ability to query the history on some model attributes, such as the update time or name of graph element. The available queries show either the attributes' presence or how they have changed through the course of the historization. Moreover, the user can analyze the EA's evolution by means of pre-defined EA smells loaded from the central EA smells catalog. A more detailed explanation of how the queries work is provided in the next section.

Queries. Two implemented queries have been realized to explore the model history. There is a *delta-based* query (cf. Fig. 2b) and a *presence-based* query. The two queries are functionally similar since checking for the presence of something can be seen as a sub-task of checking if that something has changed. If a previously present object is not present any longer, then that object has obviously been removed, which essentially summarizes how the delta-based query determines if a model element has been deleted. Checking if an element has been added is the same process but reversed, namely if it is present in the child but not the parent then it is an added element.

5   Analysis

Hitherto, we have presented the implementation to realize a historization of EA models for further analysis with EA smells addressing the Objectives 2 to 4. To prove that the presented solution meets the performance requirements of Objective 1, we conducted a set of experiments, that will be discussed next.

Transformation Time. The time required to transform the model into a history graph is shown in the scatter plot of Fig. 3a. Each point represents an average time of five different transformations of a certain version of a model, indicating a polynomial growth. Taking the average of just five executions was deemed sufficient as the transformation time never deviated more than 5% from each run. Each version differed in the number of elements it contained (16, 59, 124, 189, 254, 319, 644, 969, 1294, 1619). The elements had a fairly even split of nodes and edges.

Fetching Time. The fetching time, the time to initially load an existing history, for two histories with similar overall sizes but different make-up is shown in Fig. 3b. The histories both have around 46,000 elements but one history only represents 32 total models while the other consists of 506 smaller ones. The chart shows the results for five fetches for each history, measured in milliseconds. We can see that the fetching time for several small models is slightly higher than the fetching time for fewer large models.

Querying Time. Figure 3c compares two implemented queries when executed on a history with around 140,000 elements. The *delta query* explored the difference between two evolutions of the EA model, i.e., it identified all changes

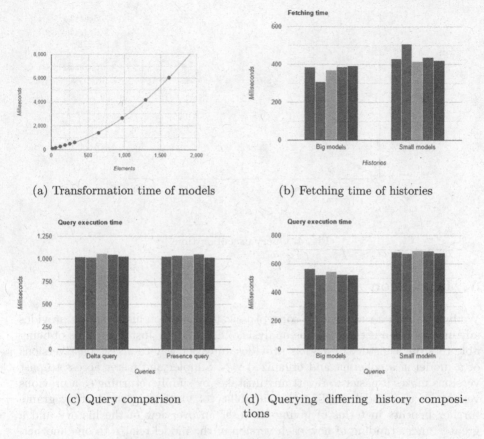

(a) Transformation time of models

(b) Fetching time of histories

(c) Query comparison

(d) Querying differing history compositions

Fig. 3. Transformation and querying analysis

between the two model evolutions. The *presence query* queried a single EA model evolution for the presence of a certain element. Therefore, each element in a single EA model evolution was assessed for a certain property and returned if found. The chart indicates that the two queries have essentially identical execution times.

Next, we elaborate the influence of the model size on the query times. Therefore, we use the same query for different sizes of models. This is illustrated in Fig. 3d. Both queried histories had about 46,000 elements in total, but one history only represented 32 models while the other consisted of 506 smaller ones. The chart shows that the history with more and smaller graphs had longer execution times when queried.

Figure 4 shows the execution time of the delta-based query and how it increases based on the element count of the history it is querying. We can derive from the figure a linear relationship between the query execution time and the element count of the queried model.

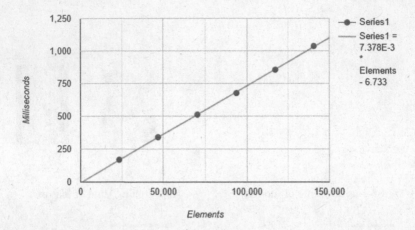

Fig. 4. Query execution time

6   Discussion

We believe even a rudimentary conceptualization of graph historization provides advantages when it comes to the analysis of EA models. Just the means of being able to store a history of models provides an easier way to access past versions of a model in a coherent and organized way. Simpler and faster access to past versions makes it easier to revert any mistakes by simply returning to a previous version of the model. Adding the capability of visualizing the history grants further benefits in terms of giving the user an overview of the history and a greater understanding of how each version of the model relates to one another. Future empirical research with our artifact will of course attest these claims.

The currently implemented queries in this work provide visual clarity of how the status of an attribute or node changed over time to ease the analysis via EA smells. Furthermore, the added functionality of the historization being generic means that a greater number of users might find the artifact helpful, especially if they are locked into a certain modeling platform and cannot for some reason switch.

The performance could be improved in a number of areas, especially the transformation time of models. The transformation time has a polynomial growth in relation to the number of model elements. The bulk of the time is spent on sorting the content of the child and then comparing that content to the content of its parent. Given a proper sorting of the content, the time complexity of the comparison should be no higher than linear since HashMaps are used to store the data, and the complexity for lookups in HashMaps is constant.

It can be argued that this polynomial growth can cause issues, due to long waiting times for large models. However, classically, the transformation of a single EA model evolution will only happen once, as afterwards the graph is already stored in the database. With that in mind, the transformation time should be tolerable for users, especially as querying on the graph representation will be performed significantly more often.

From the results, we see that the number of graphs in a history had a slightly bigger impact on the execution time of fetching and querying compared to the individual graph sizes. Accordingly, the artifact is in its current state more suitable for large models with few updates than for smaller models that might be updated more frequently. Update frequency and model size are not necessarily linked, but it might be something to take into consideration from a storage perspective since both approaches to a history will result in similar history sizes.

The functionality that should see the most use is most likely the querying of the history since varying the attribute input of the query will grant different insights. With that in mind, it is beneficial, that the query execution time grows linearly as it should stay within a tolerable range for any history with less than 500,000 elements (i.e., models far exceeding the size of typical EAs). Since the implemented queries inspect every element in the history for a certain property, it would be difficult to improve the execution time any further as long as the data structure becomes not optimized towards certain expected queries, e.g., building sets of nodes with same properties.

7   Conclusion

With this work, we aimed to contribute toward historical analysis of EA models and to provide a solution that allows a satisfactory analysis with respect to performance and efficacy.

This overall aim has been detailed into four different objectives. Objective 1 demanded that the solution should not exceed a loading time of 2 s. This objective has been partly realized, depending on the size of the input models. If the size of the model exceeds approximately 750 elements, the transformation time will be larger than 2 s with polynomial growth. However, this is still acceptable, as a single EA model evolution only needs to be transformed once and then can be queried several times by the enterprise architects. Thus, the analyst will query the model more often and our solution performs well for querying. Even for large models with more than 100,000 elements the execution time remains around 1 s.

Objective 2 is realized by the graph-presentation that is shown in Fig. 1, and Objective 3 by the integration of the solution into the existing CM2KG platform. Finally, we developed a graphical user interface that eases the exploration of the solution (cf. Sect. 4).

We believe this research establishes a foundation for several streams of future research. Firstly, it enables us in future to detect EA smells that we were not able to detect before, due to missing information. For instance, we can now detect the *Big Bang* EA smell by analyzing the number of changes between different evolutions of an EA. From a theoretical viewpoint, we want to involve enterprise architects in an empirical evaluation of our solution. This will add insights with respect to the usability, ease of use, and intention to use of our solution by practitioners. From a technical point of view, we aim to further experiment with the artifact and different implementations of transformation, fetching, and querying algorithms in order to further improve the usability. Hitherto, we have solely conducted a technical evaluation of our approach. A deeper evaluation of the functionality is missing, especially we aim for a discussion with practitioners about their concrete needs and foreseen questions towards the historization of EA models. Eventually, we intend to deploy the artifact publicly to ease testing and use by the enterprise modeling and enterprise architecture community. Besides, the source code is available on github[1].

Finally, we want to make our research easily integrate-able into enterprise architects daily working live. Therefore, we aim to integrate our approach into wide-spread tooling such as Archi [14]. Thus, the analysis capabilities will be available directly at the place in which the architect is conducting the modeling. Moreover, due to our agnostic approach relying on Knowledge Graphs, our approach can be easily integrated with existing tooling and also enables analysis of EA smells in proprietary EA model notations of existing tool vendors.

Acknowledgements. This work has been partially funded through the Erasmus+ KA220-HED project Digital Platform Enterprise (project no.: 2021-1-RO01-KA220-HED-000027576) and the Austrian Research Promotion Agency via the Austrian Competence Center for Digital Production (contract no.: 854187).

References

1. Olsen, D.H.: Enterprise architecture management challenges in the norwegian health sector. Procedia Comput. Sci. **121**, 637–645 (2017)
2. Lankhorst, M., et al.: Enterprise Architecture at Work: Modelling, Communication, and Analysis. Springer (2017). https://doi.org/10.1007/978-3-642-29651-2
3. Saint-Louis, P., Morency, M.C., Lapalme, J.: Defining enterprise architecture: a systematic literature review. In: 2017 IEEE 21st International Enterprise Distributed Object Computing Workshop (EDOCW), pp. 41–49 (2017)
4. Hacks, S., Höfert, H., Salentin, J., Yeong, Y.C., Lichter, H.: Towards the definition of enterprise architecture debts. In: 2019 IEEE 23rd International Enterprise Distributed Object Computing Workshop (EDOCW), pp. 9–16 (2019)
5. Salentin, J., Hacks, S.: Towards a catalog of enterprise architecture smells. In: 15th International Conference on Wirtschaftsinformatik (WI) (2020)
6. Barbosa, A., Santana, A., Hacks, S., von Stein, N.: A taxonomy for enterprise architecture analysis research. In: 21st International Conference on Enterprise Information Systems (2019)
7. Garg, A., Kazman, R., Chen, H.M.: Interface descriptions for enterprise architecture. Sci. Comput. Program. **61**, 4–15 (2006)
8. Panas, T., Lincke, R., Löwe, W.: Online-configuration of software visualizations with vizz3d. In: Proceedings of the 2005 ACM Symposium on Software Visualization. SoftVis 2005, pp. 173–182 (2005)
9. Chan, Y.H., Keeton, K., Ma, K.L.: Interactive visual analysis of hierarchical enterprise data. In: 2010 IEEE 12th Conference on Commerce and Enterprise Computing, pp. 180–187 (2010)

---

[1] https://github.com/rbratfors/CM2KG.

10. Smajevic, M., Bork, D.: Towards graph-based analysis of enterprise architecture models. In: Ghose, A., Horkoff, J., Silva S., Vítor, E., Parsons, J., Evermann, J. (eds.) ER 2021. LNCS, vol. 13011, pp. 199–209. Springer, Cham (2021). https://doi.org/10.1007/978-3-030-89022-3_17

11. Smajevic, M., Bork, D.: From conceptual models to knowledge graphs: a generic model transformation platform. In: ACM/IEEE International Conference on Model Driven Engineering Languages and Systems Companion, MODELS 2021 Companion, pp. 610–614. IEEE (2021)

12. Smajevic, M., Hacks, S., Bork, D.: Using knowledge graphs to detect enterprise architecture smells. In: The Practice of Enterprise Modeling - 14th IFIP WG 8.1 Working Conference, PoEM 2021, Proceedings, pp. 48–63. (2021)

13. Glaser, P.L., Ali, S.J., Sallinger, E., Bork, D.: Model-based construction of enterprise architecture knowledge graphs. In: 26th International EDOC Conference (EDOC'2022) (2022). (in press)

14. Glaser, P.L., Ali, S.J., Sallinger, E., Bork, D.: Exploring enterprise architecture knowledge graphs in archi: the eakg toolkit. In: 26th International EDOC Conference (EDOC'2022) - Tools and Demos (2022). (in press)

15. Naranjo, D., Sánchez, M.E., Villalobos, J.: Primrose: a graph-based approach for enterprise architecture analysis. In: International Conference on Enterprise Information Systems (2014)

16. Cunningham, W.: The wycash portfolio management system. OOPS Messenger **4**, 29–30 (1992)

17. Schmid, K.: On the limits of the technical debt metaphor some guidance on going beyond. In: 4th International Workshop on Managing Technical Debt, pp. 63–66 (2013)

18. Fowler, M.: Refactoring: Improving the Design of Existing Code. Addison-Wesley (2018)

19. Nuha, M.U.: Data versioning for graph databases. Master's thesis, TU Delft Electrical Engineering (2019)

20. Gómez, A., Cabot, J., Wimmer, M.: Temporalemf: a temporal metamodeling framework. In: 37th International Conference, ER 2018, Xi'an, China, 22–25 Oct 2018, Proceedings, pp. 365–381 (2018)

21. Vijitbenjaronk, W.D., Lee, J., Suzumura, T., Tanase, G.: Scalable time-versioning support for property graph databases. In: 2017 IEEE International Conference on Big Data (Big Data), pp. 1580–1589. (2017)

22. Castelltort, A., Laurent, A.: Representing history in graph-oriented NOSQL databases: a versioning system. In: Eighth International Conference on Digital Information Management (ICDIM 2013), pp. 228–234. (2013)

23. An, D.: Find out how you stack up to new industry benchmarks for mobile page speed. https://www.thinkwithgoogle.com/intl/en-ca/marketing-strategies/app-and-mobile/mobile-page-speed-new-industry-benchmarks/. Accessed 12 June 2022

24. Nah, F.: A study on tolerable waiting time: how long are web users willing to wait? Behaviour & Information Technology - Behaviour & IT 23 , p. 285 (2003)

Towards Ontology-Based Validation of EA Principles

Devid Montecchiari[1,2]([✉])[ID] and Knut Hinkelmann[1,3][ID]

[1] FHNW University of Applied Sciences and Arts Northwestern Switzerland,
Windisch, Switzerland
{devid.montecchiari,knut.hinkelmann}@fhnw.ch
[2] School of Science and Technology,
UNICAM University of Camerino, Camerino, Italy
[3] Department of Informatics, University of Pretoria, Pretoria, South Africa

Abstract. This research demonstrates the feasibility of using enterprise ontologies as representation formalism for automated validation of Enterprise Architecture (EA) principles. EA Principles are usually described in natural language, while the Enterprise Architecture is represented with graphical models. As both are intended for human interpretation, it requires humans to validate whether EA Principles are satisfied by an Enterprise Architecture. This is a complex and time-consuming process. We describe a step-by-step procedure for transforming the knowledge of Enterprise Architecture models and the vocabulary of EA Principles into the ArchiMEO ontology, which allows for automated validation. The approach is evaluated in two case studies. They confirm that an ontology-based validation of EA Principles is applicable in reality.

Keywords: Enterprise architecture · Knowledge engineering · Enterprise ontology · SBVR · EA principles

1 Introduction

Enterprise Architecture Management (EAM) is a means to deal with organizational complexity and change in an increasingly turbulent business environment [1,50]. In EAM, frameworks and modeling languages like The Open Group Architecture Framework (TOGAF) [47] and ArchiMate [46] are used to support the complexity of organizations and to support decision-making while facing enterprise transformations [13].

ArchiMate [46] can be used in the Architecture Development Method (ADM) of TOGAF [47, Sect. 31] to create enterprise architecture artifacts. These artifacts are part of the *Enterprise Continuum* and become a resource that needs to be managed and controlled [47, Sect. 31].

Enterprise Architecture (EA) principles are used together with guidelines and governance regimes to direct the EA to achieve its vision and strategy

© IFIP International Federation for Information Processing 2022
Published by Springer Nature Switzerland AG 2022
B. S. Barn and K. Sandkuhl (Eds.): PoEM 2022, LNBIP 456, pp. 66–81, 2022.
https://doi.org/10.1007/978-3-031-21488-2_5

[1, 20]. According to Greefhorst and Proper [14], EA principles feature promi-
nently in the regulative role of enterprise architectures and they provide moti-
vations for the fundamental design decisions. As such EA principles fill the gap
between high-level strategic intents and concrete designs.

While enterprise models represent the reality of the EA, EA principles pre-
scribe how the EA should be. Consequently, the EAM is strongly influenced by
the set of EA principles and their enforcement, i.e. finding deviations from the
principle in the EA [15, p. 10].

The discovery of deviations and controlling of EA principles in EA models
is called in this research *validation of enterprise principles*. While the term validation of EA principles in [14,15] refers to checking inconsistencies among the
principles set.

The validation of EA principles in EA models is a complex process, and it is
currently performed manually by the EA practitioners. This is mainly because
EA principles and EA models have different representations, which are typically
not machine-interpretable. EA principles are usually described in the natural
text, while the EA models are graphically represented. This also complicates the
required continuous monitoring process on EA, making it potentially error-prone
and time-consuming. Our research goal is to create a procedure to automatically find deviations between EA models and EA principles. This research aims
to support the validation of EA principles in enterprise models using semantic
technologies. We claim that EA models and principles can be represented using
enterprise ontologies [18,34].

The method to obtain such an automated *EA Principles Ontology-based Validation* is presented in Sect. 4. It is implemented with a step-by-step procedure
presented in Sect. 5. Finally, an implementation of the approach is shown with
an example of a case study from [2,9] in Sect. 6.

2   Literature Review

A brief background is provided referencing the definition of EA management
from Ahlemann et al. [1]. Then, the literature mainly focuses on the formalization
and representation of EA models and EA principles. Their current standard
formalization prevents an automated validation. In conclusion, relevant works
on machine interpretability of models and business rules are described.

2.1   Enterprise Architecture Management(EAM)

Ahlemann et al. [1, p. 20] provides an exhaustive EA management definition:

> *Enterprise Architecture Management is a management practice that estab-
> lishes, maintains and uses a coherent set of guidelines, architecture prin-
> ciples and governance regimes that provide direction for and practical help
> with the design and the development of an enterprise's architecture in order
> to achieve its vision and strategy.*

This definition puts the focus on establishing, maintaining, and using EA principles, guidelines, and governance regimes. EA principles can fill the gap between strategic intent and concrete decision design [14, p. 14]. EA governance is presented as a building block of a successful EAM together with the EAM organization [1]. Enterprise Architecture models are used throughout the TOGAF ADM [47, Sect. 31] and in steps described in Ahlemann et al. [1].

2.2 Formalizing Enterprise Architecture Models

According to Karagiannis & Woitsch [25], the knowledge space of models has the four dimensions *use, form, content* and *interpretation*. Originally introduced for business process models, the above is applicable for EA models, too [18].

The *use* determines which subset of the enterprise knowledge is of interest. The *form* corresponds to the metamodel of the modeling language, the *content* corresponds to the instantiations of the modeling elements and represents domain knowledge of a specific application domain. It is represented by the labels of the modeling elements. Models can be *interpreted* by humans or machines. The graphical EA models and the EA principles are cognitively adequate and intended for interpretation by humans, while machine-interpretable models have to be represented in a formal language.

Ontology-based metamodeling [20] supports modeling both in a cognitively adequate for humans and at the same time in a machine-processable way. This variant of the OMG Meta Object Facility (MOF) [35] where ontologies are used instead of UML as meta-modeling language keeps the language's abstract syntax and semantics separate from the notation (concrete syntax).

To represent the content, i.e. the domain knowledge, of a model, enterprise ontology can be used. There already exist several enterprise ontologies [5,11,31, 48]. ArchiMEO [19] is an enterprise ontology that already shows the integration of modeling language and domain knowledge. The applicability of this machine-interpretability of models has been proven for EA models [23] and other cases [19,29,40].

2.3 Enterprise Architecture Principles

According to TOGAF [47, Sect. 20.], principles - in form of rules and guidelines - play the important role of informing and supporting how an organization sets about fulfilling its mission. TOGAF provides the following distinct definitions:

- Enterprise Principles *provide "a basis for decision-making throughout an enterprise and inform how the organization sets about fulfilling its mission. These are closely related to Architecture Governance and foster the harmonisation of the enterprise decision making."*
- Architecture Principles are *"a set of principles that relate to architecture work [... and] govern the architecture process, affecting the development, maintenance, and use of the Enterprise Architecture".*

There is a convergence to describe EA principles in a textual form [7] containing *Statement, Rationale* and *Implications* as core elements [14, p. 21].

2.4 Formalizing EA Principles

EA principles are most commonly described using natural language. There are not yet tools capable of interpreting an EA principle and automatically validating if an enterprise model is consistent. To automatically validate EA principles,

– they must be *sufficiently specific* so that they can be validated for correctness and
– they must be *represented formally*, such that this validation can be done automatically.

In ArchiMate [46, Sect. 6] there is a distinction between Principles and Requirements or Constraints. While principles are more general, constraints and requirements are more concrete. This corresponds to the distinction between Policies and Business Rules in Business Motivation Modeling [36]. Business rules are concreted and expressed in such a way that they can be validated for correctness by people [43]. Business policies could be seen as tailored for modeling EA principles, from which more concrete business rules can be derived that can be validated.

According to Greefhorst & Proper [14, p. 69], there is not a common ground on how to represent EA principles, but they suggests that one can choose between informal, semi-formal and, formal representations.

– informal representations would use graphical sketches or narrative descriptions, leaving room for different interpretations
– semi-formal representations would use a controlled (graphical or textual) language, limiting the allowed semantics without a well-defined semantics
– formal representations would use a (restricted) language with well-defined semantics (e.g. Semantics of Business Vocabulary and Business Rules (SBVR))

For automatic validation, business rules - derived from EA principles - can be described *formally*. According to [8,14], SBVR is considered a promising option to formalize rules and it is a consolidated standard also in practice e.g. supporting concept modeling [43] to have a shared understanding of a domain's terminology and business logic. Comparing the possible representations of EA principles, we consider SBVR as semi-formal, while enterprise ontologies as formal (see [37, Chap. 10]).

The Goal-oriented Requirements Language (GRL) was extended to support the definition of EA principles [32] and demonstrated in a case study from a governmental organization that their goal-oriented modeling approach could be suitable for formalizing, modeling, and analyzing EA principles.

Additional notable natural language-like rule languages are RIDL [33], Lisa-D [21], ConQuer [6] and Object Role Modeling [16]. Among the above mentioned, SBVR [37] is set as a potential way to formalize EA principles as an *"SBVR-like style, might provide a balance between formality and understandability by a broad audience. This does, however, require further study and evaluation."* [14, p. 57]

2.5 Research Objective

Given the definitions of *governing statement, practicable statement* and *implementation statement* in [42], EA principles can be considered governing statement, that can be formalized in practicable statement in SBVR and ultimately could be made executable in an implementing statement. SBVR uses keywords for the phrasing of the rules and allows the definition of a vocabulary. But these rules are not executable. For rule execution there are rules languages from W3C like [27] or SWRL [22] and query languages like SPARQL [39], which use an ontology as vocabulary. Different works have also emphasized the possibility of automatically translating SBVR to OWL using design patterns and transformation rules [26, 41].

It is the objective of this research to develop a practical approach to transform EA principles represented in natural language into executable rules that can be validated over an enterprise ontology representing knowledge about the Enterprise Architecture and the application domain.

3   Research Method

The main research objective is to define a procedure to support the validation of EA models and EA principles, Automated Ontology-Based Validation of EA Principles. This study follows the Design Science Research (DSR) methodology as described by Hevner [17] as it fits for the creation of artifacts for information systems.

The design cycle started with the awareness of the problem phase, focusing on the literature research on ways to formalize and validate EA models and EA principles (Sect. 2). The findings showed that EA can be represented in Archi-Mate models and be made machine interpretable using ontologies [18], while EA principles can be semi-formally translated in SBVR [37] and then represented in an enterprise ontology. Aside from the literature review, a fictitious use case was defined and analysed to derive the requirements for the solution.

In the suggestion phase, we propose the Automated Ontology-Based Validation of EA Principles based on the literature review findings and the analysis of the case studies. The resulting tentative design suggests that an Enterprise Ontology (EO) can be used to represent both the EA principles and EA models. Hence, the Automated Ontology-Based Validation of EA Principles focuses on the knowledge available in EA models and principles (Sect. 4.1), the representation of EA models in an EO (Sect. 2.2) and finally the representation of EA principles in an EO (Sect. 4.3).

The "Step-by-Step Formalization and Validation of EA Principles" (Sect. 5) was implemented in the data sharing scenario (gathered in the awareness of the problem phase).

In the evaluation phase, the Automated Ontology-Based Validation of EA principle was implemented and evaluated in two Case Studies, proving its generality and applicability.

4 Automated Ontology-Based Validation of EA Principles

This section describes and motivates how knowledge of EA models and EA principles can be represented with an Enterprise Ontology (EO) which allows it to be validated and interpreted by machines. The analysis is based on a fictitious case about Car as a Service that was used as a teaching case. A sample architecture model for this case is provided in Fig. 1.

4.1 Knowledge in Models and EA Principles

We present how EA models and EA principles can be formally represented following the knowledge space of models of Karagiannis and Woitsch [25] with its four dimensions *use, form, content* and *interpretation* (see Sect. 2.2).

- The use determines which subset of the enterprise knowledge is of interest. In our case, it is the knowledge about EA principles and the part of the enterprise architecture models that are affected by the EA principles.
- The form corresponds to the metamodel of the modeling language. In our case, these are the elements of the ArchiMate modeling language and the text for the EA principles. In Fig. 1 there are an Application Components, an Application Function and a Data Object.
- The content corresponds to the knowledge of the application domain. It is represented by the labels of the modeling elements. We see in Fig. 1 that there are CRM, Data Migration, and Customer Data in the ArchiMate model and single source of truth in the EA principle.

The graphical EA models and the EA principles are intended for interpretation by humans. In order to validate EA principle automatically, however, the EA model and the EA principle have to be translated into a machine-interpretable format. This is where Enterprise Ontologies are used [3, 20, 44].

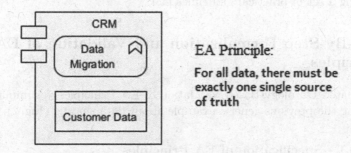

Fig. 1. A sample ArchiMate model and EA principle

4.2 Representing EA Models in an Enterprise Ontology

To represent the knowledge of EA models in an ontology, we distinguish between *metamodel ontology* and *application domain ontology*. The *metamodel ontology* contains the knowledge about the syntax and semantics of the modeling language, which corresponds to the *form* for the knowledge space (see above). We reuse the ArchiMEO ontology [19], which contains the ontology representation of ArchiMate [46].

The *application domain ontology* specifies the vocabulary that can be used for the labels of the modeling elements. It can contain common-agreed terminology like CRM but might also contain enterprise-specific terms like product names. ArchiMEO is designed as an extendable ontology that can be specialized for different use cases as shown in [10, 29, 40].

ArchiMEO [19] is chosen for its interoperability and re-usability. It is defined according to a semantically enriched Enterprise Architecture Description (seEAD) based on ArchiMate's meta-model. The seEAD conceptually links enterprise ontology concepts such as `eo:DataElement` to elements from the ArchiMate modeling language (e.g. `Data Object`). Further, it already contains different top-level ontology concepts (e.g. time, locations & etc.), and many enterprise concepts (e.g. customer, supplier, contract and many more).

4.3 Representing EA Principles in an Enterprise Ontology

EA principles can be regarded as business rules which determine the quality of an enterprise architecture. Business rules are expressed using terms that can be specified in a vocabulary consisting of concepts and relations. SBVR specifies how concepts of a vocabulary are to be interpreted in terms of formal logic [37]. Following this specification allows us to represent the vocabulary of EA Principles as an extension of the ArchiMEO ontology [19] and thus integrate them with the ontology-based representation of the EA models. However, the transition from natural language to formally represented rules has two major challenges: syntactic ambiguities and semantic informalities [4]. These could be tackled using a set of practical guidelines [43].

5   Step-By-Step Formalization and Validation of EA Principles

The Automated Ontology-Based Validation of EA Principles is summarized in 5 steps using the previous generic example about data sharing (Fig. 2).

5.1 Step 1 - Specification of EA Principles

The first step is to select and agree on a set of EA principles. TOGAF recommends several closely related principles regarding data [47, Sect. 20.6.2]:

1. Data is an asset
2. Data is shared
3. Data is easily accessible
4. Data is defined consistently throughout the enterprise.

These EA principles can be considered as *governing statements* [42]. To make them actionable, they can be translated into *practicable statements*. This is in line with the distinction between *principles* and *requirements* or *constraints* in ArchiMate [46, Sect. 6] and between *policies* and *business rules* in Business Motivation Modeling [36].

Business rules should be expressed in such a way that they can be validated for correctness by people [43]. Taking the fourth TOGAF principle (Data is defined consistently throughout the enterprise), a corresponding practical statement or Business Rule could be:

> For all data, there must be exactly one single source of truth

In a *Single Source of Truth (SSOT)* architecture, every data object is mastered (or edited) by a single application [38]. If a data object changes, its SSOT is changed and the change is propagated to other applications that use this data[1]. This rule can be validated in enterprise architecture: It is violated if the are applications that use the same data and which are not synchronized with the SSOT.

5.2   Step 2 - Creation of SBVR Rules

The above *practicable statement* is written in intelligible English, which can be interpreted and validated by humans. To make the statements machine-interpretable, they are translated into a SPARQL query that can be tested over the enterprise ontology representing the EA models. To prepare for the translation, the statements are first represented in SBVR Structured English Notation that maps mechanically to SBVR concepts [37, Appendix A]. SBVR Structured English consists of four font style elements (term, name, verb and keyword).

1. Each data object must **have** a single source of truth
2. Each single source of truth must **have** exactly one domain

The terms, names, and verbs correspond directly to classes, individuals, and properties in an ontology. The next step, therefore, deals with the representation of the EA models and domain knowledge as an enterprise ontology.

5.3   Step 3 - Formalization of the Vocabulary as an Ontology

Using SBVR rules, we stipulate a set of terms, names, verbs, and keywords in a business vocabulary. This vocabulary is now formally represented in an

---

[1] Examples of this SSOT architecture are Master Data Management systems or Cloud data services, which synchronize the data on the server with copies on various devices.

enterprise ontology. The SBVR term data object is represented according to
the ArchiMate modeling element archi:DataObject, single source of truth is
represented as eo:SSOT and domain is represented as eo:DataDomain.

```
archi:DataObject
    rdf:type owl:Class ;
    rdfs:subClassOf archi:PassiveStructureElement ;
eo:SSOT a          owl:Class ;
    rdfs:label    "single source of truth (SSOT)" .
eo:DataDomain a    owl:Class ;
    rdfs:label    "Data Domain" .
```

5.4 Step 4 - Extending EA Models and EA Principles with Domain Knowledge

Once the vocabulary of the EA Principles is represented in the enterprise ontology, it is represented how the EA Principles can be satisfied by the Enterprise Architecture.

As an example, in Fig. 2, the customer data of two applications - *Customer Relationship Management (CRM)* and *Enterprise Resource Planning (ERP)* - are synchronized by the *Master Data Management(MDM)* system. The SSOT for the customer data is stored in the MDM.

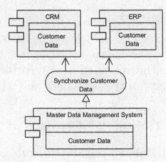

The goal of this step is to consistently extend the enterprise ontology with the relevant domain knowledge so that the EA principles can be validated. In the example of Fig. 2 the data synchronization is modeled with an *application service* which is realized by the MDM and serves the ERP and CRM (inspired by the modeling style of Wierda [49]).

Fig. 2. A MDM for customer data

Instead of using Application Services, it would also be possible to model the data synchronization using *application interfaces*.

To provide meaning to the ArchiMate models, the elements of the ArchiMate models are annotated with concepts from the enteprise ontology. As the example model is dealing with customer data, the domain ontology is extended with a new data domain class (eo:CustomerDataDomain):

```
eo:CustomerDataDomain
    a              eo:DataDomain ;
    rdfs:label     "Data Domain" ;
    eo:IsRegarding eo:Customer .
```

The customer data object in the MDM is classified as a SSOT using the object property eo:isIstanceOf, while each data object (archi:DataObject based on the language notation) can be declared as regarding a certain data domain with eo:DataObjectIsRegardingDomainData.

```
eo:isInstanceOf
    a                   owl:ObjectProperty ;
    rdfs:domain         archi:DataObject , owl:Class ;
    rdfs:label          "is istance of" ;
    rdfs:range          eo:SSOT ;
    rdfs:subPropertyOf  lo:elementIsMappedWithDOConcept .
eo:DataObjectIsRegardingDomainData
    a                   owl:ObjectProperty ;
    rdfs:domain         eo:DataObject ;
    rdfs:label          "Data Object is regarding data domain" ;
    rdfs:range          eo:DataDomain
    rdfs:subPropertyOf  eo:IsRegarding .
```

5.5   Step 5 - Formalization of the SBVR Rules

Using scripts and queries to manipulate and analyze models is a functionality
of many modeling tools [12]. The representation of models using an ontology
language and annotating them with domain knowledge provides additional reasoning functionality. Depending on the kind of reasoning, different rule and query
languages may be used. As we are dealing with the validation of rules representing constraints, SHACL may be the go-to language for validating RDF graphs,
defining constraints over RDF/OWL and embedding rules in the ontology [27].
Alternatively, the validity of a model according to a business rule can be tested
by phrasing the rule as a query using the query language as SPARQL [39].

6   Evaluation

The steps described in the previous section have been implemented and tested in
two different case studies: a Swiss University [9] and a Swiss Bank [2]. EA principles and EA models were stipulated and created via interviews with different
stakeholders of the two companies. In both cases, it was possible to formalize
and validate EA principles in an automated way confirming the applicability
of the approach. The EA models for the case studies were created using the
agile and ontology-aided modeling environment AOAME [30]. In the following
section, we show the implementation and validation of a selected EA principle
of the university use case.

6.1   Case Description

The case study is about the administration process of the master theses (MT) in
the master of Science in Business Information Systems[2]. The focus on students'
data management is crucial in this process. Figure 3 shows a part of the application architecture. Students can register to master thesis courses each semester
via the Evento application. This application has an *API* to export the list of
students enrolled. The API is consumed by the learning management system
Moodle, in which the courses are hosted. Moodle allows the manual registration
of students, which may cause inconsistent data.

---

[2] https://www.fhnw.ch/en/degree-programmes/business/msc-bis.

At the beginning of the master thesis, the students stipulate a MT agreement with their supervisors in a MS Sharepoint online form at the start of each semester. This list is not kept automatically in sync in Moodle as students can decide to postpone their registration during the first weeks after the start of the semester. Therefore a MT registration list in Excel is manually updated for consolidating the two data objects as an SSOT.

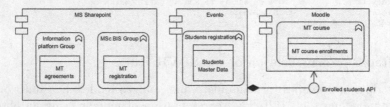

Fig. 3. Master thesis administration application architecture

6.2 Implemented Approach

The ArchiMEO ontology was used as metamodel for the ArchiMate models e.g. data object is automatically translated as AD conceptually links enterprise ontology concepts such `archi:DataObject`. In AOAME model elements can be annotated with concepts from the domain ontology via its intuitive graphical interface, right-clicking on the modeling element and choosing properties (and concepts) from the ArchiMEO ontology (center of Fig. 4).

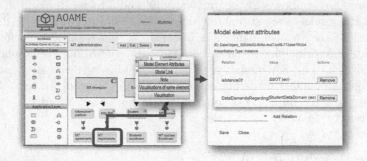

Fig. 4. Semantic annotations on ArchiMate elements in AOAME

As an example, the following is the result of the annotations for the data object MT registrations.

```
mod:DataObject_32534b52-948d-4bd7-bdf8-773dde7f6004
     a                       mod:ConceptualElement , archi:DataObject ;
     eo:DataObjectIsRegardingDomainData  eo:StudentDataDomain ;
     eo:isIstanceOf          eo:SSOT .
```

In **Step 1**, in alignment with the EA principles described in Sect. 5, the EA principle to validate is that "data must be defined consistently throughout the enterprise". In this case there is no a master data management system that synchronizes the students data but, data are stored in different applications, allowing repetitions. Hence, discrepancies between students data in the different applications are possible by design.

In **Step 2**, in agreement with the stakeholders, we identified the SBVR rule: Exactly one data object must be the single source of truth of <u>students data</u>. Having this rule, multiple data objects regarding students can be stored in different applications, however exactly one should be considered a SSOT.

In **step 3**, a new data domain is introduced in ArchiMEO and declared as (`Eo:StudentDataDomain`). The concept of customer is declared as `eo:Student` so that it is possible to declared the (`Eo:StudentDataDomain`) as a data domain regarding students data.

In **Step 4**, the EA model is represented and annotated in AOAME a view is presented in the left side of Fig. 4. Each Data Object has been annotated with the student data domain, while the MT registration is declared as the SSOT (right side of Fig. 4).

In **Step 5**, the SBVR rules are formalized. The following SPARQL query is a representation of the SBVR rule from step 2.

```
SELECT ?DataDomain (COUNT(*) AS ?SingleSourceOfTruthDataElement ) WHERE {
    ?DataObj     eo:isIstanceOf                          eo:SSOT .
    ?Shape       mod:shapeVisualisesConceptualElement    ?DataObj .
    ?DataObj     eo:DataObjectIsRegardingDomainData      ?DataDomain .
} GROUP BY ?DataDomain
HAVING (?SingleSourceOfTruthDataElement=1)
```

The query is executed in the webapp of Apache Jena Fuseki used as triplestore in AOAME [28]. Having modelled both the models (Fig. 2 and 3) in AOAME, the query results (Fig. 5 show that exactly one SSOT is annotated for each data domain. In other words, there exist exactly one modelled Data Object regarding student data which is classified as the SSOT.

	DataDomain	SingleSourceOfTruthDataElement
1	eo:CustomerDataDomain	"1"^^xsd:integer
2	eo:StudentDataDomain	"1"^^xsd:integer

Fig. 5. Query result in the Apache Jena Fuseki

7   Conclusion and Future Work

The main research contribution is an ontology-based approach for automatic validation of EA Principles. Human-interpretable graphical EA models and text-based EA Principles are translated into executable semantical representation based on Enterprise Ontology.

Following the step-by-step procedure shown in Sect. 5, ArchiMate models are represented in an ontology and enhanced with domain knowledge, and business rules are translated into *implementing statements* written as queries in SPARQL. The approach was implemented by extending the ArchiMEO ontology [19] to capture domain and language knowledge for the EA principles validation.

The current research contribution prepares the ground for validating EA principles using different enterprise modeling languages like BPMN for business processes are ER diagrams for data models - simply by extending an enterprise ontology with the concepts for the languages' metamodels. This supports the creation of an hybrid knowledge base integrating different modeling languages and ontologies like in Karagiannis & Buchmann [24].

Currently, the step-by-step manual procedure for the ontology-based validation of EA principles is not fully automated. The automation of the remaining manual steps in the approaches requires further research. However, it is already proven in the literature that SBVR rules could be automatically transformed into an OWL ontology and SWRL rules [41, 45].

References

1. Ahlemann, F., Stettiner, E., Messerschmidt, M., Legner, C. (eds.): Strategic Enterprise Architecture Management: Challenges, Best Practices, and Future Developments. Springer Science+Business Media, Berlin, Heidelberg (2012)
2. Ahmed, S.: Modelling and Validation of Enterprise Architecture Principles for Swiss Banks. Master's thesis, Fachhochschule Nordwestschweiz FHNW (2022)
3. Antunes, G., Bakhshandeh, M., Mayer, R., Borbinha, J., Caetano, A.: Using ontologies for enterprise architecture integration and analysis. Complex Syst. Inform. Model. Q. **1**, 1 (2014)
4. Bajwa, I.S., Lee, M.G., Bordbar, B.: Sbvr business rules generation from natural language specification. In: 2011 AAAI Spring Symposium Series. Citeseer (2011)
5. Bertolazzi, P., Krusich, C., Missikoff, M.: An approach to the definition of a core enterprise ontology: CEO. In: OES-SEO 2001, International Workshop on Open Enterprise Solutions: Systems, Experiences, and Organizations, pp. 14–15 (2001)
6. Bloesch, A.C., Halpin, T.A.: ConQuer: a conceptual query language. In: Thalheim, B. (ed.) ER 1996. LNCS, vol. 1157, pp. 121–133. Springer, Heidelberg (1996). https://doi.org/10.1007/BFb0019919
7. Borgers, M., Harmsen, F.: Strengthen the architecture principle definition and its characteristics-a survey encompassing 27 years of architecture principle literature. In: ICEIS, vol. 2, pp. 607–622 (2018)
8. Bridgeland, D.M., Zahavi, R.: Business Modeling: A Practical Guide to Realizing Business Value. Morgan Kaufmann (2008)
9. Di Ianni, M.: Automated Validation of Enterprise Architecture Principles. Master's thesis, Fachhochschule Nordwestschweiz FHNW (2022)
10. Emmenegger, S., Laurenzi, E., Thönssen, B.: Improving supply-chain-management based on semantically enriched risk descriptions. In: Proceedings of 4th Conference on Knowledge Management and Information Sharing (KMIS2012). Barcelona (2012)
11. Fox, M.S., Barbuceanu, M., Gruninger, M.: An organisation ontology for enterprise modeling: Preliminary concepts for linking structure and behaviour. Comput. indust. **29**(1–2), 123–134 (1996)

12. Ghiran, A.M., Buchmann, R.A.: The model-driven enterprise data fabric: a proposal based on conceptual modelling and knowledge graphs. In: Douligeris, C., Karagiannis, D., Apostolou, D. (eds.) KSEM 2019. LNCS (LNAI), vol. 11775, pp. 572–583. Springer, Cham (2019). https://doi.org/10.1007/978-3-030-29551-6_51

13. van Gils, B., Proper, H.A.: Enterprise modelling in the age of digital transformation. In: Buchmann, R.A., Karagiannis, D., Kirikova, M. (eds.) PoEM 2018. LNBIP, vol. 335, pp. 257–273. Springer, Cham (2018). https://doi.org/10.1007/978-3-030-02302-7_16

14. Greefhorst, D., Proper, E.: Architecture Principles: The Cornerstones of Enterprise Architecture. Springer (2011). https://doi.org/10.1007/978-3-642-20279-7

15. Haki, M.K., Legner, C.: Enterprise architecture principles in research and practice: insights from an exploratory analysis. In: European Conference on Information Systems (ECIS 2013) Completed Research vol. 204 (2013)

16. Halpin, T.: Object-Role Modeling Fundamentals: A Practical Guide to Data Modeling with ORM. Technics Publications (2015)

17. Hevner, A.R.: A three cycle view of design science research. Scandinavian J. Inf. Syst. 19(2), 4 (2007)

18. Hinkelmann, K., Gerber, A., Karagiannis, D., Thoenssen, B., van der Merwe, A., Woitsch, R.: A new paradigm for the continuous alignment of business and it: combining enterprise architecture modelling and enterprise ontology. Comput. Indust. 79, 77–86 (2016)

19. Hinkelmann., K., Laurenzi., E., Martin., A., Montecchiari., D., Spahic., M., Thönssen., B.: Archimeo: a standardized enterprise ontology based on the archimate conceptual model. In: Proceedings of the 8th International Conference on Model-Driven Engineering and Software Development - Volume 1: MODELSWARD, pp. 417–424. INSTICC, SciTePress (2020). https://doi.org/10.5220/0009000204170424

20. Hinkelmann, K., Laurenzi, E., Martin, A., Thönssen, B.: Ontology-based metamodeling. In: Dornberger, R. (ed.) Business Information Systems and Technology 4.0. SSDC, vol. 141, pp. 177–194. Springer, Cham (2018). https://doi.org/10.1007/978-3-319-74322-6_12

21. ter Hofstede, A.H.M., Proper, H.A., van der Weide, T.P.: Formal definition of a conceptual language for the description and manipulation of information models. Inf. Syst. 18(7), 489–523 (1993)

22. Horrocks, I., Patel-Schneider, P.F., Boley, H., Tabet, S., Grosof, B., Dean, M., et al.: SWRL: A semantic web rule language combining OWL and RuleML. W3C Member Submission 21(79), 1–31 (2004)

23. Kang, D., Lee, J., Choi, S., Kim, K.: An ontology-based enterprise architecture. Expert Syst. Appl. 37(2), 1456–1464 (2010)

24. Karagiannis, D., Buchmann, R.A.: A proposal for deploying hybrid knowledge bases: the ADOxx-to-GraphDB interoperability case. In: Hawaii International Conference on System Sciences 2018 (HICSS-51) (2018)

25. Karagiannis, D., Woitsch, R.: Knowledge engineering in business process management. In: vom Brocke, J., Rosemann, M. (eds.) Handbook on Business Process Management 2. IHIS, pp. 623–648. Springer, Heidelberg (2015). https://doi.org/10.1007/978-3-642-45103-4_26

26. Karpovic, J., Nemuraite, L.: Transforming SBVR business semantics into web ontology language owl2: main concepts. Inf. Technol. 27–29 (2011)

27. Knublauch, H., Kontokostas, D.: Shapes constraint language (SHACL). Technical report, W3C (2017). https://www.w3.org/TR/shacl/

28. Laurenzi, E., Hinkelmann, K., van der Merwe, A.: An agile and ontology-aided modeling environment. In: Buchmann, R.A., Karagiannis, D., Kirikova, M. (eds.) PoEM 2018. LNBIP, vol. 335, pp. 221–237. Springer, Cham (2018). https://doi.org/10.1007/978-3-030-02302-7_14

29. Laurenzi, E., Hinkelmann, K., Montecchiari, D., Goel, M.: Agile visualization in design thinking. In: Dornberger, R. (ed.) New Trends in Business Information Systems and Technology. SSDC, vol. 294, pp. 31–47. Springer, Cham (2021). https://doi.org/10.1007/978-3-030-48332-6_3

30. Laurenzi, E., et al.: An Agile and Ontology-Aided Approach for Domain-Specific Adaptations of Modelling Languages. Ph.D. thesis, University of Pretoria (2018)

31. Leppänen, M.: A context-based enterprise ontology. In: Abramowicz, W. (ed.) BIS 2007. LNCS, vol. 4439, pp. 273–286. Springer, Heidelberg (2007). https://doi.org/10.1007/978-3-540-72035-5_21

32. Marosin, D., van Zee, M., Ghanavati, S.: Formalizing and modeling enterprise architecture (EA) principles with goal-oriented requirements language (GRL). In: Nurcan, S., Soffer, P., Bajec, M., Eder, J. (eds.) CAiSE 2016. LNCS, vol. 9694, pp. 205–220. Springer, Cham (2016). https://doi.org/10.1007/978-3-319-39696-5_13

33. Meersman, R.: The RIDL conceptual language. Technical report, Research report, International Centre for Information Analysis Services, Brussels, Belgium (1982)

34. Montecchiari, D.: Ontology-based validation of enterprise architecture principles in enterprise models. In: BIR 2021 Workshops and Doctoral Consortium, co-located with 20th International Conference on Perspectives in Business Informatics Research, 22–24 Sept 2021, Vienna, Austria (2021). http://ceur-ws.org/Vol-2991/

35. OMG: Meta object facility (MOF) core specification, version 2.4.2. Technical report, Object Management Group (2014). https://www.omg.org/spec/MOF/2.4.2/PDF

36. OMG: Business motivation model(bmm) 1.3. Technical report, Object Management Group (2015). https://www.omg.org/spec/BMM/1.3/PDF

37. OMG: Semantics of business vocabulary and business rules, version 1.5. Technical report, Object Management Group (2019). https://www.omg.org/spec/SBVR/1.5/PDF

38. Pang, Ca., Szafron, D.: Single Source of Truth (SSOT) for Service Oriented Architecture (SOA). In: Franch, X., Ghose, A.K., Lewis, G.A., Bhiri, S. (eds.) ICSOC 2014. LNCS, vol. 8831, pp. 575–589. Springer, Heidelberg (2014). https://doi.org/10.1007/978-3-662-45391-9_50

39. Pérez, J., Arenas, M., Gutierrez, C.: Semantics and complexity of SPARQL. ACM Trans. Database Syst. **34**(3), 1–45 (2009)

40. Peter, M., Montecchiari, D., Hinkelmann, K., Grivas, S.G.: Ontology-based visualization for business model design. In: Grabis, J., Bork, D. (eds.) PoEM 2020. LNBIP, vol. 400, pp. 244–258. Springer, Cham (2020). https://doi.org/10.1007/978-3-030-63479-7_17

41. Reynares, E., Caliusco, M.L., Galli, M.R.: A set of ontology design patterns for reengineering SBVR statements into OWL/SWRL ontologies. Expert Syst. Appl. **42**(5), 2680–2690 (2015)

42. Ross: Basic RuleSpeak guidelines. Do's and Don'ts in Expressing Natural-Language (2009)

43. Ross, R.G.: Business Knowledge Blueprints: Enable Your Data to Speak the Language of the Business (Issue 2). In Business Rule Solutions LLC (2020)

44. Smajevic, M., Hacks, S., Bork, D.: Using knowledge graphs to detect enterprise architecture smells. In: Serral, E., Stirna, J., Ralyté, J., Grabis, J. (eds.) PoEM 2021. LNBIP, vol. 432, pp. 48–63. Springer, Cham (2021). https://doi.org/10.1007/978-3-030-91279-6_4

45. Sukys, N.: Paradauskas, Sinkevicius: Transformation framework for SBVR based semantic queries in business information systems. Proceedings BUSTECH (2012)

46. The Open Group: ArchiMate 3.1 Specification (2009)

47. The Open Group: TOGAF 9 - The Open Group Architecture Framework, vol. 9 (2009)

48. Uschold, M., King, M., Moralee, S., Zorgios, Y.: The Enterprise Ontology the Knowledge Engineering Review, vol. 13. Special Issue on Putting Ontologies to Use (1998)

49. Wierda, G.: Mastering ArchiMate Edition III: a serious introduction to the Archi-Mate enterprise architecture modeling language. R&A (2017)

50. Zachman, J.A.: A framework for information systems architecture. IBM Syst. J. **26**(3), 276–292 (1987)

Ontological Analysis and Redesign of Security Modeling in ArchiMate

Ítalo Oliveira[1]([⊠]), Tiago Prince Sales[1], João Paulo A. Almeida[2],
Riccardo Baratella[1], Mattia Fumagalli[1], and Giancarlo Guizzardi[1,3]

[1] Conceptual and Cognitive Modeling Research Group (CORE),
Free University of Bozen-Bolzano, Bolzano, Italy
`{idasilvaoliveira,tprincesales,rbaratella,mfumagalli,gguizzardi}@unibz.it`
[2] Ontology and Conceptual Modeling Research Group (NEMO),
Federal University of Espírito Santo, Vitória, Brazil
`jpalmeida@ieee.org`
[3] Services & Cybersecurity Group, University of Twente, Enschede, The Netherlands

Abstract. Enterprise Risk Management and security have become a fundamental part of Enterprise Architecture, so several frameworks and modeling languages have been designed to support the activities associated with these areas. ArchiMate's Risk and Security Overlay is one of such proposals, endorsed by The Open Group. We investigate the capabilities of the proposed security-related constructs in ArchiMate with regard to the necessities of enterprise security modeling. Our analysis relies on a well-founded reference ontology of security to uncover ambiguity, missing modeling elements, and other deficiencies of the security modeling capabilities in ArchiMate. Based on this ontologically-founded analysis, we propose a redesign of security aspects of ArchiMate to overcome its original limitations.

Keywords: Security modeling · Enterprise architecture · ArchiMate · Ontological analysis · Unified foundational ontology

1 Introduction

Enterprise architecture refers to principles, methods, and models that are used in the design and implementation of an enterprise's organizational structure, business processes, information systems, and infrastructure [7]. Risks are pervasive throughout the activities of any enterprise, so it is important to create security mechanisms to control certain risks that are particularly threatening to an organization's objectives. Enterprise Risk Management is exactly about this process of identification, evaluation, treatment, and communication regarding these risks, as described by ISO 31000, an International Standard for Risk Management [6]. The TOGAF® Series Guide to "Integrating Risk and Security within

Work Supported By Accenture Israel Cybersecurity Labs

a TOGAF Enterprise Architecture" [16] states that the Security Architecture is a cross-cutting matter, ubiquitous throughout the entire Enterprise Architecture. It is understood as a coherent collection of views, viewpoints, and artifacts, including security, privacy, and operational risk perspectives, along with related topics like security objectives and security services. The Security Architecture affects and informs the Business, Data, Application, and Technology Architectures [16]. Because of that, Enterprise Risk Management has, naturally, become a key aspect of Enterprise Architecture, as seen by the *Risk and Security Overlay* (RSO) of ArchiMate [1], an attempt to introduce risk and security concepts into ArchiMate language – the Open Group's open and independent conceptual modeling language for Enterprise Architecture [15].

Though the RSO is based on risk and security frameworks (COSO, ISO, TOGAF, and SABES) [1], it has already been shown to have some limitations concerning its conceptualization of risk concepts [12], including ambiguity and missing modeling elements that negatively impact the capabilities of the RSO to support enterprise risk and security modeling. Through an ontological analysis founded upon the *Unified Foundational Ontology* (UFO) [4] and the *Common Ontology of Value and Risk* (COVER) [11], researchers have shown, for instance, a *construct overload* on the VULNERABILITY construct, which collapses actual vulnerabilities with assessments about them, and a *construct deficit* to represent THREAT CAPABILITIES [12]. Based on the results of this analysis, an ontologically well-founded redesign of RSO was proposed to overcome the identified problems in the risk-related elements [12]. Here, employing a similar methodology of ontological analysis (tracing back to [4,10]), we further investigate the modeling capabilities of the *security* elements of RSO: the notions of CONTROL OBJECTIVE, SECURITY REQUIREMENT, SECURITY PRINCIPLE, CONTROL MEASURE, and IMPLEMENTED CONTROL MEASURE. Our analysis is grounded in the *Reference Ontology of Security Engineering* (ROSE) [9], which is a UFO-based core ontology for safety and security; particularly, ROSE provides an elucidation of the notion of security mechanism. Based on the ontological analysis of security modeling constructs of RSO with ROSE, we propose a redesign of the concerned language fragment, taking advantage of the improved risk-related elements by the previous work [12].

The remainder of this paper is structured as follows: in Sect. 2, we provide an overview of the RSO focusing on security elements. In the same section, we present the redesigned version of the RSO with respect to risk elements, which will be the starting point of our own proposal. In Sect. 3, we briefly present our ontological foundations regarding value, risk, and security, which serves as the conceptual basis for the analysis in Sect. 4. The results of the analysis are used to redesign the RSO in Sect. 5. We conclude with a discussion on related work in Sect. 6 and final remarks in Sect. 7.

2 Security Modeling in Archimate

We present here the current security modeling constructs proposed for the ArchiMate language as part of the Risk and Security Overlay [1] along with the redesigned risk elements that resulted from the ontological analysis in [12].

2.1   The Original ArchiMate Risk and Security Overlay

The most updated version of the RSO was developed by a joint project of The Open Group ArchiMate Forum and The Open Group Security Forum [1], accommodating changes to the ArchiMate language in Version 3.1 of the standard. The RSO was designed through ArchiMate language customization mechanisms, in particular the specialization of both ArchiMate Core and Motivation and Strategy elements, and additional risk and security-specific attributes [1].

Table 1 summarizes the security elements according to the specialized ArchiMate elements. A CONTROL OBJECTIVE (or security objective) is a desired state of security, a high-level goal that should be realized by a SECURITY REQUIREMENT (or control requirement), which is, during the risk analysis process, a specification of an action or set of actions that should be executed or that must be implemented as part of the control, treatment, and mitigation of a particular risk [1]. A CONTROL OBJECTIVE is associated with risk assessment, so that, for example, if the risk of workplace accident is assessed as unacceptable, then the organization could decide to reduce it as its CONTROL OBJECTIVE. To achieve this goal, the organization could define that its employees should wear personal protective equipment as SECURITY REQUIREMENT. RSO proposes the representation of CONTROL OBJECTIVE and SECURITY REQUIREMENT as specializations of the ArchiMate constructs of GOAL and REQUIREMENT, respectively.

Table 1. Summary of security elements in ArchiMate's Risk and Security Overlay (RSO)

RSO element	ArchiMate element
Control objective	Goal
Security requirement	Requirement
Security principle	Principle
(Required) control measure	Requirement
Implemented control measure	Core Element

The notion of SECURITY PRINCIPLE is less developed in the RSO white paper [1]. A PRINCIPLE in ArchiMate represents a statement of intent defining a general property that applies to any system in a certain context in the architecture [15]. Similarly to REQUIREMENTS, PRINCIPLES defines the intended properties of systems. But PRINCIPLES are wider in scope and more abstract than REQUIREMENTS. For example, the PRINCIPLE "Information management processes comply with all relevant laws, policies, and regulations" is realized by the REQUIREMENTS that are imposed by the actual laws, policies, and regulations that apply to the specific system under design [15]. A SECURITY PRINCIPLE is related to the notion of policy and ArchiMate Motivation elements, though the RSO offers neither an explicit definition of it nor its usage in an example. The white paper also notes that the ArchiMate language does not have the concept of operational policy [1].

According to the RSO, a required CONTROL MEASURE, also called risk control, treatment or mitigation, specializes SECURITY REQUIREMENT, and it is a proposed action, device, procedure, or technique that reduces a threat, a vulnerability, or an attack by eliminating or preventing it, by minimizing the harm it can cause, or by discovering and reporting it so that corrective action can be taken [1]. An IMPLEMENTED CONTROL MEASURE is the deployment of a CONTROL MEASURE. Depending on the kind of control, almost any core concept or combination of core elements of ArchiMate can be used to model the implementation of a CONTROL MEASURE. A CONTROL MEASURE may also be realized by a grouping of a set of core elements as its implementation [1].

Figure 1 summarizes how RSO proposes to represent risk and security elements in ArchiMate [1]. An IMPLEMENTED CONTROL MEASURE is associated with an ASSET AT RISK, which can be a RESOURCE or a core element of ArchiMate. An IMPLEMENTED CONTROL MEASURE influences negatively a VULNERABILITY as an ASSESSMENT, in the sense that it makes the emergence of a THREAT EVENT and the consequent LOSS EVENT associated with that VULNERABILITY less probable.

To exemplify how the RSO can be used, we present two examples extracted from [1], highlighting the assumptions that the white paper calls "common characteristics shared by entities in risk management domains". The examples refer to the case of the Coldhard Steel company, illustrating the stereotyping of ArchiMate Motivation elements as risk elements. Figure 2 represents the risk of losing production due to machine failure. A power supply assembly is an ASSET AT RISK that fails when the power fluctuates (a THREAT EVENT). This power assembly failure causes the failure of other machines, characterizing a loss for the organization (a LOSS EVENT), associated to the RISK of production loss. Then, the CONTROL OBJECTIVE is defined as an adequate peak power supply capacity, which means that the organization seeks to reduce this risk, which should be done by the CONTROL MEASURE of replacing the power supply assembly. By this example, we notice some of the aforementioned characteristics: the asset is exposed to a threat or a risk due to its vulnerability, but, at the same time, the asset posses a control requirement and, indeed, participates in the realization of its own CONTROL MEASURE.

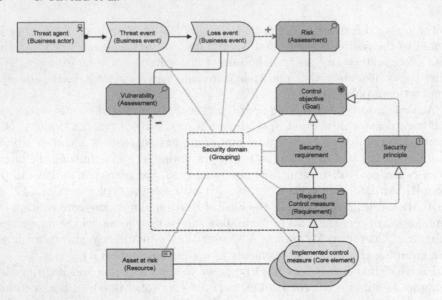

Fig. 1. Mapping of risk and security elements to the ArchiMate language [1]

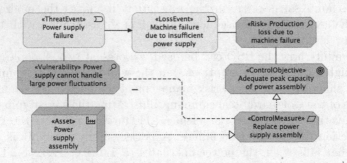

Fig. 2. Example from the case of the Coldhard Steel company [1]

The second example (Fig. 3) illustrates a risk mitigation approach – continuous improvement of machine reliability – applied across the entire Coldhard Steel risk management domain. The implementation of control measures is grouped by RISK MITIGATION DOMAIN, aimed at negatively influencing the vulnerability of inadequate power supply. This implementation involves several core elements of ArchiMate, such as CONTRACT, OUTCOME, BUSINESS PROCESS, and EQUIPMENT.

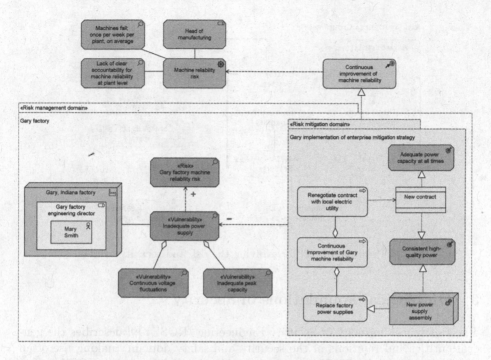

Fig. 3. Mitigation of machine failure risk at Coldhard Steel gary factory [1]

2.2   Redesigned Risk Elements of ArchiMate Based on COVER

In [12], the authors performed an ontological analysis of the risk aspects of the RSO based on the Common Ontology of Value and Risk (COVER), proposing a redesign of part of the RSO to address the limitations identified by the analysis. Figure 4 shows the proposal of [12] for evolving the RSO, while Table 2 shows the full representation of risk concepts in ArchiMate based on COVER. This representation will be the basis of our own proposal concerning security aspects of ArchiMate.

A HAZARD ASSESSMENT, proposed to represent UFO situations that activate threat capabilities, is an identified state of affairs that increases the likelihood of a THREAT EVENT and, consequently, of a LOSS EVENT. The occurrence of these events depends on the vulnerabilities of an ASSET AT RISK or of a THREAT ENABLER and the (threat) capabilities involving THREAT AGENT. All of this forms the RISK EXPERIENCE of a RISK SUBJECT, whose intention or GOAL is harmed by a LOSS EVENT. This experience may be assessed by a RISK ASSESSOR (who may be the same subject as the RISK SUBJECT) through a RISK ASSESSMENT (e.g., that determines that the RISK is unacceptable).

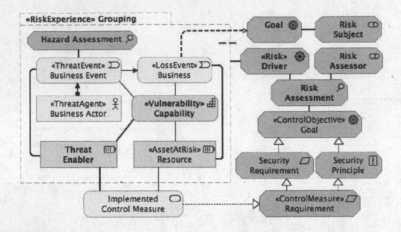

Fig. 4. Proposal of [12] for evolving the risk and security overlay.

3   Ontological Foundations of Security

The Reference Ontology of Security Engineering (ROSE) [9] describes the general entities and relations of the security and safety domain, making use of an adapted version of COVER to capture value and risk domain[1]. ROSE understands the domain of security as the *intersection* between the domain of value and risk, understood under the terms of COVER [11], and the theory of prevention [2], which describes, in UFO's terms, how certain types of event are prevented or interrupted due to the occurrence of other events of certain types.

Table 2. Representation of risk concepts in ArchiMate based on COVER

COVER concept	Representation in ArchiMate
VULNERABILITY	Capability stereotyped with «Vulnerability»
THREAT OBJECT	Structure Element stereotyped with «ThreatAgent»
THREAT EVENT	Event stereotyped with «ThreatEvent»
HAZARD ASSESSMENT	Assessment stereotyped with «HazardAssessment»
LOSS EVENT	Event stereotyped with «LossEvent»
INTENTION	Goal
RISK SUBJECT	Stakeholder associated with a Goal that is negatively impacted by a «LossEvent»
OBJECT AT RISK	Structure Element stereotyped with «AssetAtRisk»
THREAT ENABLER	Structure Element associated with a «ThreatEvent» or a «LossEvent»
RISK EXPERIENCE	Grouping stereotyped with «RiskExperience»
RISK	Driver stereotyped with «Risk»
RISK ASSESSMENT	Assessment associated with a «Risk»
RISK ASSESSOR	Stakeholder associated with a Risk Assessment

---

[1] Files related to ROSE can be found in the following public repository: https://github.com/unibz-core/security-ontology.

From this perspective, security mechanisms create value by protecting certain goals from risk events. In COVER, Value is a relational property that emerges from the relations between capacities of certain objects and the goals of an agent. The manifestations of these capacities are events that bring about a situation (a state of affairs) that impacts or satisfies the goal of a given agent – the goal is understood as the propositional content of an intention [5]. Risk is the anti-value: risk events are the manifestations of capacities, vulnerabilities, and, sometimes, intentions that inhere in an agent; these events bring about a situation that hurts the goal of a given agent. Just like value, security is also a relational property that emerges from the relations between the capabilities of objects and the goals of an agent; however, manifestations of these capabilities bring about a situation that impacts the goal of an agent in a very specific way: preventing risk events [9]. Using the prevention theory described in [2], ROSE understands that THREAT CAPABILITY, VULNERABILITY, and, sometimes, INTENTION are dispositions associated with types whose instances maintain a *mutual activation partnership* to each other. This means that a THREAT OBJECT can only manifest its THREAT CAPABILITY if a VULNERABILITY can be exploited; if the THREAT OBJECT creates an ATTACK (an action, a kind of event), then the INTENTION is also required. Analogously, a VULNERABILITY is only manifested in the presence of a THREAT CAPABILITY. From a security point of view, the importance of this *generic dependence* relation among these entities is that it determines some ways by which security measures can work: the removal of any of them from the situation that could activate them all together implies the prevention of the associated RISK EVENT. Figure 5 represents the risk aspects of ROSE in OntoUML language; this part is basically an adaptation and extension of COVER, clearly showing the dependence between intentions, capabilities, and vulnerabilities.

A SECURITY MECHANISM is always designed by an AGENT called the SECURITY DESIGNER to be a *countermeasure to* events of certain type (RISK EVENT TYPE) [2,9]. When an object is made to be a countermeasure to certain types of events, it aggregates capabilities whose manifestations ultimately prevent these events in a systematic fashion. The AGENT creating a SECURITY MECHANISM is not necessarily the one protected by its proper functioning, i.e., the PROTECTED SUBJECT. Nonetheless, both agents have INTENTIONS that are positively impacted by this proper functioning. For example, the government designs policies for public safety, the functioning of such policies satisfies some goal the government had when it designed them, but also satisfies the goal of people who want to be safe. Sometimes, the PROTECTED SUBJECT is the same AGENT as the SECURITY DESIGNER, such as when a person places an electric fence surrounding her own house. A SECURITY MECHANISM is an object, which may be a simple physical object like a wall, a high-tech air defense system like the Israeli Iron Dome, an AGENT like a policeman, a social entity like a security standard or anti-COVID-19 rules, that bears capabilities called CONTROL CAPABILITY. The manifestation of this kind of capability is a PROTECTION EVENT, specialized in CONTROL CHAIN EVENT and CONTROL EVENT, where the former can cause the latter. The CONTROL EVENT is of a type (CONTROL EVENT TYPE) that prevents, directly or indirectly, events of certain type (RISK EVENT TYPE). This is so because the control events bring about a CONTROLLED SITUATION, which is of a type that is *incompatible with* the situations of the type that trigger risk events of certain types. Since risk events are specialized in THREAT EVENT and LOSS EVENT, the CONTROLLED SITUATION TYPE is incompatible with the THREATENING SITUATION TYPE or with LOSS TRIGGERING SITUATION TYPE. Figure 6 shows this ontological unpacking of the notion of Security Mechanism [9].

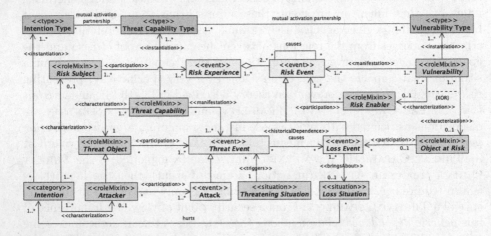

Fig. 5. Risk aspects of ROSE [9]. The colors used signal the corresponding UFO categories: object types are represented in pink, intrinsic aspect types in light blue, situation types in orange, event types in yellow, higher-order types in a darker blue (Color figure online)

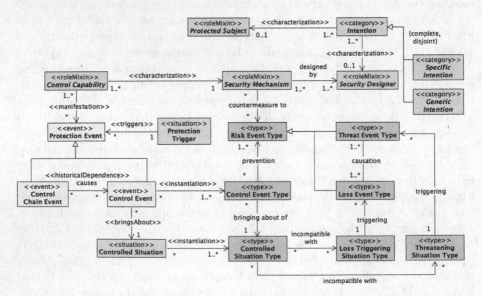

Fig. 6. Security mechanism in ROSE [9]

4   Ontologically-Founded Analysis of Security Modeling

ArchiMate is a modeling language for Enterprise Architecture. The RSO enriches ArchiMate with risk and security elements to support Enterprise Risk Management and security. It is known that one of the key success factors behind the use of a modeling language is its ability to provide its target users with a set of modeling primitives that can directly express important domain abstractions [4]. In other words, the more the grammar of a domain-specific modeling language corresponds to the ontology of the domain, the more capable the language is of modeling domain scenarios accurately. An ontological analysis is "the evaluation of a modeling grammar, from the viewpoint of a predefined and well-established ontology" [10], which is, in our case, ROSE [9] concerning the security domain. Ideally, according to Rosemann *et al.* [10], the modeling grammars should be isomorphic to their underlying ontology, that is, the interpretation from the modeling constructs to the ontology concepts should be bijective. This is a desirable characteristic because it prevents certain types of issues that affect the modeling capability of the language: (a) *ontological incompleteness* (or *construct deficit*), which is the lack of a grammatical construct for an existing ontological concept; (b) *construct overload*, which occurs when one grammatical construct represents more than one ontological construct; (c) *construct redundancy*, which happens when more than one grammatical construct represents the same ontological construct; (d) *construct excess*, when there is a grammatical construct that does not map to any ontological construct [10]. With the support of this framework, we identify shortcomings concerning the security modeling capability of the RSO.

Redundant Intentions and Lack of Clarity. The notions of CONTROL OBJECTIVE, SECURITY REQUIREMENT, CONTROL MEASURE, and SECURITY PRINCIPLE, all reflect a desired state of affairs that guides the actions of some agent. As we interpret the RSO, there are two relevant aspects among these distinctions: (1) a distinction between an end and a means to this end; that is the meaning behind, for example, the statement that a SECURITY REQUIREMENT (a means) realizes a CONTROL OBJECTIVE (an end); and (2) the generality and abstractness of these intentions, in the sense that, for example, CONTROL OBJECTIVE is more general than CONTROL MEASURE; concerning this generality and abstractness, it is not clear where SECURITY PRINCIPLE should be placed, since in Fig. 1 SECURITY PRINCIPLE realizes CONTROL OBJECTIVE, though the documentation of ArchiMate suggests PRINCIPLE has a higher level of generality and abstraction, which means the realization relation should be the inverse. The white paper [1] does not provide an example employing SECURITY PRINCIPLE or even SECURITY REQUIREMENT, making use solely of CONTROL OBJECTIVE, CONTROL MEASURE, and IMPLEMENTED CONTROL MEASURE. Furthermore, no distinction is made regarding how CONTROL MEASURE specializes SECURITY REQUIREMENT. The means-end distinction is relational: an end targeted by a means may be a means to another end. For example, protecting the technical infrastructure from damage may be an end targeted by control measures, but it may also be a means to achieve mandatory legal requirements. Because of all that, those distinct notions of the RSO seem to be a case of construct redundancy, since different security modeling constructs represent the same ontological concept. The redundant constructs (particularly, SECURITY REQUIREMENT and SECURITY PRINCIPLE) do not seem to play any practical role in security modeling[2]. We refer to this as *Limitation L1*.

Underspecification of Implemented Control Measures. An IMPLEMENTED CONTROL MEASURE can be any ArchiMate core element or multiple core elements grouped in a cluster, as seen in Fig. 3. This would look like a construct overload, since a single construct collapses the object, its capability, and the event that is the manifestation of this capability. However, it is actually a strategy of representation via a supertype, so it is not an ontological problem by itself. The issue relies on the fact that this strategy offers no guidance to the modeler on what the implementation of a control measure should look like. In other words, the device of IMPLEMENTED CONTROL MEASURE is too generic and suffers from underspecification. In contrast, ROSE unfolds the notion of security mechanism in a general pattern that distinctively shows the difference between objects (PROTECTED SUBJECT, SECURITY DESIGNER, SECURITY MECHANISM), their modes and capabilities (INTENTION, CONTROL CAPABILITY), the associated events and situations. The lack of this richness of the domain may be better classified as a construct deficit. This is aggravated by the assumption that the asset itself realizes its own control measure (see Fig. 2), suggesting a confusion between the OBJECT AT RISK and elements of the pattern of SECURITY MECHANISM. We term this issue *Limitation L2*.

Lack of Distinction Between Baseline Architecture and Target Architecture. The implementation and migration concepts of ArchiMate are used to describe how an architecture will be realized over time through changes [7], providing the means to represent a baseline and a target architecture. The existence of these concepts in ArchiMate is justified by the importance of accounting for changes in the process of evolution of an enterprise. The introduction of a security mechanism is one of these changes. However, the RSO does not make use of this characteristic of ArchiMate, simply showing that security entities have a negative influence on VULNERABILITY. The redesigned RSO (see Fig. 4) connects IMPLEMENTED CONTROL MEASURE to THREAT ENABLER and ASSET AT RISK, in order to express the impact on the threat event or the loss event. Still, no account of change is provided, as it would be expected from the capabilities of ArchiMate language by the means of constructs showing different PLATEAUS from the baseline architecture to the target architecture. We call this lack of use of temporal aspects of ArchiMate *Limitation L3*.

Modeling the Subjects in the Security Domain. ROSE highlights there is a subject whose INTENTION is positively impacted by the effects of a SECURITY MECHANISM, the PROTECTED SUBJECT. Considering the risk domain, it is clear

---

[2] Actually, we can wonder whether the distinction of several of ArchiMate's Motivation Elements is (or not) redundant, such as GOAL, OUTCOME, REQUIREMENT, and PRINCIPLE, but this issue is outside the scope of our paper.

that this subject must be a proper subtype of the RISK SUBJECT, which appears in the redesigned version of the RSO, as seen in Fig. 4. In addition, another subject has not only his or her intentions positively impacted by the effects of a SECURITY MECHANISM, but is also responsible for the creation or introduction of the mechanism – often due to legal or contractual reasons, such as when someone is hired to install an electric fence. This is what ROSE calls the SECURITY DESIGNER. Sometimes the PROTECTED SUBJECT and the SECURITY DESIGNER are the same individual, while sometimes this is not the case. The original RSO presents none of that, whereas these subjects are not part of the scope of the redesigned version of the RSO. In summary, a case of construct deficit. We call this *Limitation L4*.

Triggering Conditions of Protection Events. The manifestation of the capability of a SECURITY MECHANISM occurs due to a PROTECTION TRIGGER, a certain state of affairs that activates that capability. This represents environmental conditions that affect the manifestation of a CONTROL CAPABILITY. For instance, a circuit breaker manifests its capability of interrupting a current flow when a fault condition is detected (heating or magnetic effects of electric current). In the redesigned RSO, there is an analogous notion for THREAT EVENT, a threatening circumstance mapped as an assessment called HAZARD ASSESSMENT [12]. They are particular configurations of the world that allow or increase the probability of the occurrence of a THREAT EVENT. The advantage of explicitly accounting for the situations that trigger the PROTECTION EVENT is that we can represent how several environmental factors increase the effectiveness of the SECURITY MECHANISM, assuming its effectiveness is directly connected to how likely it works properly, manifesting the PROTECTION EVENT. This whole dimension is neglected by the RSO, a case of construct deficit – *Limitation L5*.

Interdependence Relation Among Risk Capabilities. As shown by ROSE, in its risk aspects (Fig. 5), the manifestations of threat capabilities, vulnerabilities and, sometimes, intentions depend on the presence of each other. From this perspective, for example, it makes no sense to say that there is an ongoing threat without the simultaneous participation of a vulnerability. More importantly, from the security modeling point of view, recognizing this generic dependence relation among these entities allows for different strategies of protection or mitigation, since the removal of any of these capabilities or intentions would result in the prevention of the threat or loss event. Again, this dimension is not considered by the RSO, which refers to the efficacy of the control measure as simply influencing negatively a vulnerability. Doing so, the RSO says nothing about the multiple patterns of prevention uncovered by ROSE. Therefore, a case of construct deficit, *Limitation L6*.

5   Redesigning the Security Elements of ArchiMate

To address the identified shortcomings of security modeling in ArchiMate, we now propose a redesign of the security-related portion of the RSO, which also

follows its original strategy of only using existing ArchiMate constructs. Since *L1*
concerns a case of construct redundancy, we retain only the required constructs.
So we retain CONTROL OBJECTIVE as a goal and CONTROL MEASURE as a
required means to achieve this goal. Considering this distinction from ROSE's
perspective, we can conclude that the former is associated with a PROTECTED
SUBJECT, while the latter is associated with a SECURITY DESIGNER, the one
responsible for introducing the SECURITY MECHANISM. For example, a company
has a CONTROL OBJECTIVE of protecting customer's data from cyberattacks.
Based on an assessment, a series of CONTROL MEASURES should be implemented
by the company's cybersecurity team, playing the role of SECURITY DESIGNER;
both the company and the customers may be regarded as PROTECTED SUB-
JECTS, since they have assets at risk that should be protected.

L4 is the absence of these two subjects, so we propose to introduce them,
respectively, as a STAKEHOLDER and a BUSINESS ROLE. The PROTECTED SUB-
JECT specializes RISK SUBJECT, though some RISK SUBJECTS might not be
PROTECTED SUBJECTS due to lack of protection. Similarly, *L6* is the absence
of a dependence relation among THREAT CAPABILITIES, VULNERABILITIES, and
INTENTIONS (GOAL in ArchiMate), a limitation that is easily solved by adding
ArchiMate's associations among these entities. To address *L5*, the introduction of
ROSE's concept of PROTECTION TRIGGER follows the previous work [12], which
uses ASSESSMENT to represent THREATENING (or HAZARDOUS) SITUATIONS. So
PROTECTION TRIGGER becomes CONTROL ASSESSMENT.

Limitations L2 and *L3* are treated together: the baseline architecture reflects
the state of the organization before the implementation of a security mechanism,
and the target architecture shows the impact of the implementation of the security mechanism. At baseline, following a proposal for a pattern language for value
modeling in ArchiMate [13], there is a LIKELIHOOD associated with the causal
emergence of a THREAT EVENT and a LOSS EVENT. The dependence relations
among risk entities are also shown, so that it should be clear that interfering
in one of them would affect the likelihood of happening events like these. This
is exactly what a SECURITY MECHANISM does in a systematic fashion, following the ROSE and the theory of prevention [2,9][3]. But the implementation of
a SECURITY MECHANISM is carried out by a SECURITY DESIGNER through the
WORK PACKAGE device of ArchiMate's migration layer, oriented by an identified gap in the baseline architecture. Once a SECURITY MECHANISM is implemented, the target architecture may show a different configuration of the risk
entities that are interdependent, as well as a decreased likelihood concerning
the emergence of a THREAT EVENT or a LOSS EVENT. Because of that, RISK
ASSESSMENT may also be different, maybe evaluating the risk is now acceptable. Similarly, the required CONTROL MEASURE might change. The pattern of
SECURITY MECHANISM from ROSE is translated in ArchiMate as a Structure
Element that holds a capability whose manifestation is an event that negatively
influences the likelihood of THREAT EVENT or a LOSS EVENT. This pattern

---

[3] Naturally, employing the theory of prevention in ArchiMate requires adaptation,
considering ArchiMate does not distinguish the instance level from the type level.

follows the value modeling pattern in ArchiMate proposed by [13], since security is a matter of specific creation of value through the prevention of risks. Figure 7 shows our proposal to evolve the security aspects of the RSO, highlighting in bold the constructs and relations we propose. Table 3 shows our proposal of the representation of security concepts in ArchiMate based on ROSE.

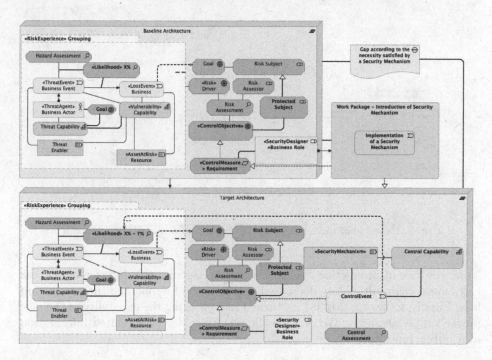

Fig. 7. Proposal for evolving the security aspects of the Risk and Security Overlay of ArchiMate

Figure 8 exemplifies our proposal using the same example from the RSO involving a LOSS EVENT of production loss caused by a THREAT EVENT of power fluctuation with intermediate steps in between. Notice that there is a certain likelihood associated with the causation between the power fluctuation and the power supply failure. The business owner is the RISK SUBJECT, and the RISK ASSESSMENT is that the risk of production loss is unacceptable. Considering this risk experience in the baseline architecture, therefore before the introduction of a SECURITY MECHANISM, the CONTROL OBJECTIVE is defined to be an adequate peak capability of power assembly, realized by a CONTROL MEASURE of replacing power supply assembly. This is the responsibility of a technician, the SECURITY DESIGNER. In the target architecture, we see some changes concerning the risk entities: the new power supply assembly is able to handle large power fluctuations, decreasing the likelihood of power supply failure; the original power supply assembly was totally removed from the scene, which means its vulnerability was also removed from scene. This is one of the ways of prevention [2].

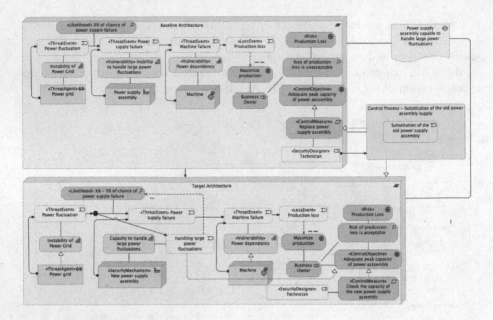

Fig. 8. Example of modeling the introduction of a security mechanism

Now, the risk of production loss is acceptable, because this interference in the risk causal chain ultimately decreased the chances of happening the production loss. Finally, CONTROL MEASURE turned into checking the capability of the new power supply assembly. We provide the resulting files with related information in a public repository[4].

6   Related Work

The closest related works to ours are proposals of modeling Enterprise Risk Management and security through ArchiMate, as seen by ArchiMate's Risk and Security Overlay. The research conducted by Mayer and his collaborators [8] is one example of these proposals. They propose a conceptual model for Information System Security Risk Management, which is then integrated with enterprise architecture through ArchiMate's RSO. Their model contains four "risk treatment-related concepts": risk treatment, security requirement, control. These concepts are mapped into RSO metamodel without revision, which means that the problems we have shown remain untouched, such as construct redundancy and construct deficits.

Another related proposal is the Master thesis by Sander van den Bosch [3]. Based on Zachman Framework and SABSA Model, he proposes a metamodel describing risk and security elements, which are the following: vulnerability, threat, risk, security mechanism, and security policy. Then he employs them

---

[4] See: https://github.com/unibz-core/security-archimate.

Table 3. Representation of security concepts in ArchiMate based on ROSE

Ontology concept	Representation in ArchiMate
Protected Subject	A specialization of Risk Subject associated with a «ControlObjective»
Security Designer	Business Role associated with «ControlMeasure» and assigned to the implementation of a Security Mechanism
Security Mechanism	Structure Element (Business Agent, Resource) stereotyped with «SecurityMechanism»
Control Capability	Capability associated with Control Event and *SecurityMechanism*
Protection Trigger	Assessment stereopyed with «ControlAssessment»
Protection Event	Control Event that realizes «ControlObjective» and it is associated with «SecurityMechanism»

to extend ArchiMate towards "Secure Enterprise Architecture approach". The resulting language and the metamodel are validated by interviews with experts from both the enterprise architecture and the security discipline. The Master thesis by José Miguel Lino Teixeira [14] goes in a similar direction, but it maps ISO 22301 and ISO 31000 concepts into ArchiMate concepts, then introducing risk and security concepts. For example, the concept *Risk Source* from ISO 31000 is defined as an "Element which alone or in combination has the intrinsic potential to give rise to risk". The authors understands that "Risk can come from every layer of the ArchiMate, and we can assume that all elements can be a source of risk", including BUSINESS ACTOR, DRIVER, and RESOURCE. Although both proposals present interesting results, their analysis of security are not grounded in any well-founded ontology like ROSE, which is founded in UFO. As a consequence, their analysis suffer from a degree of informality, and certain modeling patterns and security elements are missing, such as the ones presented previously.

7   Final Remarks

We presented an ontologically-founded analysis of the security modeling fragment of ArchiMate's Risk and Security Overlay (RSO). This analysis, grounded in the *Reference Ontology of Security Engineering* (ROSE) [9], allowed us to clarify the real-world semantics underlying the security-related constructs of the overlay, as well as to unveil several deficiencies in its modeling capabilities, including both redundancy and deficit of constructs. We then addressed these issues by redesigning the security modeling aspects of the RSO, making it more precise and expressive. The proposed redesign supports the representation of several important elements of Enterprise Risk Management and security that the original RSO neglects, including patterns of security mechanism, the subjects involved in it, the interdependence relations among risk entities, and the interaction between security and ArchiMate's baseline and target architecture. In doing so, we fill the gap left by a previous work that analyzed the risk and value aspects of ArchiMate [12,13]. Therefore, we expect to contribute to the ontology-based modeling of enterprise risk and security in a more comprehensive manner. In future work, we intend to provide more examples in ArchiMate showing different patterns described by the theory of prevention [2] and to offer support for computational simulations of scenarios in Enterprise Risk Management and security.

References

1. Band, I., et al.: How to model enterprise risk management and security with the archimate language. The Open Group white paper (W172), vol. 9 (2019)
2. Baratella, R., Fumagalli, M., Oliveira, Í., Guizzardi, G.: Understanding and modeling prevention. In: Guizzardi, R., Ralyte, J., Franch, X. (eds.) International Conference on Research Challenges in Information Science, LNBIP, vol. 446, pp. 389–405. Springer (2022). https://doi.org/10.1007/978-3-031-05760-1_23
3. van den Bosch, S.: Designing Secure Enterprise Architectures A comprehensive approach: framework, method, and modelling language. Master's thesis (2014)
4. Guizzardi, G.: Ontological foundations for structural conceptual models (2005)
5. Guizzardi, G., et al.: Grounding software domain ontologies in the Unified Foundational Ontology (UFO): the case of the ODE software process ontology. In: Ibero-American Conference on Software Engineering, pp. 127–140 (2008)
6. ISO: ISO 31000:2018 - Risk management - Guidelines (2018)
7. Lankhorst, M.: Enterprise Architecture at Work: Modelling, Communication and Analysis. Springer (2017)
8. Mayer, N., Feltus, C.: Evaluation of the risk and security overlay of archimate to model information system security risks. In: 2017 IEEE 21st International Enterprise Distributed Object Computing Workshop (EDOCW), pp. 106–116. IEEE (2017)
9. Oliveira, Í., et al.: An ontology of security from a risk treatment perspective. In: Chakravarthy, U., Mohania, M., Ralyté, J. (eds.) Conceptual Modeling. ER 2022. LNCS, vol. 13607. Springer, Cham (2022). https://doi.org/10.1007/978-3-031-17995-2_26
10. Rosemann, M., et al.: A reference methodology for conducting ontological analyses. In: Atzeni, P., Chu, W., Lu, H., Zhou, S., Ling, T.-W. (eds.) ER 2004. LNCS, vol. 3288, pp. 110–121. Springer, Heidelberg (2004). https://doi.org/10.1007/978-3-540-30464-7_10
11. Sales, T.P., et al.: The common ontology of value and risk. In: Trujillo, J.C., et al.(eds.) ER 2018. LNCS, vol. 11157, pp. 121–135. Springer, Cham (2018). https://doi.org/10.1007/978-3-030-00847-5_11
12. Sales, T.P., et al.: Ontological analysis and redesign of risk modeling in ArchiMate. In: Intl. Enterprise Distributed Object Computing Conference, pp. 154–163 (2018)
13. Sales, T.P., et al.: A pattern language for value modeling in ArchiMate. In: Giorgini, P., Weber, B. (eds.) CAiSE 2019. LNCS, vol. 11483, pp. 230–245. Springer, Cham (2019). https://doi.org/10.1007/978-3-030-21290-2_15
14. Teixeira, J.M.L.: Modelling Risk Management using ArchiMate. Master's thesis (2017)
15. The Open Group: Archimate® 3.1 specification. https://pubs.opengroup.org/architecture/archimate3-doc/
16. The Open Group: Integrating risk and security within a togaf® enterprise architecture. The Open Group Guide white paper (2019). www.opengroup.org/library/g152

Modeling Capabilities and Ecosystems

Foundations of Capability Maps – A Conceptual Comparison

Anders W. Tell[⊠] [iD] and Martin Henkel [iD]

Department of Computer and Systems Sciences, Stockholm University, Stockholm, Sweden
{andersw,martinh}@dsv.su.se

Abstract. Capability maps aim to provide a business or organization with an overview of what it can achieve. As such, capability maps are touted as means for business innovation and planning. However, several types of capability maps exist, with different conceptual backgrounds and levels of integration with enterprise architecture frameworks. In this paper, we characterize and compare three capability maps - Beimborn, VDML, and TOGAF. We base the comparison on a capability map analysis model. Using the analysis model, we highlight the differences in how the capability maps are integrated into enterprise architecture frameworks and linked to concepts such as organizational units, processes, and business models.

Keywords: Capability map · Capability analysis · Work-oriented approach · Capability pattern

1 Introduction

Capabilities, and capability maps, have been put forward as a way to analyze businesses and organizations and to perform strategic planning and management. Even though several different definitions exist, a capability in the field of modeling commonly refers to an organization's potential to reach a goal [13] or, generally the substantial possibility of a possessor to achieve a result through a lead-to mechanism using sources [16]. As a foundation for an organization's capabilities are the resources that an organization has [11] and its potential to use them. One important aim of a capability map is to provide an overview of an organization's capabilities, typically in an easy-to-grasp visual form. The visualized capability map provides further means for analyzing capabilities and their relationships [2].

Several approaches exist for creating and documenting capability maps, founded on different theories and connected to various enterprise architecture frameworks. For example, some maps are based on descriptions grounded in a resource-based view [2], where a map essentially provides an overview of valuable resources. At the same time, other approaches have conceptual similarities to business process models.

Although there exists research literature covering the concept of capability, there is a lack of literature covering the general characterization of capability maps. This creates

B. S. Barn and K. Sandkuhl (Eds.): PoEM 2022, LNBIP 456, pp. 101–117, 2022.
https://doi.org/10.1007/978-3-031-21488-2_7

problems when trying to understand, evaluate and select a type of capability map to apply. This paper addresses this problem by developing a capability map analysis model.

In this paper, the developed analysis model is used to compare and contrast three types of capability maps, Beimborn [2], VDML [10], and TOGAF [17]. The comparison, based on the capability map analysis model in Sect. 3, examines three parts of the capability maps: 1) its use of the capability construct, 2) capability interrelationships and types in the map, and 3) how the capability map is designed and described to be situated, instantiated and used. The first part of the analytical model is based on a capability pattern previously published [16], outlining six different constituents of capabilities. The second part is based on a capability map pattern presented in this paper. The third part is based on an extension of the work-oriented approach [15], outlining the needed roles and the work they can perform with the examined maps.

The contribution of this paper is the comparison of three different kinds of capability maps and the analytical model in itself. The analytical model can be used by enterprise architecture framework builders to analyze capability maps in the presence of related information products such as process maps, and by other actors or stakeholders to evaluate the utility of capability maps.

The research literature that covers capability maps is scarce, although the general topic of capabilities is big. Therefore this paper includes a selection of three approaches to capability maps with different profiles that cover varying aspects. The selection of the three maps to compare (Beimborn, VDML, and TOGAF) represent a spectrum of choices – Beimborn being a fully stand-alone capability map, and VDML is intricately integrated with numerous concepts, such as REA and value streams. At the same time, TOGAF forms a larger EA framework. Other approaches exist that provide the ability to model capabilities, such as CDD [13]; however, these do not claim to be maps of capabilities explicitly but are more focused on the intricacies of capabilities, such as their inner workings or their context.

2 Background

While there has been recent research on the concept of capabilities and their use in enterprise modeling, comparatively little work has been published on the use of capability maps. However, the study and application of both capabilities and capability maps show the potential use of the concept of capability in several areas.

Several sources point out the benefit of capability maps due to their capacity to visualize and give an overview of an organization in one model. This provides an organization with the capacity to review capability relationships [18] and offers a "one-page" overview of an organization [9]. Figure 1 shows an example of a capability map, illustrating an organization with main capabilities, Innovation, Acquisition, and Exploitation, and their respective sub-capabilities.

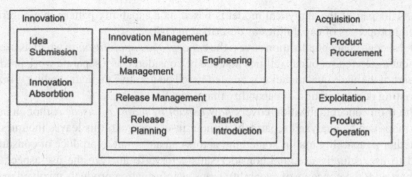

Fig. 1. Example of a capability map, excerpt from VDML

While the map in its basic form can be used as means for identifying opportunities and challenges [17, 20], it may also be used as a base for further exploration and visualization. For example, a "capability heat-map" [7, 17] may be created by highlighting or coloring the capabilities that are problematic and need decisions on actions to take.

The application of the maps for strategic decision-making is pointed out by several sources [2, 9]. Other application areas have been IT capability analysis [12] and the more general use in Enterprise Architecture Management [8]. Regardless of application areas, we have found no sources that compare different types of capability maps and their foundations.

3   Analytical Model

This section presents the capability map analysis model that this paper is based on. The analytical model consists of three parts: conceptualizations of capability, capability map, and capabilities in-use.

In this paper, the studied capability map approaches were analyzed using the grounded research method [21]. The documents specifying each approach provided the data from which the capability map characterization in Sect. 3.3 was generated through iterative thematic coding, while the first and third parts are based on existing work as described in Sect. 3.1. Using the documentation of each approach for the analysis meant that we went beyond analyzing just the presentation (that is, the notation). The coding was performed using the MAXQDA software for qualitative research, which was also used to mark text and collect information related to the other characterizations in the analysis model.

3.1   Overview of the Analytical Model

The first conceptualization covers the *concept of capability*, which is considered an important part of strategic planning and enterprise architecture frameworks. In these contexts, it is clear that not only one capability is identified, analyzed, and planned but a set of interrelated capabilities that are associated with a planning context or architectural scope. This part of the analytical model is based on a capability pattern that describes essential properties of capabilities as described in [14].

The second conceptualization covers the *concept of a capability map* which is used to represent a selected set of capabilities that can be considered as a separate work product. This part of the analytical model was created based on iterative thematic coding utilizing the existing documentation of capability maps, see Sect. 3.3.

The third conceptualization covers *how capability maps are used*. Although capability maps can be analyzed separately without in-use context, this leaves the question of whether a capability map is something actors can and want to produce or consumers intend to use, actually use, and consider satisfactory. To analyze the use-aspect, this third part adds the concepts of capability maps as information products involved in creation, production, and consumption. This part of the analysis model is based on the work-oriented approach [15].

Figure 2 shows how the three parts of the analysis framework relate to concepts of architectural description as defined in ISO 42010 [6]. Stakeholders' concerns are covered by the third part of the model. The capability maps concepts cover the ISO concepts of Viewpoint and Model Kind, while the capability constitutes an Element.

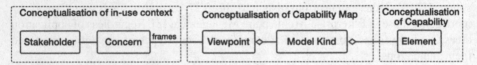

Fig. 2. Illustration of the analysis model parts together with ISO 42010 [6] elements

3.2 Conceptualization of a Capability

The central construct in a capability map is capability, which has been recognized as a part of business and enterprise architecture frameworks. Unfortunately, each framework provides specific conceptualizations using different underlying theories, thus making comparative analysis difficult.

Therefore the conceptualization of capability is chosen based on the 'general capability pattern' that identifies six (6) key parts that characterize a capability in general [16].

According to the capability pattern [16] a capability can be characterized by the six parts: "a <substantial> <possibility> of <possessor> to <result> by/with <source> through <lead-to>":

- **Possessor:** the portion of reality to which the capability is attributed to, owned by, or accessed by. Examples: organization, person, machine, enterprise, or system.
- **Possibility:** a possibility and modality for something to come into existence by some source through a lead-to mechanism. Examples: capacity, or disposition.
- **Source:** the input factors of a capability, the causes, which participate in a thematic 'source' role. Examples: things, assets, facilities, resources, people, knowledge, processes, machines, or culture.

- **Result:** the to-part, which participates in a determinant thematic 'product' role; the accomplishment, the achievement, effect, and consequence. Examples: activity is done, delivered goods, performed service, or fulfillment of objective.
- **Lead-to:** the way source(s) can lead to the result. Examples: natural process, mechanisms, prescribed or described work, causality, or mathematical formula.
- **Substantiality:** the strength of the lead-to mechanism, and source factors. Examples: capacity of sources, or demonstrated achievement of results.

Based on the capability pattern prototypical kinds of capability can be defined.

- *Processual Capability*: A capability where the 'lead-to' characteristic is based on and grounded in well-formulated processes, activities, functions, or tasks.
- *Abstract Capability*: A capability where one or more characteristics are defined abstractly or without details, such as a capability that is defined in terms of "what" (Fig. 3).

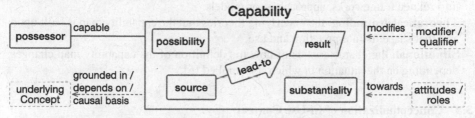

Fig. 3. Key characteristics of the capability pattern

The following characteristics concerns how a capability is related to its surrounding, the causal basis, theoretical grounding, and adaptation to situations where it is used.

- **Grounding and causal basis:** each of the characteristics of the capability pattern is *grounded* in something that constitutes the causal basis. For example, a 'possessor' can be grounded in an organization, a 'source' can be grounded in a specific car or in an abstract resource, or a lead-to can be grounded in a mechanism or process.
- **Theoretical grounding:** the underlying theories that the capability is built upon and that shape its interpretation and use.
- **Situational:** the characteristics of how the definition of the capability changes depending on the situation in which it is applied [5, 14].

3.3 Conceptualization of a Capability Map

While the capability pattern allows the analysis of a capability, there is also a need to analyze a set of capabilities that form a capability map. Thus, we here introduce a *capability map pattern* that characterizes capability maps.

In general, a capability map can be characterized as a "model and an information product that contains a select set of organized capabilities and relationships."

- **Selection:** the principle that determines which capabilities and relationships can or must be included or excluded from the capability map. Note that there exist infinite kinds of capabilities [16], although only some kinds of capabilities are interesting for actors in the work they do. Furthermore, some capability theories explicitly include reasoning about which capabilities are important and should be included.
- **Relationships:** the characterization of relationships between capabilities.
- Note that the relationships are grounded on an underlying causal basis. An example is the output-input connections that are derived from and grounded in inputs and outputs of some actions or functions.
- **Structure:** the principle that determines how the sets of capabilities and relationships are structured. For example: in a hierarchy or as levels.

The following characteristics concerns how a capability map is related to its surrounding, the integration, theoretical grounding, and adaptation to situations where it is used.

- **Pragmatic integration:** the characterization of how a capability map is integrated into related frameworks, approaches, or models.
- **Theoretical grounding:** the underlying theories that the capability map is built upon and that shape its interpretation and use.
- **Situational:** the characteristics of how the definition of the capability map changes depending on the situation in which it is applied [5].

3.4 Conceptualization of In-Use Context

The conceptualization of capability maps in-use provides anchoring and representation of a capability map treated as an information product used in situations relevant to actors playing different roles. The conceptualization enables the analysis of precise information needs deriving from actors' questions and actions, production and consumption of information products, and features and affordances of information products offered by producers to meet consumers' stated information needs.

The conceptualization is an extension of the Work Oriented Approach (WOA) introduced in "Productization of Business Models by Adding Situational Knowledge" [15]. The WOA has gone through design iterations since its introduction, where it has been strengthened and clarified. We here introduce the concept of 'work statement' to represent both work aspects and use requirements. Furthermore, we add the archetypical role of 'creator' to handle better the creation and innovation of information product kinds.

WOA extends traditional stakeholder analysis and management approaches such as the one TOGAF incorporates. WOA enables the capture of detailed stakeholders' concerns, doings, decisions, questions, results, and information needs through work statements so that the creation, production, and consumption of information products can be designed and evaluated with more relevance and precision.

WOA supports multi-perspective analysis of capability maps and analysis of situations with shared capability maps where actors agree on the content and use of capability maps, or analysis of capability maps that represent the past, present, or future.

Based on the expanded WOA, the in-use analysis includes the following essential characteristics that we apply to capability maps:

- **Work-to-be-done:** represents a work practice where actors are asking questions, acting, having information needs, creating results, or achieving objectives. The work-to-be-done shares features with the Jobs-to-be-Done theory, which has made significant contributions to innovation, design, and product development [3, 19] and with the work practices field [1].
- **Work statement:** represent the details of a work-to-be-done such as an actor participating in a work-to-be-done, an artifact or information product participating, an actor asking a question based on available information, an actor making a decision, an actor using an artifact, an actor experiencing a problem and a pain, an actor is having information needs, etcetera. A work-to-be-done can be described and detailed using several work statements.

  - *Stated by*: A work statement is *stated by* an actor, which can be different from the actor represented in the work statement. This enables analysis of who said what and asymmetries, such as when a producer claims that a consumer is satisfied but the consumer reports other experiences [15].

- **Information product:** is an entity that participates in work actors do together with others. A capability map is considered an information product.
- **Roles and relationships:** In an information production situation can multiple actors or stakeholders that play different roles be identified [15]. WOA represents roles in a *roles and relationship model* where each role is associated with work-to-be-done.

In a typical information production situation, three archetypal roles can be identified:

- *Creator*, is a role that creates new *types* of information products. Examples: a new model kind, a new type of algorithm, or a new kind of capability map. A creator can be a researcher or innovator bringing a novel product type to the market.
- *Producer*, is a role that produces *instances* of a kind of information product. Examples: model, application of an algorithm, or capability map. A producer can be a seller that offers features and affordances from a value proposition.
- *Consumer*, is a role that consumes and uses *instances* of a kind of information product that is produced by producers. A consumer can be a buyer of information products matching their needs.

4 Research Results

In this section, the results of the application of the analysis model are presented in a compact format to fit the limited set of pages available for this paper.

4.1 The Studied Capability and Capability Map Constructs

The first approach is described in the research paper "Capability-oriented Modeling of the Firm" by Beimborn in 2005 [2], which is one of the first papers considering the construct of capability maps as an analytical tool. Interestingly it provides a self-contained information product based on the core theories of the Resource-based view of the firm and the Competence-based view of strategic management. It can complement existing modeling approaches and process improvement frameworks, which can be useful to analysts and users.

The second approach is the Value Delivery Modeling Language v1.1 from 2018 (VDML), created by members of the Object Management Group [10]. In this approach, the capability map and capability constructs are integrated with a large, formal, and highly integrated meta-model that covers commonly used concepts such as organizational units, collaborations, value streams, and activities.

The third approach is the TOGAF framework with Business Capabilities v2 from The Open Group [17] in 2022, which is widely used in the field of enterprise architecture. In this approach, capability concerns are framed in a capability viewpoint in the business architecture part of TOGAF, and (business) capability maps are diagrams and architectural work products. The capability construct is part of the TOGAF Enterprise Metamodel.

The approaches define the concept of capability and capability maps similarly, see Table 1.

Table 1. Definitions of analyzed capability and capability maps and shared characteristics

Aspect	Beimborn	VDML	TOGAF
Capability Definition	"a particular ability or capacity that a business may possess or exchange in order to enable a specific purpose or outcome"	"ability to perform a particular kind of work and deliver desired value"	"a particular ability that a business may possess or exchange to achieve a specific purpose."

(continued)

Table 1. (*continued*)

Aspect	Beimborn	VDML	TOGAF
Capability Map Definition	*"a nested hierarchy of capabilities and a taxonomic diagram that describes the interplay of capabilities while doing business"*	The capability map construct is defined indirectly through 'CapabilityLibrary' *"a hierarchy of capabilities required for the enterprise to deliver the desired results along with assessment of the importance and performance of these capabilities"*	*"complete, stable set of business capabilities (along with all of their defining characteristics) that covers the business, enterprise, or organizational unit in question."*
Theoretical grounding of Capabilities and Capability Maps	*Directly based on:* Resource-based view of the firm (RBV), Competence-based view of strategic management (CBV), Business Process Reengineering (BPR)	*Directly integrated with:* Value Networks, Resources, Events, Agents (REA), e3value, Value Stream, Cube Business Model, Possession, Ownership, Availability (POA), BMM Strategic Planning, Balanced Scorecard and Strategy Map, and BPMN	*Indirectly based on:* Process models, function mapping, value stream mapping, service orientation, capability-based planning, project portfolio management, Competences
Pragmatic Integration of Capability Map	Self-contained use	Integrated as a party of the Value Delivery Model	Integrated with TOGAF Architecture Framework as an Artifact and Diagram in a Capability (Map) Viewpoint

Definitions: What can be noted from the analysis and coding is first that all three define capability with reference to '*ability*' that is undefined. A further study of the documents shows that all three consider capabilities as - *what* the business does and not how, and that capabilities are more *stable* than corresponding processes and functions. Moreover, as noted in the table, Beimborn and VDML both directly connect a capability map to a hierarchy of capabilities, while TOGAF more loosely refers to a capability map as a set of capabilities.

The Beimborn and TOGAF define capability as one construct but VDML spreads the construct over several entities, Capability Definition, Capability Category, Capability Method, and Capability Offer, which can incur difficulties in understanding capability maps and increase the effort for creating capability maps.

Theoretical Grounding: The analyzed capability and capability map constructs are based on, integrated with, or informed by several theories and methods (see Table 1). Beimborn has directly specified the theoretical basis, while VDML has focused on integrating the underlying meta-model with a number of related approaches, and TOGAF is more indirectly inspired by concepts such as value streams and processes.

Pragmatic Integration: Even though Beimborn suggests the capability map is used in a larger methodology the capability map can be considered as a self-contained work product, while VDML and TOGAF capability maps are integrated as a part of much larger frameworks thus limiting use separately from the enclosing framework.

4.2   Characterization of Capability Constructs

The analysis was conducted using the capability pattern as a high-level coding structure. The results per capability pattern part are summarized in Table 2. As a general observation, the approaches define the concept of capability in a similar way.

Table 2. Summary of capability characteristics

Characteristics	Beimborn	VDML	TOGAF
Possessor	Business, Firm	Organizational unit	Business, Enterprise, Organizational unit
Possibility	*Unclear*	*Unclear*	*Unclear*
Lead-to	Ability, capacity, patterns of actions, function, knowledge	Function, collaboration, activity network, capability method, performers. Practices	Activity, process
Source	People, workflow, technology, information, capabilities	Resources, people with particular skills and knowledge, intellectual property, practices, facilities, tools, equipment, energy, resources, performers, actors, and services	Information, people, actors, business units, partners, resources, tools, materials, assets, IT systems, applications, assets, enablers, tools, and materials

(*continued*)

Table 2. (*continued*)

Characteristics	Beimborn	VDML	TOGAF
Result	Purpose. Outcome, information, influence	Values, deliverables, products, services	Purpose, outcome, information, deliverable, output, thing
Substantiality	Capacity, Service level, Strategic indicators, Functional Measurements	Measured Characteristics on Activity, Resource, Ports, ResourceUse, Capability Offer	Metrics on Capabilities

Possessor: The approaches are clear that a capability is related to the business or organizational units. However, they differ in descriptions of which entity is the possessor of the capability and if the organizational units are linked to or owns the capability, or if the capability is derived from the organizational unit. None of the approaches has a graphical syntax for expressing clearly what/who is the possessor.

Possibility: It is unclear how all three approaches relate to the modality of the achievement of the results. The definitions are based on 'ability' that is undefined and this creates uncertainty about which modality the capability constructs represent for example 'can do', 'do', or 'ought to do'.

Lead-To: All three approaches are based on the concept of 'ability' as that which leads to some results. However, all three distinctly define that it are well-formulated processes, functions, activities, or patterns of actions that are the real engines underpinning capabilities, thus the approaches are based on processual capabilities.

Source: All three approaches include many kinds of sources and results where most of them are well-known inputs and outputs found in traditional processes maps. Beimborn and VDML attach inputs (source) and outputs (results) to the capabilities where outputs can connect to inputs in capability maps.

Result: Interestingly, none of the three approaches and their results is directly connected to any performance framework or purpose structure that includes changes, benefits, outcomes, impacts, objectives, or goals such as Benefit Realization, Balanced Scorecards, or Goal models. VDML provides an indirect link between capabilities and activities that adds values but not directly to other kinds of values. TOGAF provides indirect links between capabilities and the realization of values streams, and to course-of-actions that appear not to be documented in any artefact or diagram.

Substantiality: In VDML and TOGAF it is possible to attach measurements on capabilities that can be shown in heatmap diagrams. VDML takes one step further and attaches Measured Characteristics to more entities including input and output ports. Beimborn incorporates a Capability Cockpit that presents capability-related strategic indicators such as inimitability and functional measurements such as delivery time.

4.3   Characterization of Capability Map Constructs

The analyzed approaches define capability maps in the following ways (see Table 3).

Selection: All three approaches select (abstract) processual capability in their maps. Beimborn focuses on deriving capabilities from process maps. VDML and TOGAF are open-ended where selected capabilities are chosen based on analysis of elements such as organization, value stream, strategic and financial plans, and business models.

Both Beimborn and TOGAF discuss different criteria relating to capabilities such as the characterization of a capability as strategic or core, inimitability, consumption of significant financial resources, and capabilities that are required to create and deliver value to their customers. Furthermore, TOGAF per definition focuses on selecting a complete and stable set of capabilities that covers the *whole scope* of the business, enterprise, or organizational unit in question, which can create large capability maps.

Interestingly, the capability maps include capabilities that deliver *desired* values or achieve or enable a *specific* purpose or outcome, which may not be all kinds of capabilities that are relevant to stakeholders' work and information needs.

Table 3. Summary of capability map characteristics

Aspect	Beimborn	VDML	TOGAF
Selection	Processual capabilities, Derived from process models	Processual capabilities, Open-ended, based on analysis	Processual capabilities, Open-ended, based on analysis, Stable, Complete
Relationships	{superior C, granular, sub C}, {output, connect, input}, {C, support, C}, {C, control, C}, {C, links to, business partners C}	{broad C classify narrow C},{output, connect, input}, and{C, support, C}	{superior, granular, sub}, {broad C classify narrow C}
Structure	Hierarchy with predefined top levels, Dependencies between capabilities	Open-ended hierarchy (level of details), Dependencies between capabilities	Open-ended hierarchy with stratification, and leveling processes, Dependencies between capabilities,

Relationships: All approaches provide hierarchical relationships between capabilities. Furthermore, Beimborn and VDML provide interconnected capability maps through dependencies that are grounded in the relationship between underlying activities and their inputs and outputs.

Structure: All approaches structure the capabilities in two dimensions, hierarchically with increasing levels of details and through dependencies. Beimborn provides an upper structure with five generic capabilities that are present in almost every company (developing products and services, client interaction, fulfilling customer demands, managing and controlling the enterprise, and collaborative activities), and unlimited lower levels. VDML and TOGAF provide open-ended structuring that depends on aspects such as the modelled organization, products or lines of business, value streams, activities, and the capabilities offered by organization units. TOGAF provides two primary processes for organizing capability maps, stratification, and leveling. TOGAF interestingly use extensively very broad scoped "management" oriented capabilities as examples for upper levels.

Situational: No approach provides a direct adaptation mechanism for the capability map or capability constructs. Although, the Architecture Development Method in TOGAF enables the use of situational method engineering and the creation of situated capability viewpoints and situated capability model kinds.

4.4 Conceptualization of In-Use Context

The three approaches provide different depths and levels of detail in their descriptions of how capabilities and capability maps are intended to be used. Beimborn and VDML provide little information about usage, while TOGAF provides a full capability-based planning method (Table 4).

Table 4. Summary of roles, work-to-be-done, and work statements

Aspect	Beimborn	VDML	TOGAF
Creators	Authors of paper	Object Management Group Members	The Open Group members
Producers	*Business Process Analyst* *Capability Analyst*	Business leader & analyst, Information systems analyst & designer *Consumers can participate in production*	(Enterprise) Architect Senior business leaders, Senior executives *Identified stakeholders can participate in production*
Consumers	Manager Decision maker	Business people, Executive, Business architect, Business leader & analyst, Operational designer, Manager, Information Systems Analyst, designer	(Enterprise) Architects Identified stakeholders, such as CxO, Program Management Office, Executive, Line Management, Business Process/Functional Expert, Suppliers, Planner

(continued)

Table 4. (*continued*)

Aspect	Beimborn	VDML	TOGAF
Participating information products	Capability Map Process Map	Value Delivery Model with Capability Library, Business Item Library, Value Library, Role Library, Practice Library	Business Capability Map, Business Capabilities catalog, *Matrixes*: Capability / Organization, Strategy / Capability, Capability / Organization, Value Stream / Capability, Stakeholder catalog
Examples of work statements for the Work to be done of Producers and Consumers as stated by the Creator	Present a consistent picture of a firm's capabilities Analyze optimization opportunities Evaluate process outsourcing potential Locate performance problems	Present an abstraction of the operation of an enterprise for business executives Design or re-design business model Discover opportunities to consolidate or outsource	Present self-contained view of the business Identify, build, source, deploy, change, restructure capabilities Identify opportunities for business improvement or investment Analyze contribution of capabilities to strategy, value streams, revenues, and costs

What can be noted from the general analysis and coding is that all three archetypical roles can be identified. Most if not all work statements are stated by the creators although Beimborn presents a case study where authors (creators) also are producers. Works statements stated by consumers have not been presented.

Most of the work statements are in general in nature without details about actual questions a capability map should answer, or the information needs deriving from decisions and actions performed by producers or consumers as stated by themselves.

An interesting question can be posed regarding how TOGAF treats capabilities in the capability-based planning method, is a TOGAF's capability defined and used in the same manner as a (business) component since both share the same compositional structure and that both can be identified, build, sourced, financed deployed, restructured, etcetera?

5   Discussion

The three analyzed capability and capability maps share many features, although they are structured differently when looking at the details.

They share the view that a capability is an abstraction of what a business does and that a capability is something to talk about, analyze, invest in, and manage.

They also share a problem. The inclusion of the 'ability' in the definitions is problematic since 'ability' is undefined, and in dictionaries, it is considered a synonym for 'capability'. Therefore, all three capability definitions are either *under-defined* or *circular*. Secondly, in western languages, and ontologies, there are clear distinctions between modalities and tenses such as 'did do', 'doing now', 'can do, 'is allowed to do', or 'desire to do'. Also, 'ability' is in natural languages associated with the possibility-modality 'can do' and not with 'do'. Thus, being unclear on 'ability' and modalities can create *cognitive dissonance* amongst ordinary people.

The three analyzed approaches focus primarily on capability maps' content and structure, assuming that processual-oriented capability maps are useful.

However, in the paper "Business Capability Maps: Current Practices and Use Cases for Enterprise Architecture Management" from 2018 [8], the authors report challenges with the use of (business) capability maps, such as lack of understanding (64% of organizations), business capabilities differ from business process thinking and require a mind shift within the organization, missing acceptance (44%), production challenges, business stakeholders are not familiar with BCM (64%), and the concept is hard to understand by stakeholders in organizations (64%). The reported challenges raise interesting questions.

- The relative similarity and closeness between capability maps and process/functional models raise some questions, is a capability map significantly different from an abstract process map or a mere mirror, what additional knowledge is added by a capability map compared to a process model, and what relative advantages do a capability map provide compared to other available kinds of information products, methodologies, or theories?
- The processual nature of the approaches raises the question, are there other kinds of capabilities than processual that are important to people in the work they do? Examples; risk-based capabilities when risk management is important, unwanted or undesired capabilities that can influence the triple bottom line such as pollution, or capabilities that transcend process boundaries such as the pricing process [4].
- The size and complexity of VDML and TOGAF raise the questions, of whether a simple and self-contained capability map based on RBV or CBV such as Beimborn can be easier to understand and simpler to produce and consume, and if the VDMLs and TOGAFs approaches can create a cognitive overload for consumers that are not also producers or enterprise architects due to the many aspects to think about.
- All three approaches focus primarily on presenting capability maps from creator and producer points of view, however, can the utility of capability maps be evaluated without the views of the consumers (buyers) being asked for and evaluated?

These questions are hard to answer by analyzing the inherent characteristic of capabilities and capability maps since the answers are related to how the capabilities and capability maps form parts of the work-to-be-done of different roles. A creator, inventor, or researcher can create an artifact that is valuable in their mind but does the intended producers and consumers intend to use, use and recommend the artifact to others? A conceptualization of in-use, such as the work-oriented approach, provides a balanced approach that can address the questions and other in-use qualities.

6 Conclusions

In this paper, we presented an analytical model that can be used to describe aspects of capability maps. The model's three parts may be applied to discern details of how capabilities, the capability map, and its intended use are described and structured. The model was applied to three kinds of capability maps, highlighting their similarities and differences. Looking closer at how capabilities are defined and used in the maps shows that they all have a process-based view of capabilities. Moreover, all three are documented from the Creator's perspective, with less attention paid to how the maps can be used.

The findings from applying the analytical model provide arguments for future research on capability maps and the map's relative advantage compared to adjacent information products such as abstract process maps, actors' pragmatic intentions to use maps, and the actual use of maps by actors playing different roles in the light of the questions raised in Sect. 5.

Furthermore, the WOA provides a research vehicle where situational use of capability maps can be explored in relation to the varying roles actors play and the actual work actors do, as expressed by themselves or others.

The sample of three capability map approaches with different characteristics limits general conclusions, which provides an opportunity for future research.

References

1. Adler, E., Pouliot, V.: International practices: introduction and framework. Cambridge Stud. Int. Relat. **119**, 3–35 (2011)
2. Beimborn, D., et al.: Capability-oriented Modeling of the Firm. Presented at the (2005)
3. Christensen, C.M., et al.: Know Your Customers' "Jobs to Be Done. https://hbr.org/2016/09/know-your-customers-jobs-to-be-done
4. Dutta, S., et al.: Pricing process as a capability: a resource-based perspective. Strateg. Manag. J. **24**(7), 615–630 (2003). https://doi.org/10.1002/smj.323
5. Henderson-Sellers, B., et al.: Situational Method Engineering. Springer (2014). https://doi.org/10.1007/978-3-642-41467-1
6. ISO/IEC: IEEE: 42010:2011 Systems and software engineering—Architecture description. ISO/IEC (2011)
7. Keller, W.: Using capability models for strategic alignment. In: Simon, D., Schmidt, C. (eds.) Business architecture management. MP, pp. 107–122. Springer, Cham (2015). https://doi.org/10.1007/978-3-319-14571-6_6
8. Khosroshahi, P.A., et al.: Business capability maps: current practices and use cases for enterprise architecture management. In: Proceedings of the 51st Hawaii International Conference on System Sciences (2018). https://doi.org/10.24251/hicss.2018.581
9. Kurnia, S., et al.: Artifacts, activities, benefits and blockers: exploring enterprise architecture practice in depth. In: Proceedings of the 53rd Hawaii International Conference on System Sciences (2020). https://doi.org/10.24251/hicss.2020.687
10. Object Management Group: Value Delivery Modeling Language, 1.1
11. Offerman, T., et al.: Business capabilities: a systematic literature review and a research agenda. In: 2017 International Conference on Engineering, Technology and Innovation, pp. 383–393 (2017). https://doi.org/10.1109/ice.2017.8279911

12. Mina, R., Mirsalari, S.R.: IT capability evaluation through the IT capability map. J. Inf. Syst. **4**, 32, 207 (2021). https://doi.org/10.29252/jist.8.32.207

13. Stirna, J., Grabis, J., Henkel, M., Zdravkovic, J.: Capability driven development – an approach to support evolving organizations. In: Sandkuhl, K., Seigerroth, U., Stirna, J. (eds.) PoEM 2012. LNBIP, vol. 134, pp. 117–131. Springer, Heidelberg (2012). https://doi.org/10.1007/978-3-642-34549-4_9

14. Tell, A.W., Henkel, M., Perjons, E.: A method for situating capability viewpoints. In: Řepa, V., Bruckner, T. (eds.) BIR 2016. LNBIP, vol. 261, pp. 278–293. Springer, Cham (2016). https://doi.org/10.1007/978-3-319-45321-7_20

15. Tell, A.W.: Productization of business models by adding situational knowledge. In: 4th International Workshop on Value Modelling and Business Ontologies (2019)

16. Tell, A.W.: What capability is not. In: Johansson, B., Andersson, B., Holmberg, N. (eds.) BIR 2014. LNBIP, vol. 194, pp. 128–142. Springer, Cham (2014). https://doi.org/10.1007/978-3-319-11370-8_10

17. The Open Group: TOGAF - Business Capabilities, Version 2. https://pubs.opengroup.org/togaf-standard/business-architecture/business-capabilities.html. Accessed 2022

18. Ulrich, W., Rosen, M.: The Business Capability Map: The "Rosetta Stone" of Business/It Alignment. https://www.cutter.com

19. Ulwick, A.W.: Jobs To Be Done: Theory to Practice. Idea Bite Press (2016)

20. Barroero, T., Motta, G., Pignatelli, G.: Business capabilities centric enterprise architecture. In: Bernus, P., Doumeingts, G., Fox, M. (eds.) EAI2N 2010. IAICT, vol. 326, pp. 32–43. Springer, Heidelberg (2010). https://doi.org/10.1007/978-3-642-15509-3_4

21. Birks, M., Mills, J.: Grounded Theory: A Practical Guide. Sage (2015)

Applying and Evaluating the KYKLOS Method

Georgios Koutsopoulos[✉] [ID], Anna Andersson, Janis Stirna[ID], and Martin Henkel[ID]

Department of Computer and Systems Sciences, Stockholm University, Postbox 7003, 164 07 Kista, Sweden
{georgios,js,martinh}@dsv.su.se, anna.anderson@live.se

Abstract. Organizations are dealing with a continuous need to adapt to their dynamic environments by changing their business capabilities. KYKLOS is a recently developed modeling method aiming to provide methodological and tool support for the phenomenon of capability change in organizations. This paper reports on a case study used to demonstrate and evaluate KYKLOS. The case study has been performed in a company in the ERP system consulting domain, and the results have been used to evaluate the method using two groups of evaluators, a business user group and a group of modeling experts. The paper reports the insights and findings that validate and motivate future research about the method and the different perspectives between the two groups of evaluators.

Keywords: Capability management · Method evaluation · Enterprise modeling · Change management

1 Introduction

Modern organizations are continuously encountering challenges associated with almost constant change in the environments they operate in. The high level of dynamism that is observed in business environments leads to a required pace of change that surpasses the pace of change in organizations with which they can easily cope [1]. This situation results in a need for additional adaptability. In practice, organizations need to change business offerings that they are capable of, which makes the concept of organizational capability relevant. The concept of capability has been defined in various ways in the literature (c.f. for instance [2]). We defined capability as a set of resources and behaviors, whose configuration bears the ability and capacity to enable the potential to create value by fulfilling a goal within a context. Capability management is a way to tackle complexity stemming from turbulent business contexts [3]. The reason is that capability management provides the necessary methodological guidance for improving the flexibility and productivity, especially when it is applied in digital organizations [4].

The task of supporting organizations during the phenomenon of capability change can be facilitated by Enterprise Modeling (EM) because it supports developing a multi-perspective view on the organizational design. The concept of capability offers a context-dependent extension for dealing with business variability and change to EM. In this

© IFIP International Federation for Information Processing 2022
Published by Springer Nature Switzerland AG 2022
B. S. Barn and K. Sandkuhl (Eds.): PoEM 2022, LNBIP 456, pp. 118–133, 2022.
https://doi.org/10.1007/978-3-031-21488-2_8

regard, as identified in previous steps of our research, a variety of generic or domain-specific capability modeling methods and approaches exist [5]. To our knowledge, hitherto, there are no approaches specifically designed for the domain of changing organizational capabilities. This gap resulted in the development of the KYKLOS method [6], aiming to provide methodological and tool support for organizations undergoing changes or needing to, by focusing on organizational capabilities.

Concerning engineering modeling methods, regardless of the design and development framework, a common requirement is that every method is to be used by people in order to solve practical problems [7]. Another commonality in every method design and development project is that the designed artifact needs to be demonstrated, and evaluated by its intended users. KYKLOS is no exception. It needs to be demonstrated and evaluated by its users. Therefore, the aim of this paper is *to have KYKLOS demonstrated, and evaluated* by its potential users, which consist mainly of business and modeling experts. Including both business experts and modeling experts allows *comparing the two groups*, leading to an *understanding of the knowledge needed to use the method* and also gives *input for future development of the method*. The differentiating groups of evaluators provide the opportunity *to explore reasons behind the differences between the groups, and potential means to bridge the gap*. As a ground for the demonstration and evaluation, a case study has been conducted in a Swedish company operating within the ERP system implementation and consulting domain and is undergoing a challenging shift in its customers' preferences which requires adaptation of its business capabilities.

The rest of the paper is structured as follows. Section 2 provides an overview of the background, including a KYKLOS overview. Section 3 describes the research methodology. Section 4 presents the case study and the application of the method. Section 5 presents the evaluation results. Sections 6 and 7 discuss the findings and provide concluding remarks respectively.

2   Background

2.1   Background on Modeling Methods and Evaluation Activities

The purpose of modeling activities is to describe specific aspects of the world by applying abstraction. For specific domains, specific attributes of the entities that comprise the domain are represented in a conceptualization, for example, a meta-model, and a specific state of affairs of the domain that is expressed using a conceptualization is called a model [8]. The construction of a model requires guidance in the form of a modeling method. A method's components are a modeling technique and the mechanisms and algorithms that work on the created model [9]. The modeling technique, in return, consists of a modeling language and a modeling procedure. The description of the necessary steps for applying the method is the modeling procedure. Syntax, semantics and notation are the parts that comprise the modeling language. The syntax describes the rules and elements for developing a model, the semantics describe the meaning of a language, and the notation concerns the visualization of the language [9].

Modeling methods are often developed within design frameworks, for example, Design Science Research [10] and Design Thinking [11]. What is common among every approach is that the developed method needs to be evaluated before a design project is finalized. Evaluation activities can take place in various formats [7]. Initially, an evaluation can be summative or formative, which refers to the assessment of completed or still developing artifacts respectively. Additionally, an evaluation can be naturalistic, meaning that it has been conducted in the case's natural environment, with a real case, real users, and a real problem, or artificial, meaning that the evaluation is not bound in reality. One last classification of evaluation activities exists between activities that require an artifact to be used before evaluating it, namely *ex post*, and the activities concerning artifacts that may not be fully developed and are evaluated on a conceptual level without being used. These activities are called *ex ante* [7].

The diversity of design projects results in a need for diverse evaluation approaches and strategies. The Framework for Evaluation in Design Science (FEDS) [12], is an approach that includes four evaluation strategies for a wide spectrum of design projects. The first distinct strategy in FEDS, Quick and Simple, concerns small and simple designs with low social and technical risks involved. It often starts with no to minimum formative evaluations and often consists of one single summative evaluation. It has low cost and produces quick project conclusion, but is not reasonable when design risks exist. The second strategy, namely Human Risk and Effectiveness, which is also the strategy used in this study, is selected when the main design risk in a project is user-oriented, it is relatively cheap to evaluate naturalistically and the focus is on evaluating if the benefits of the artifact will still accrue when it is placed in operation, even if complications exist regarding social and human difficulties in adoption and use of the artifact. It emphasizes initial formative and artificial evaluations that gradually progress to summative naturalistic ones. The third, Technical Risk and Efficacy, concerns projects with technically-oriented risk, expensive to evaluate naturalistically and establish that the utility of the artifact depends on the artifact itself. It commonly emphasizes on artificial formative and summative evaluations, only relying on naturalistic ones by the end of the project due to the cost. The last strategy, Purely Technical, is selected for purely technical artifacts with no social aspects or ones that are not meant to be used but in the far future. Since a purely technical artifact or one that does not plan to involve users soon, this strategy focuses on artificial evaluations over naturalistic ones [12].

2.2 Overview of KYKLOS

KYKLOS is a domain-specific modeling method that has been introduced in [6] and is developed within a PhD project [2]. It aims to provide methodological and tool support for managing changing capabilities in organizations. Its development was based on a previously published set of requirements [13], which summarized in the following requirement areas, (i) Context, (ii) Intentions, (iii) Decision-making, (iv) Configuration components, (v) Transitions, (vi) Ownership, and (vii) Capability dependencies. Presenting the KYKLOS language to its full extent is not feasible in this paper, therefore, we refer to [6] for the syntax and semantics, and to Table 1 for the semantics. KYKLOS has been implemented in a tool via the ADOxx meta-modeling platform [6].

The modeling procedure of KYKLOS consists of the following four phases [6]. (i) *Foundation*, describing the base of the analysis, as the identified main changing capability, the one(s) supporting it, and all the capability outcomes. (ii) *Observation*, which concerns the identification of the need to change, as context elements, with associated monitored factors which are relevant to the capability's performance, and are expressed and connected to the capability as measurable KPIs. (iii) *Decision alternatives*, which is about analyzing alternative capability configurations that fulfill the same set of intentions and address the need to change. In parallel, all the required and available components, in terms of resources and processes, are identified per configuration, along with their ownership and allocation status. (iv) *Delivery of change*, in which the change is captured as a transition between configurations.

Table 1. The KYKLOS semantics, from [6].

Concept	Description
Capability	A set of resources and behaviors, whose configuration bears the ability and capacity to enable the potential to create value by fulfilling a goal within a context
Configuration	The set of resources that comprise the capability along with the behavior elements that deliver it. A capability may have several different configurations but only one may be active at any given moment in time
Resource	Any human, infrastructure, knowledge, equipment, financial or reputation asset that can be used by an organization to enable the capability's realization. It can be allocated to one or more capability configurations, based on its capacity
Resource pool	The complete set of an organization's available resources
Context	All the factors that form the setting in which a capability exists, are relevant to its performance and within which the capability is perceived
Outcome	The result of the capability's realization. Comparing it to KPIs and Intention elements can provide insight on whether a capability change is necessary or not
KPI	A present measurable value that expresses an important aspect of the context that a capability depends on to reach the desired outcome. Used to assess the efficiency of the capability's realization when compared with outcome values
Monitored Factor	A context factor that has been identified and associated to a capability's performance and is being observed in relation to the capability. It is usually expressed as a KPI
Intention element	An abstract element that includes all the concepts that refer to the intentions governing the capability, for example, goals, problems or requirements
Goal	A desirable state that an organization aims to achieve. It is a type of Intention element
Problem	An undesirable condition that an organization aims to avoid or tackle. It is a type of Intention element
Requirement	A necessary state that an organization has to fulfill. It is a type of Intention element
Process	A behavior element that consists of activities aiming to fulfill a certain goal
Change	Change represents the transition from one configuration to another. It can be described using several change properties. A capability change is finalized when a configuration's activity state is modified

Delivering the change enables an inactive configuration, while disabling an active one, and vice versa for retiring a capability. For introducing a new capability, the transition follows from a configuration which can be considered missing, to an active one. The description of change captures its attributes, in terms of (i) control, (ii) scope, (iii) frequency, (iv) stride, (v) time, (vi) tempo, (vii) desire, and (viii) intention [6]. The procedure can be iterative. The KYKLOS notation is presented in Table 2.

Table 2. The KYKLOS notation [14].

3   Methodology

This paper is part of a PhD project aiming to develop methodological and tool support for organizations whose capabilities are changing or need to. Driven by DSR [10], and in particular, the framework of [7], it consists of five steps – (i) Explicate problem, (ii) Define requirements, (iii) Develop artifact, (iv) Demonstrate artifact, and (v) Evaluate artifact. This paper concerns the last two steps. A case study has been employed, based on the Human Risk and Effectiveness strategy of FEDS, since the artifact has user-oriented and social challenges, and, it has been subjected previously to artificial ex ante formative evaluation, in [15]. The case study has been conducted for demonstrating and evaluating the KYKLOS method. The results have been used to evaluate the method.

The method was *demonstrated* using a case study [16] in an organization which will be described in Sect. 4. Regarding the data collection for the case study, four initial online individual guided interviews [17] were conducted for framing the problem and the current and desired states of the company. The initial interviews were followed by three four-hour modeling sessions with an analyst-driven approach, where the main author acted as the analyst and method expert, applying and guiding the KYKLOS modeling procedure.

For every interview, the participant's role in the company and the role's association to change initiatives guided the discussion. The participants were employees of the organization with various roles associated to the given change, in particular, the director of the company, the head of customer success, the responsible for strategic initiatives of DI, and a data scientist. The participants have been selected using a purposive and convenience sampling. The company's specialization is directly related to changes, since it an essential aspect of their services to customers. The company's understanding of changing capabilities is not limited to its own capabilities, but its understanding of the customers' organizations is also valuable and relevant to KYKLOS.

Regarding the *evaluation* step, this paper concerns the evaluation of the KYKLOS method, which is *summative*, since the artifact is developed to a reasonably stable version 1.0, *naturalistic*, since the case study, the problem, and the users are real, and *ex post* because the evaluation took place after using the artifact. A series of nine workshops was held to evaluate the results of applying the method in the given case study, with a total of 21 respondents participating as evaluators. The groups of evaluators were classified in two main categories, the business group and the group of modeling experts. The former group consisted of 10 employees of the case study company and the latter of 11 individuals with modeling expertise representing various companies and universities. The business group, comprised of DI employees, was involved in the evaluation that used the case study, since it concerns their own organization. The director and head of customer success participated in the evaluation as well, and the rest of the group consisted of a solution architect and seven consultants. The expert group, even if it has not been directly involved in the case study, is suitable for evaluating KYKLOS due to their extensive familiarity and knowledge of modeling methods. It consisted of 10 expert researchers and teachers in enterprise and conceptual modeling, affiliated with universities in Sweden and Latvia, and one expert modeler from a private organization is the United States.

Four workshops were held for the business group, all online and with one to five participating evaluators, and five for the expert group, two online and three physical ones, with one to six evaluators per workshop. The workshops consisted of a presentation of the method's aims, semantics, syntax and tool, a thorough explanation of the goals, model, and analysis of the case study, and the evaluation, consisting of discussion, comments and a questionnaire for evaluating the method. For the expert group, live demonstration of the tool was also included, along with tool use during the physically conducted workshops.

The questionnaire was based on the Method Evaluation Model (MEM) [18], which consists of specific method aspects to be evaluated. MEM has been derived from the Technology Acceptance Model (TAM) [19]. The questionnaire consisted of 15 Likert-scale questions (Q1–15), which are inspired from and reflect on MEM's evaluation aspects – the method's Perceived Ease of Use (Q1–3), Actual Efficiency (Q4), Actual Effectiveness (Q5–11), which concerns whether the method fulfills its requirements, Perceived Usefulness (Q12–13), and Intention to Use (Q14–15). MEM also includes the Actual Usage aspect, however, the recent development of KYKLOS, without any actual usage so far, apart from the case studies conducted for demonstration and evaluation purposes, does not provide fruitful ground for assessment. The results have been primarily analyzed quantitatively using descriptive statistics and correlations, using means and t-tests. We opted for treating the data from the Likert scale questions as interval data, thereby enabling the use of means and t-tests. According to [21], they "are sufficiently robust to yield largely unbiased answers that are acceptably close to "the truth" when analyzing Likert scale responses". This practice is often recommended, especially when the measured concepts concern less concrete concepts [20], "with no fear of "coming to the wrong conclusion"" [21]. For the secondary qualitative analysis of documented comments stated during the workshops, descriptive coding [22] and thematic analysis [23] have been employed.

4 The Case Study

The case study concerns an ERP and IT consulting company in Sweden. In compliance with the company's desire to remain anonymous, we will refer to it as Digital Intelligence (DI). It is an SME, established over 20 years ago, with several offices countrywide, and specialized in selling ERP products and also consulting its clients regarding the ERP products, and, in particular, their operational aspect, and the purchase of specific customizations. The clients are given support during their digital transformations via software systems and other IT solutions. Various change initiatives have been implemented in DI over the years. Their aim was to retain DI's market share, with a focus not only on the services provided to the customers, but also to the company's structure.

As far as the specific change is concerned, the initial challenge was to identify and frame the problem. The only input and motivation, was a recently noticed shift in the requirements of its customer base. The customers used to request consulting services that were limited to equipping a specific solution but now, the customers are displaying the tendency to request a wider supply of services, specifically, they request from DI an assessment on a wide spectrum of dimensions in order to support the customer's decision on the optimal IT solution. Consequently, DI has identified an emerging need to monitor and assess its provided services, which led to a needed adaptation of DI's capabilities, a fact that indicates the case's suitability for applying KYKLOS.

4.1 Case Analysis

The gap between the value delivered by DI's capabilities and the clients' requests was clear. Driven by KYKLOS's method phases, the initial focal point of the analysis was to identify the company's capabilities that are associated to the provision of insightful ERP sales, whether the gap can be bridged, and how this can be achieved. DI's work procedures were thoroughly explored and it was revealed that, in practice, the required change is the evolution of ERP sales by inclusion insight on the customers' needs. In essence, this means extending the operational consulting with strategic consulting.

During the foundation phase of KYKLOS, ERP sale is identified as the main capability that is affected by this change. The supporting capabilities that are related to this change are Consulting and Customer assessment, along with Product acquisition and Company role clarification, which bear an indirect relevance. Completing the foundation phase, the outcomes of the capability have also been modeled, as shown in Fig. 1.

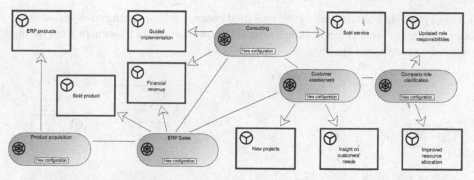

Fig. 1. The capabilities and their outcomes, captured during foundation.

The observation phase resulted in identifying the change motivators, which are both intention and context elements. Regarding the intention elements, they are the generic goals To run a successful business, the identified problem that the customers are lacking strategic guidance, and their related elements, as shown in Fig. 2. Context elements like Industry trends and Automation of sales processes have been captured, and the Satisfaction of customers has also been identified as a change motivator.

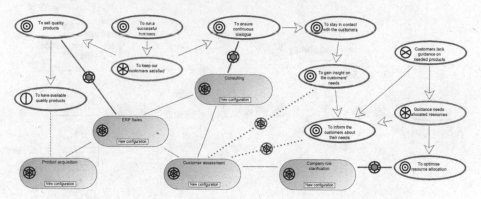

Fig. 2. The capabilities and intention elements, captured during observation.

During the decision phase, different configurations of the capabilities and their required components were identified along with the existing available resources of the company. The configuration of ERP sale with limited insight requires salespersons, offices, salaries, and specific human resource roles like Key account manager, along with the established communication processes between the company and clients. The transition to insightful sales requires insight on the customers' needs. Instead of completing the analysis, the missing component provided the opportunity to explore how the insight can be acquired.

Improved proactive is a configuration planned to replace Proactive, which has, in return, replaced the Reactive configuration of the Customer assessment capability (Fig. 3) and can provide the Insight knowledge resource as its outcome. However, this transition was not possible because, among the specified components of the Improved proactivity configuration, a Facilitation working method (Knowledge) and a training process for the method were required but missing.

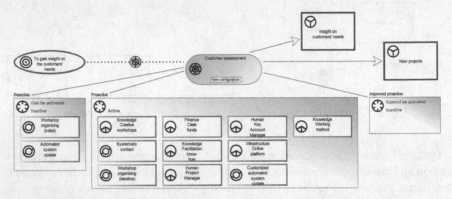

Fig. 3. The capability, its configurations, outcomes, and allocated resources.

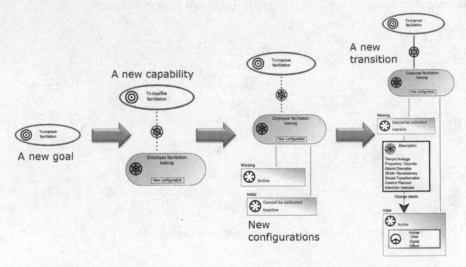

Fig. 4. Step-wise introduction of a new capability in the case study

These missing components are required because the facilitation, in other words the interaction between the customer and employee, was identified as lacking structure, a fact that resulted in the inability to gain deep insight on the customers' needs, which is required for improving the ERP Sale capability. Additional exploration revealed that these resources, as outcomes, can be acquired via the introduction of a new capability, the Employee facilitation training, which fulfills a new goal element that is introduced in the model, along with all configurations and transition of the new capability, as shown in Fig. 4.

A noteworthy fact is that the components required for the realization of this capability are existing in the company, and temporary reallocation can result in the desired strategic consulting and insightful sales. Finally, all the transitions and their attributes were captured in the delivery phase of the modeling procedure. In this way, all the above-mentioned elements were captured and the KYKLOS model was completed, in a model deemed as too large to present here.

5 Evaluation Results

This section will present the evaluation results, per group, per evaluation aspect, and overall. The evaluators responded to Likert-scale questions, which were formed as statements about the method, with the values 1 to 5 being assigned to the labels "Strongly disagree" to "Strongly agree" respectively. Initially, the collected dataset's reliability was analyzed using Cronbach's alpha, ensuring the quality of the results with an $a = .95$. The construct validity of the questionnaire was tested using bivariate correlations and all the items were validated with scores $<.05$, with one exception (Q11). The description of the findings follows, per evaluation aspect, along with a visualization of the results in a set of diagrams that depicts the overall evaluation results (Fig. 5a), the results of the group of modeling experts (Fig. 5b), the results of the business group (Fig. 5c), and the means of the groups (Fig. 5d), for each part of the questionnaire.

Perceived Ease of Use: The initial three questions of the questionnaire assessed the method's Perceived Ease of Use according to MEM, and were specified for KYKLOS by asking about the clarity of the method's phases (Q1), the clarity of its modeling procedure (Q2), and the ease to use it overall (Q3). For the business group, the responses ranged from 2.7 to 3.0/5, resulting in negative to neutral scores for KYKLOS's ease of use. On the contrary, the group of modeling experts evaluated this aspect of the method with 4.0 to 4.5/5, which results in a clearly positive score for the given aspect. Overall, combining the results of the entire group of evaluators results in scores that range between 3.4 to 3.8/5, which results in an overall positive response regarding KYKLOS's ease of use. The comments of the two groups are indicative of their responses. To illustrate, one business evaluator mentioned "for me, that do not have any experience in this type of modeling I found this method hard to understand.", but a comment from the expert group was "the method itself is not hard to follow if you have some experience in capability modelling".

Actual Efficiency: In order to evaluate the actual efficiency of a method, MEM suggests assessing the quantitative aspects of applying the method, in terms of time, cost and effort. However, taking into consideration that there are no other methods specifically designed for the domain of changing capabilities, this aspect was evaluated by comparing KYKLOS with every evaluator's known methods that may be used for tackling the given problem. Therefore, the evaluators were asked whether the method reduces the effort required for modeling changing capabilities (Q4). For the business group of evaluators, the responses produced a score of 3.2/5, showing a positive result which is slightly higher than neutral, supported by statements like "I think it would take quite a while to model a complex organization" and "I think this model is too time consuming". The group of modeling experts produced a value of 4.0/5 for the same aspect, a result that shows a clearly positive viewpoint. An interesting comment about the effort came from an expert stating "effort reduction is not an issue; the issue is getting a better result and KYKLOS could be useful here". In total, the evaluation results in a score of 3.6/5 for the reduced effort required using KYKLOS.

Actual Effectiveness: MEM defines the actual effectiveness of a method as the degree to which it achieves its objectives. So, for this aspect, the requirement areas of KYKLOS (c.f. [13] for details) were used, asking the evaluators whether KYKLOS is effective for modeling the following areas that are associated to changing capabilities: (i) Context (Q5), (ii) Intentions (Q6), (iii) Decision-making (Q7), (iv) Configuration components (Q8), (v) Transitions (Q9), (vi) Ownership (Q10), and (vii) Capability dependencies (Q11).

Q11 was identified as an item with low validity and has been removed from the statistical analyses. The results from the business group of evaluators ranged between 3.0 and 3.8/5, in other words, the requirements of KYKLOS scores ranged from neutral to different grades of positive, as shown in Fig. 5b. The lowest score was received by Ownership and the highest one by Configuration components. A comment indicating the group's response was "some of the (modeling) components were a little bit confusing". Regarding the expert group, the scores were higher, ranging from 4.1/5 which was assigned to Context, to 4.6/5, which was the score of Configuration components. The expert group focused on specific model elements as this comment illustrates – "the pool concept and notation is interesting and probably useful in many situations.". The combined results provided a range of scores between 3.6 and 4.2/5, which shows an overall positive response to the effectiveness of the method.

Q11, which is not part of the quantitative analyses, got the 3rd higher score among the questionnaire items. Despite the fact that Q11 has been removed from the statistical analyses for reasons of research rigor, there were comments supporting the high scores that capability associations and dependencies received. So, even if it cannot be evaluated quantitatively, qualitatively, this aspect was approved, a fact which can be supported by comments like "the capability relationships can be used for capability mapping in Enterprise Architecture projects", and "I agree with the idea that only one main capability and the supporting ones exist per model because it helps avoid complexity".

A notable observation associated to the perceived ease of use and actual effectiveness is that both groups expressed difficulties regarding sources of potential confusion, however, the business group expressed generic comments about the method overall, while the group of experts expressed difficulties regarding specific components of KYKLOS. For example, comments from the expert group about the notation "the hardest part, at least for me, would be to follow the expected notation that is not a standard modelling notation", the Resource pool, "more clarification on the resource pool can be beneficial", and the ownership "was not sure about ownership, there are resource elements in modelling notation, but resources are meant to describe the ownership for capabilities?". An example of the business group's generic comments states "if I were to look at the finished model I think it is quite complex and there are several other modelling techniques that are easier to grasp". There were also neutral statements, like "I think that compared to a lot of other models, it quite detailed focused. Which could be both a positive thing and a negative one", coming from the business group.

Perceived Usefulness: For evaluating the perceived usefulness of KYKLOS, the evaluators were asked to assess whether they perceive the concepts included in the method as adequate for modeling the phenomenon of capability change (Q12), and if, as a whole, they perceive the method to be useful for the given domain (Q13). The business group's scores were 2.9 and 3.3/5 respectively, while the expert modeler group's scores were higher for these questions too; 4.4 and 4.3/5 respectively. The comments coming from the two groups were as diverse as the scores, for example "I'm not sure how we could use this model.", from the business group, and "it fills a necessary niche in the modeling world." or "it is very useful for large companies with so many projects running at the same time." from the expert group. The combined results of the entire group of evaluators were 3.7/5 for the concept set and 3.8/5 for the overall usefulness, resulting in a positive response in general.

Intention to Use: As suggested by MEM, the objects that were used for evaluating the method's intention to use consisted of a statement about the overall intention to use KYKLOS for modeling changing capabilities (Q14), and another one about the preference to use KYKLOS in comparison to other available methods known to the evaluators (Q15). The business group responded negatively to both questions, with scores of 2.3 and 2.1/5 respectively, which was supported by statements like "I will probably choose to use a simpler model". On the contrary, the expert modelers responded positively, evaluating Q14 with 3.7/5 and Q15 with 3.9/5, supported by statements like "for any future capability modeling, I would utilize the KYKLOS method.". The overall results regarding the intention to use KYKLOS show a neutral response of 3.0/5 for both questions. A specific aspect of the method that was discussed was the tool, which was mentioned as a motivational factor for using the method, in comments like "I'd use KYKLOS, since it has a responsive UI and does allow to create a clean model.". Given the significant differences in this aspect, it should be taken into consideration that a new method is still part of a familiar area for the experts, however, for the business group, their interest in using the method could only be seen from a perspective of extending their personal methodological toolbox, based on their specific roles in the company.

Assigning weights of -2 to 2 to the responses "Strongly disagree" to "Strongly agree" respectively, enabled a different perspective on the analysis, and allowed identifying that the highest rated question was the Configuration components with a score of 25 and the Intent to Use and Preference shared the lowest position sharing the score of 1. Regarding the responses per group, the business group's weighted scores ranged between -9 and 8 and the expert group's between 8 and 18. This is also reflected in the means of the responses; Components has a score of 4.2/5 and Intent to Use and Preference shared a 3.0/5. Regarding all the means of the responses per group, they ranged between 2.1 and 3.8/5 for the business group and 3.7 and 4.6/5 for the group of expert modelers. The differences of the two groups are also reflected in the means, which are shown in Fig. 5d. The group results were tested with Independent Samples T-Tests and all group differences were identified as significant (sig. 2-tailed $<.05$) for all the items of the questionnaire with the exception of Capability dependencies.

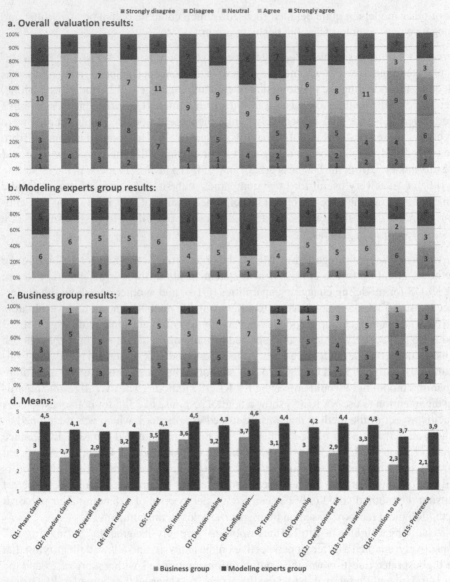

Fig. 5. The evaluation results overall (5a), for the group of modeling experts (5b), the business group (5c), and the compared means of the two groups (5d).

6 Discussion

Initially, the demonstration activity provided the opportunity to show that KYKLOS has potentials to be not only effective for capturing and documenting one or more changing capabilities, but also facilitates the analysis of the capabilities via their configurations, to a degree that enables making suggestions for improvements, thus, it also supports decision-making. In particular, in the DI case, by the use of KYKLOS, the thorough exploration of the configurations of the supporting capabilities indicated weaknesses that could be mitigated by reallocating resources, a fact which led to the suggestion for introducing a new capability, the Employee facilitation training. In this way, KYKLOS was applied to the case study and its feasibility was proved, which is the aim of the demonstration step in DSR [7].

Regarding the evaluation, the method has been deemed useful but, for the business group, there are difficulties concerning the adoption and use, which is in line with the Human Risk and Effectiveness strategy, whose activities aim to ensure that the method is still beneficial "on the long run", despite the difficulties, according to FEDS [12]. This relates to an important aspect of the results, which is the significant differences that have been identified between the two groups of evaluators, which were not expected during the design phase of the research. All the evaluation aspects received a higher score from the expert group, a fact indicating that previous modeling experience is a desired attribute for every potential KYKLOS user. This has also been mentioned in comments from the business group, for example "I am not sure everyone is able to apply this model, I think it does require previous knowledge of modelling.", "I think the model is difficult to communicate to outsiders.", and "I think it is important to have in mind that training and education will be an important part when companies are going to use this model.", while there were no similar comments from the expert group.

Overall, both groups are positive about the effectiveness, efficiency, and usefulness of the method, but disagree on the ease and intention to use it, a fact which is indicated by the larger differences in the respective scores. For the research team of KYKLOS, this raises the issue of complexity of the method. On the one hand, this paper identified that the current version of the method should be communicated to users with modeling experience and avoid non-experts, since the response from the business group of evaluators indicates several encountered difficulties, in terms of understanding, applying and benefiting from the method. In this way, the complexity of the method, which reflects the actual complexity of the domain of capability change, will remain intact, without sacrificing any of the descriptive power of KYKLOS. This will also mean that the target group of the KYKLOS users will be significantly delimited. On the other hand, efforts also can be put on bridging the gap between user categories. Potential solutions to this issue can be the development of structured method training, a KYKLOS "light" version with reduced complexity and available modeling elements, that can be used for a higher level of models for changing capabilities, or a canvas-based approach, hiding the details of the modeling language, that can be used as a pre-modeling step for KYKLOS. The first solution, does not really bridge the gap methodologically, because it aims to convert non-experts to experts, however, the other two could provide valid bridging solutions, but the fact that these approaches will result in reduced descriptive power or increased analyst workload should not be ignored. The significant differentiation between expert and non-expert users of a modeling method, along with ways to bridge their gap, is a topic worthy of further research. The expert modelers also expressed wishes for using existing enterprise models as inputs to KYKLOS models, as well as suggested various functional improvements to the method and tool, such as the ability to create capability views, capability maps, and to decompose capabilities.

Therefore, the contribution of this paper has not been limited only to the demonstration and evaluation of KYKLOS, but also to raising new directions for future research. Another topic that has been raised during the workshops and has been derived from the discussion around the usefulness of the method, was the scope flexibility of KYKLOS. One evaluator from the business group mentioned that "it feels like it might not capture everything needed to model changing capabilities, the human factor e.g.", followed by the question "would it be possible to change the model's scope from an organizational perspective to an individual?". Currently, this is outside the scope of the method, however, it motivates the exploration of potential KYKLOS extensions to support this aspect of change. Researching whether the perspective of individual capabilities can be integrated with the current KYKLOS structure and converting the method to a new version with a flexible scope is a challenge for the KYKLOS research team or any researcher with an interest in the given area.

7   Conclusions

KYKLOS, which is a domain-specific modeling method designed for supporting organizations during the change of their capabilities, has been demonstrated and evaluated and the results of these activities have been reported in this paper. The method has been applied on a case study in a Swedish company in the IT domain, where the potentials of KYKLOS both as a modeling and a decision-supporting method have been confirmed. A group of business experts from the company and a group of modeling experts have participated in a series of workshops where the method was evaluated via its application. Overall, the two groups agreed that the method is efficient, effective and useful, however, the business group disagreed on the ease and intention to use it. Both in agreements and disagreements, the group scores were significantly different. The evaluation also raised the topics of complexity and scope flexibility for KYKLOS.

Acknowledgements. We would like to express our gratitude to the case study company and all the participants of the evaluation workshops for their time, effort, and valuable feedback.

References

1. Burke, W.W.: Organization Change: Theory and Practice. Sage Publications (2017)
2. Koutsopoulos, G.: Managing Capability Change in Organizations: Foundations for a Modeling Approach (2020). http://urn.kb.se/resolve?urn=urn:nbn:se:su:diva-185231
3. Wißotzki, M.: Capability Management Guide. Springer, Wiesbaden (2018)
4. Sandkuhl, K., Stirna, J. (eds.): Capability Management in Digital Enterprises. Springer, Cham (2018). https://doi.org/10.1007/978-3-319-90424-5
5. Koutsopoulos, G., Henkel, M., Stirna, J.: An analysis of capability meta-models for expressing dynamic business transformation. Softw. Syst. Model. **20**(1), 147–174 (2020). https://doi.org/10.1007/s10270-020-00843-0
6. Koutsopoulos, G., Henkel, M., Stirna, J.: Modeling the phenomenon of capability change: the KYKLOS method. In: Karagiannis, D., Lee, M., Hinkelmann, K., Utz, W. (eds.) Domain-Specific Conceptual Modeling, pp. 265–288. Springer, Cham (2022)

7. Johannesson, P., Perjons, E.: An Introduction to Design Science. Springer, Cham (2014). https://doi.org/10.1007/978-3-319-10632-8
8. Guizzardi, G.: Ontological foundations for structural conceptual models (2005)
9. Karagiannis, D., Kühn, H.: Metamodelling platforms. In: Bauknecht, K., Tjoa, A.M., Quirch-mayr, G. (eds.) EC-Web 2002. LNCS, vol. 2455, pp. 182–182. Springer, Heidelberg (2002). https://doi.org/10.1007/3-540-45705-4_19
10. Hevner, A., March, S.T., Park, J., Ram, S.: Design science in information systems research. MIS Q. **28**, 75–105 (2004). https://doi.org/10.2307/25148625
11. Dorst, K.: The core of 'design thinking' and its application. Des. Stud. **32**, 521–532 (2011). https://doi.org/10.1016/j.destud.2011.07.006
12. Venable, J., Pries-Heje, J., Baskerville, R.: FEDS: a framework for evaluation in design science research. Eur. J. Inf. Syst. **25**, 77–89 (2016)
13. Koutsopoulos, G., Henkel, M., Stirna, J.: Requirements for observing, deciding, and delivering capability change. In: Gordijn, J., Guédria, W., Proper, H.A. (eds.) PoEM 2019. LNBIP, vol. 369, pp. 20–35. Springer, Cham (2019). https://doi.org/10.1007/978-3-030-35151-9_2
14. Koutsopoulos, G., Henkel, M.: An experience report on the implementation of the KYKLOS modeling method. In: Serral, E., Stirna, J., Ralyté, J., Grabis, J. (eds.) PoEM 2021. LNBIP, vol. 432, pp. 103–118. Springer, Cham (2021). https://doi.org/10.1007/978-3-030-91279-6_8
15. Koutsopoulos, G., Henkel, M., Stirna, J.: Improvements on capability modeling by imple-menting expert knowledge about organizational change. In: Grabis, J., Bork, D. (eds.) PoEM 2020. LNBIP, vol. 400, pp. 171–185. Springer, Cham (2020). https://doi.org/10.1007/978-3-030-63479-7_12
16. Yin, R.K.: Case Study Research: Design and Methods. Sage Publications, Thousand Oaks, Calif (2003)
17. Gubrium, J., Holstein, J., Marvasti, A., McKinney, K.: The SAGE Handbook of Interview Research: The Complexity of the Craft. SAGE Publications, Inc., 2455 Teller Road, Thousand Oaks California 91320 United States (2012). https://doi.org/10.4135/9781452218403
18. Moody, D.L.: The method evaluation model: a theoretical model for validating information systems design methods. In: Proceedings of the 11th European Conference on Information Systems, 16–21 June 2003, pp. 1327–1336. Naples, Italy (2003)
19. Davis, F.D.: Perceived usefulness, perceived ease of use, and user acceptance of information technology. MIS Q. **13**, 319 (1989). https://doi.org/10.2307/249008
20. Sullivan, G.M., Artino, A.R.: Analyzing and interpreting data from likert-type scales. J. Grad. Med. Educ. **5**, 541–542 (2013)
21. Norman, G.: Likert scales, levels of measurement and the "laws" of statistics. Adv. Health Sci. Educ. **15**, 625–632 (2010). https://doi.org/10.1007/s10459-010-9222-y
22. Saldaña, J.: The Coding Manual for Qualitative Researchers. Sage, Los Angeles, Calif (2009)
23. Braun, V., Clarke, V.: Using thematic analysis in psychology. Qual. Res. Psychol. **3**, 77–101 (2006). https://doi.org/10.1191/1478088706qp063oa

Using Tangible Modeling to Create an e^3value Conceptual Model for Digital Ecosystems

Nedo Bartels[1]([✉])(iD), Roel Wieringa[2](iD), Matthias Koch[1](iD), Karina Villela[1](iD), Daniel Suzumura[1](iD), and Jaap Gordijn[2,3](iD)

[1] Fraunhofer IESE, Kaiserslautern, Germany
{nedo.bartels,matthias.koch,karina.villela,
daniel.suzumura}@iese.fraunhofer.de
[2] The Value Engineers, Soest, The Netherlands
{roel,jaap}@thevalueengineers.nl
[3] Vrije Universiteit, Amsterdam, The Netherlands
j.gordijn@vu.nl

Abstract. The design of digital platforms and ecosystems is a challenging problem that involves technical, organizational, and business aspects. In this context, modeling languages for creating conceptualizations are crucial to support the design of comprehensive ecosystems. However, the creation of conceptual models requires the input and expertise of practitioners, who usually do not have the time to learn modeling languages. In this paper, we explore how to overcome this challenge by combining a tangible design approach for ecosystems, named the Tangible Ecosystem Design (TED) methodology, with a value modeling approach named the e^3value methodology. We created and analyzed a TED Service Map and a corresponding e^3value model to formulate lessons learned based on a comparison of models. Our results suggest that (1) the design process of a value model can benefit from tangible modeling and (2) model elements can be partially transferred from TED models to e^3value models. The contribution of this paper provides lessons learned that can be used to derive e^3value models from the TED approach and thereby lower entry barriers for conceptual models of complex ecosystems.

Keywords: e^3value · Tangible ecosystem design · Tangible modeling · Value modeling · Business models · Digital ecosystems

1 Introduction

Regardless of the domain, the emergence of digital platforms and ecosystems is changing markets and sectors [21]. As a consequence, companies try to (re-)define their own business strategies regarding how to create and capture values [27]. We define a *digital ecosystem* as a 'collection of companies that work cooperatively and competitively to satisfy customer needs' [16] by providing digital products or

© IFIP International Federation for Information Processing 2022
Published by Springer Nature Switzerland AG 2022
B. S. Barn and K. Sandkuhl (Eds.): PoEM 2022, LNBIP 456, pp. 134–148, 2022.
https://doi.org/10.1007/978-3-031-21488-2_9

services. Here, we consider a *digital platform* as a specific kind of an *ecosystem*, with the addition that the platform offers platform services used frequently by all actors of an ecosystem. A digital platform is offered by one or more *asset broker(s)*, which enable the exchange of *assets* between their *asset providers* and *asset consumers*. Often, but not necessarily, a platform is provided by a single party such as Airbnb, Uber, eBay, etc. [14].

For digital ecosystems, a *business model* can be designed that conceptualizes how economic value is created, distributed, and consumed in a network of parties. The e^3value methodology [5] allows the notion of models as an abstraction of reality according to a certain conceptualization [8]. A challenge to be faced is how to transfer the use of the e^3value methodology to practitioners, e.g., how to facilitate wide-spread adoption of the methodology in the field. One of the problems experienced, according to the developers of e^3value, is that practitioners find it hard to develop precise and accurate conceptual models in general. The same holds for e^3value, despite the effort of its developers to keep the complexity of the e^3value methodology to the bare minimum [4].

One easy-to-use method for designing business models is the Business Model Canvas (BMC) [20]. However, BMC is (1) intended for business cases with one focal actor and its direct key partners and key customers, whereas we are interested in full ecosystems (because digital innovation affects all parties in an ecosystem, not just one), and (2) is restricted in its expressive power (nine building blocks without formal syntax or semantics do not cover a full ecosystem). As a consequence, BMC is not very suitable for carrying out various kinds of analyses such as ecosystem-wide net cash flow analysis, risk and fraud analysis, etc. We argue that applying these analyses techniques should be an intrinsic part of any ecosystem (re-)design process, and should also be integrated with the conceptualization technique(s) used. Current methods and frameworks lack guidance for tacking the complex and long-term task of ecosystem design [28].

Because people find it hard to conceptualize ecosystems in general [23] and to use e^3value in particular, the question arises of whether we can offer people assistance to do so. A solution that we explore in this paper is the combination of c^3value methodology, and *tangible modeling*, specifically the *Tangible Ecosystem Design* (TED) methodology [17], which uses Playmobil® toys like figures, cars, and objects together with a set of print templates to design digital ecosystems systematically. Experience has shown that the TED methodology makes ecosystem concepts more concrete and understandable, as well as making the process of designing ecosystems easier for participants [17,18].

Similar to [11], we propose tangible modeling and the use of physical components as a design approach to support the subsequent ecosystem modeling process. This paper explores the relationship between TED and e^3value to the extent that a TED *Service Map* (SM) model (see Sect. 4) can be used to derive and initiate an e^3value model (see Sect. 5) to make the process of the e^3value methodology more accessible to practitioners. Therefore, our *research question* is: What are the semantic similarities between a TED Service Map model and an e^3value model?

This paper is structured as follows. In Sect. 2, we introduce relevant related work. Sect. 3 presents the study design. Then Sects. 4 and 5 introduce the two methodologies used in the paper, namely TED and e^3value. Sect. 6 presents the core of the paper, i.e., how a TED Service Map model can be related to an e^3value model, showing a set of lessons learned. Finally, Sect. 7 presents our conclusion and future work.

2   Related Work

In the past, the conceptual modeling and requirements engineering community have proposed a large portfolio of modeling techniques. They developed languages such as e^3value [5], i^* [24], BPMN [19], SSN [1], SEAM [3], and the UML [7] family to mention but a few, and studied how to use these techniques in *combination* for the purpose of understanding ecosystems (see e.g. [10,15,23,25]). These techniques are perceived as useful for creating *conceptual models* for modeling ecosystems, but practitioners often find them hard to use [13]. There are multiple reasons for this (see the observations of [23]), but similar to [12], we claim that conceptualization (of what all these techniques do) is hard by *nature*, requires effort and handling, and practitioners do not have the time to learn a modeling language. Evidence provided by [12] shows that tangible modeling languages, i.e., languages whose concepts are represented by physical objects, such as plastic toy figures, have positive effects on collaborative modeling efforts and can lead to better conceptual models [6,17,22]. The experiments of [12] indicate a beneficial impact of *iconicity* (similarity between sign and object) on participants' understanding, modeling speed, and model quality, which can be enhanced by the *tangibility* of physical objects. Moreover, according to [6], practitioners achieve a better understanding, there is greater consensus, and rate of adoption of the results is higher.

Based on existing literature indicating the potential of tangible modeling for the ecosystem design process [2,6,11,13], we identified a lack of research on approaches and experiences that demonstrate the combination of tangible modeling with value modeling techniques for the design process of digital ecosystems. Therefore, we are exploring for the first time the combination of tangible modeling of TED, which uses physical artifacts to represent actors and exchanges within a digital ecosystem, and the value modeling approach of e^3value.

3   Relating TED and e^3value: Study Design

The goal of this paper is to understand how tangible modeling in general, and TED in particular, relates to value modeling, e.g., e^3value. Although we chose to combine TED and e^3value because we are familiar with both methodologies, we do not rule out other approaches. Understanding this relationship is important for using tangible modeling as a tool to lower the barriers for practitioners to create meaningful and correct e^3value models. Given the nature of TED SM models, we expect semantic overlap of a TED SM model with an e^3value model, and hence the TED SM model is useful input for an e^3value model. To establish this, our research followed three steps. (1) To find out whether TED and e^3value can be meaningfully related, a real-life project carried out by Fraunhofer IESE was used. The aim of the project was to develop a digital ecosystem for a mobility platform. In order to understand all technical, organizational, and business aspects of the digital ecosystem, a series of TED workshops with stakeholders was carried out, resulting in a number of tangible models, including the TED SM model (see Sect. 4). Since the design process of the TED SM model is not part of this work, the workshops are not presented in detail. (2) Taking the TED SM model for the digital ecosystem of the mobility platform, researchers from Fraunhofer IESE and *The Value Engineers* (TVE) jointly developed the corresponding e^3value model. This development was led by e^3value experts. The result is a valid e^3value model (Sect. 5) to the corresponding e^3value methodology. (3) The two models the TED SM model and the e^3value model were compared in order to derive similarities. Our observations on the similarities between the TED SM model and the e^3value model are formulated as lessons learned (see Sect. 6.5) and need to be evaluated in the future.

Since ecosystem modeling can be considered as a design problem, and thus a case of Design Science [9], we intend to use our formulated findings to provide design guidelines for deriving an e^3value model from a TED SM model in the future.

4   The TED Methodology for Ecosystem Design

The goal of the *Tangible Ecosystem Design* (TED) methodology is to support the design of *digital ecosystems*, which are socio-technical systems connecting multiple, typically independent providers and consumers of assets. The TED methodology is an interactive workshop approach to help ecosystem initiators identify and understand interactions and exchanges among their actors. By combining touchable Playmobil® toy figures with proven creativity techniques, TED can be used to design a tangible, concrete, and touchable model of a digital ecosystem (see, e.g., Fig. 1). The TED methodology consists of three components, which are ideally conducted in interactive workshops. These workshops can be held together in presence or virtually - associated materials exist for both scenarios [26]. The three components of the TED methodology are:

1. *Service Blueprint.* The goal of the Service Blueprint is to map the activities and interactions of the platform users and systems and to define a user journey (e.g., user opens app, user registers, user sets payment method, etc.). In doing so, the workshop participants also define various processes and activities along their user journey via different layers: (1) user activities, (2) interactive system activities, (3) system activities in the background, and (4) organizational or contractual prerequisites. An example of a service blueprint can be found in [26].
2. *Service Map* (SM). The goal of the SM model is to determine the roles of the actors in the digital ecosystem, to work out the exchanges between them, and

Fig. 1. Impressions of a TED workshop.

to define a possible revenue model. The elements of the SM primarily include actors and different kinds of flows such as money-, asset-, and data flows, and contractual relationships. It has been shown in the TED workshops that a process-like mindset helps participants to model complex exchanges in the SM. However, the SM is not a process model. A representation of a TED SM model can be seen in Fig. 2.

3. *Motivation Matrix.* The aim of the Motivation Matrix is to identify the benefits and values for each actor participating in the digital ecosystem. For each actor, a comparison is made between what is expected through participation and what the digital ecosystem actually enables. A representation of a Motivation Matrix can be seen in [26].

In terms of scope, this paper focuses mainly on the TED SM model, as it defines the ecosystem actors and its interactions similar to a value model in e^3value. Figure 2 presents a TED SM model for Airbnb.

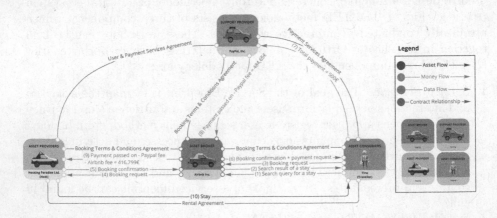

Fig. 2. Example representation of a TED SM using the example of Airbnb

5 The e^3value Methodology for Ecosystem Value Modeling

The e^3value methodology creates a value model that represents a network of actors that create, transfer, and consume things of economic value. We assume that the reader is familiar with e^3value, otherwise, we refer to [5]. To illustrate e^3value and TED with common knowledge, Fig. 2 and Fig. 3 present a simplified version of Airbnb. Similar to the TED model in Fig. 2, the value model in Fig. 3 shows the interactions between the Airbnb platform and its hosts, visitors, and the payment service PayPal.

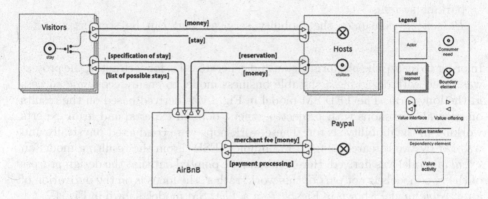

Fig. 3. Example representation of an e^3value model using the example of Airbnb

6 Relating the TED SM to e^3value: The Mobility Platform

We will first present the use case we considered and then show the corresponding TED SM model and e^3value model. We will discuss the correspondences between the two models and then formulate them as lessons learned.

6.1 Use Case – Digital Platform for Mobility Services

The goal of the considered mobility platform is to build an open-source, standardized platform to enable innovative mobility services. Therefore, local trip planners (referred to as *multimodal mobility operator*) can use the mobility platform as a marketplace to combine mobility services (e.g. taxi cabs), data sources (e.g., traffic situation), and mobility process services (e.g., parking systems) to promote innovative mobility services to passengers. The vision of the mobility platform is to (1) create a marketplace for innovative mobility services, (2) ensure interoperability between different modes of mobility, and (3) make it easier for passengers to use bundled mobility services and trips. From a technical perspective, the mobility platform should be based on open-source components and semantic web technologies. The mobility platform includes the following actors:

- *Mobility platform:* provides the digital platform and the marketplace, which connects mobility services with, mobility-related data sources and process services.
- *Multimodal mobility operator:* offers a trip planning service for the intelligent bundling of mobility services to enable passengers to get a complete mobility solution.
- *Mobility provider:* provides a single (or multiple) mobility service(s), such as taxi cabs, buses, trains, and e-scooters, to transport passengers.
- *Data provider:* offers mobility-related data sources, such as traffic and weather situation or local events that affect mobility conditions.
- *Processing service provider:* offers mobility-related process services, such as parking systems.
- *Passenger:* consumes the mobility services, and can be seen as an end-customer.

In order to realize the platform vision and generate value for each actor, the project was faced with designing a suitable business model to ensure economic success in the long term. The TED SM model in Fig. 4 was derived based on the results on several workshops with project partners, domain experts, and legal experts working in the mobility sector. These workshops were conducted physically and was led by two researchers from Fraunhofer IESE. From the resulting model an e^3value model was derived. Here, it should be pointed out that the design process of the two models is not part of this work; rather, the focus is on the derivation of an e^3value model, shown in Fig. 5, from a TED SM model, shown in Fig. 4.

6.2 TED SM Model for the Mobility Ecosystem

We will briefly summarize the TED SM model based on the numbered flow sequences 1–4 in Fig. 4. 1st *flow sequence: passenger's request for mobility services.* The passenger makes a mobility request to the multimodal mobility operator, who then forwards this request to the mobility platform. The mobility platform then requests the best travel mode from the processing service providers, the current traffic situation from the data provider, and corresponding mobility offers from the mobility providers. 2nd *flow sequence: actors' response via mobility platform.* Relevant traffic data and process travel modes as well as the available mobility offers are then sent via the mobility platform to the multimodal mobility operator, who bundles them into a complete mobility offer and forwards this to the passenger. 3rd *flow sequence: booking process.* The passenger confirms the compiled mobility offer by initiating a booking with the multimodal mobility provider. The multimodal mobility provider sends the booking data to the mobility providers, who in turn issue their access authorization to the mobility services. 4th *flow sequence: payment process.* The payment process takes place in parallel with the booking process. The passenger pays the total price per booked trip to the multimodal mobility provider. The multimodal mobility provider retains a portion and passes the remaining amount on to the mobility service providers for their mobility services. The data and process service providers are paid by the multimodal mobility provider for providing traffic data and travel mode. In addition, the mobility

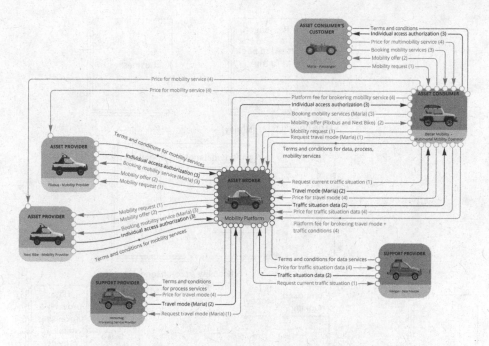

Fig. 4. TED SM model of the mobility ecosystem.

platform receives a brokering fee from the multimodal mobility provider for the brokering of (1) mobility services, and (2) data and process services.

6.3 The e^3value Model of the Mobility Ecosystem

Researchers from Fraunhofer IESE and TVE designed a possible e^3value model for the TED SM model. The design process was led by e^3value experts to ensure that the resulting model is correct. We need correct models to do proper similarity analysis between TED SM and e^3value models. The resulting value model is depicted in Fig. 5. For the sake of simplicity, those actors that fulfill similar roles were grouped together in the e^3value model; accordingly, a total of four market segments and one mobility platform as actor were modeled.

Starting with the passenger, there are two value transfers to the multimodal mobility operator, which clarifies the core exchange of a trip booking and money. Here, the multimodal mobility operator enables the value exchange by composing a trip from bookable mobility services (e.g., taxi cabs, buses, e-scooter) and listed mobility information (e.g., best mobility offer during rush hour). The core of the e^3value model is the mobility platform with its value activities *listing* and *booking* and its ten value transfers. For the listing, mobility-related data from data providers is linked with the mobility offer data (e.g., seat availability) of mobility providers. For this, the data providers get paid by the multimodal mobility provider by means of a fee. The mobility providers use the platform primarily to acquire customers for their mobility services and to process bookings. Payment

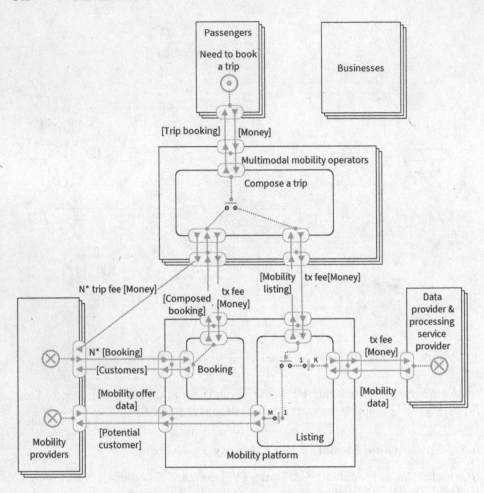

Fig. 5. e^3value model of the mobility ecosystem

to mobility providers is not made through the mobility platform. In addition, the multimodal mobility operator pays the mobility platform a transaction-based brokerage fee for the use of the booking and listing functions.

6.4 Evaluation of the TED SM Model and the e^3value Model

Discussions were held with three experts who have knowledge of both ecosystem modeling and the project. In the discussions, both the TED SM model and the e^3value model were compared in order to validate overall model meaningfulness as well as semantic similarities and differences.

The experts discussed the completeness of the two models in terms of whether the support providers should be considered together as in Fig. 5 or separately (see data provider and processing service provider in Fig. 4). However, all three experts considered the e^3value model (Fig. 5) designed from the TED SM model (Fig. 4) as coherent and reasonable, and agreed that TED SM models and e^3value models have semantic overlaps. We assume that following a TED Service Map model can partly lead to an e^3value model.

6.5   Analysis of TED SM Model and e^3value Model Correspondences

We formulated the similarities between the TED SM and an e^3value model as a set of lessons learned (see Table 1, and the subsequent discussion), which summarizes the experience we gained. These lessons learned were found by carefully analyzing both the TED SM and the corresponding e^3value model for semantic similarity.

To assess whether modeling elements of an e^3value model can result from a TED SM model, we formulated our lessons learned using three gradations: (1) *can lead*, in the case of a clear transfer from TED to e^3value; (2) *can partially lead*; in the case of a potential transfer, and (3) *not considered* in TED, in the case of no transfer. The structure of Table 1 is inspired by the guidelines of [25] regarding correspondence between BPMN and e^3value models.

Table 1. Lessons learned – from TED Service Map model to e^3value model

ID	TED elements	e^3value elements	Lessons learned
L1		Actor / Market segment	Specified actors in TED SM *can lead* to actors and market segments in e^3value.
L2	Asset Flow / Money Flow	Value transfer	TED SM asset flows, and money flows *can partially lead* to value transfers in e^3value.
L3	Asset Flow / Money Flow	Value interface	TED SM asset flows, and money flows *can partially lead* to value interfaces in e^3value.
L4	Asset Flow / Money Flow	Value offering	TED SM asset flows, and money flows *can lead* to value ports in e^3value.
L5	Contract Relationship	Actor A — Actor B / Value Transaction	TED SM contract relationships *can partially lead* to value transactions in e^3value.
L6		Consumer need / Boundary element	TED SM actors *can partially lead* to consumer needs and boundary elements in e^3value.
L7	Data Flow	Value activity	TED SM data flows *can partially lead* to value activities in e^3value.
L8	n/a	AND dependency / OR dependency / Cardinality dependency	e^3value dependency elements are *not considered* in TED SM.

Observations Extracted from the Use Case. In the following, we present the lessons we learned from the comparison between the TED SM model and the e^3value model in the context of the mobility ecosystem under consideration:

L1 *Specified actors in TED SM can lead to actors and market segments in e^3value.* The defined actors can be transferred directly into an e^3value model. One characteristic of the TED SM is the fine-grained classification of the different actors of a digital ecosystem. At the core of this classification is the fact that a concrete actor in a digital ecosystem can be an asset broker (e.g., Airbnb lodging platform) or a platform provider (e.g., Airbnb, Inc.), an asset provider (e.g., host), an asset consumer (e.g., traveler), a support provider (e.g., PayPal Holdings, Inc.), or a competitor (e.g., booking.com). Here, an actor can potentially switch roles (e.g. a host can also be a traveler and vice versa). Moreover, an actor can perform both roles at the same time, e.g., asset broker and platform operator are the same. Both TED and e^3value represent actors in an ecosystem, and by classifying them in TED, it is possible to accomplish almost a one-to-one translation of relevant market segments and actors in exchange in an e^3value model. A minor difference is that in the TED SM model, actors are made concrete with names in order to reflect a real-world case as tangibly as possible. In an e^3value model, a more abstract perspective is taken for defining actors. When creating the e^3value model, we found that the clear stakeholder classification in TED is conducive to the explicit determination of value transfers in e^3value (e.g., "Maria" as an asset consumer in Fig. 4 and "passenger" who want to consume mobility in Fig. 5. The same applies to "Flixbus" as an asset provider and "mobility providers" who want to sell mobility services).

L2 *TED SM asset flows, and money flows can partially lead to value transfers in e^3value.* Following asset flows and money flows in the TED SM model could partially help to model corresponding value transfers in the e^3value model. A *value transfer* is a concept within the e^3value methodology in which actors/entities exchange something of economic value. In an e^3value model, it is explicitly asked *what* exactly is exchanged and less *how* it is traded, as is the case with process models [5]. In a TED SM model, the transfer of economic value is represented by asset flows and money flows; however, the flows are represented in a more physical way, and show the direct exchange between actors, and less the actual value transfer. A value transfer can be derived from a TED SM model if an economic exchange can be indicated clearly between two actors. For example, the passenger pays a price (gives money) and gets an individual access authorization (gets mobility) to the mobility service from the multimodal mobility operator. However, when an economic exchange is split between actors and thus cannot be identified easily in a TED SM model, the transfer to an e^3value model is limited. Example: the mobility provider gives individual access authorization to the mobility platform but receives money from the multimodal mobility operator. Furthermore, we assume that data flows cannot be used to derive comprehensive value transfers, but can only complement other asset and money flows to indicate relevant information for value transfers in an e^3value model (e.g., mobility offer/request flow between mobility provider and mobility platform in Fig. 4).

L3 *TED SM asset flows, and money flows can partially lead to value interfaces in e^3value.* The paths of asset flows and money flows in a TED SM model can be used to indicate value interfaces in an e^3value model. A value interface groups all value ports and value offerings that are connected to a value transfer. A value interface is characterized by two aspects: *economic reciprocity* describes that an actor is willing to exchange a value object for another value object via its ports; and the exchange of value objects takes place *atomically* at the value interface level [5]. In a TED SM model, the concept of reciprocity is not described explicitly, but value transfers and thus value interfaces can be derived partially based on asset and money flows between two actors. TED data flows can further specify a considered value transfer.

L4 *TED SM asset flows, and money flows can lead to value ports in e^3value.* Following the directions of asset flows and money flows in a TED SM model can be partially used to model value ports in an e^3value model. A single *value port* of an actor is a willingness to provide or request value objects to or from other actors. All in-going and out-going value ports in combination create a *bundle* of value objects in a value interface [5]. The TED flow directions, indicated by the arrowhead, can be transmitted one-to-one as an in-going or out-going value port in e^3value (e.g., value ports in Fig. 5 between passengers and multimodal mobility provider, and the asset flow and money flow direction in Fig. 4).

L5 *TED SM contract relationships can partially lead to value transactions in e^3value.* A contractual relationship in a TED SM model can partially lead to a set of value transfers between actors. A *value transaction* is the set of value transfers between at least two actors, when a value interface is triggered (e.g. confirmation of a purchase on a website). In a TED SM model, contractual relationships includes, e.g., terms and conditions, and specify the contractual exchange of values between two parties (e.g. Maria as a passenger confirms the contractual condition to pay the price for the multimobility service and thus receives individual access to a mobility service).

L6 *TED SM actors can partially lead to consumer needs and boundary elements in e^3value.* The actor specification in TED can be used as a starting point to indicate customer needs and boundary elements in e^3value. A *customer need* is a lack of something valuable that the actor wants to acquire. A *boundary element* represents the limit of the scope of a value model [5]. Here, it can be assumed that asset consumers mostly have a customer need, while asset providers or support providers have boundary elements.

L7 *TED SM data flows can partially lead to value activities in e^3value.* We experienced that data flows are helpful to indicate value activities in e^3value. A *value activity* is a task performed by an actor that potentially results in a benefit for the actor. The data flows in TED SM implicitly show interactions between actors and allow making inferences about value activities in

e^3value (e.g., see the platform service *booking* in Fig. 5 and the data flow *booking mobility service* between mobility provider and mobility platform in Fig. 4).

L8 e^3value *dependency elements are not considered in TED SM.* Dependency elements, i.e. AND/OR and cardinality operators, can not be derived from a TED SM model. AND/OR and cardinality dependencies are purely logical constructions, represent no time ordering, and clarify how input conditions must occur so that an output state appears (e.g., a train passenger's need is satisfied when the passenger gets ONE ride AND food OR drink). In a TED SM model, there are no dependency paths, especially since no logical connectors such as AND/OR operators are defined. A TED SM model does not consider an *internal perspective* for each actor. An internal perspective of value creation is more likely to be represented in a *TED Service Blueprint model*, which is not part of the scope of this paper.

Limitations. The results of this paper aim to facilitate ecosystem modeling, but the work is project-specific and can be generalized only to a limited extent. The lessons learned presented need to be tested with practitioners in the future to assess their usefulness. While initial discussions with experts confirm that the designed conceptual models are reasonable and that the combination of tangible and value modeling has potential, we would like to strengthen our results by further validations.

In the future, multiple use cases are required to uncover missing relations that might not have been addressed in this work. The Airbnb example in Fig. 2 and Fig. 3 serves only for methodological explanation, however, it helps to illustrate *L2*; the difference between a physical flow in TED and an economic exchange in e^3value. In the TED SM model, three parties are physically connected as the traveler transfers money to the Airbnb lodging platform via PayPal. Compared to the e^3value model, only a single value transfer between the Airbnb lodging platform and PayPal is modeled to focus on the economic exchange: PayPal provides its payment service and receives money. Further investigation is needed in order to ascertain the accuracy of tangible modeling for e^3value models.

7   Conclusion and Future Work

We analyzed the semantic overlaps between the elements of TED SM models and e^3value models in a real-life project in the mobility sector. This work is ongoing research and our findings are based on a single case. However, our preliminary insights indicate that the design process of a value model can be improved from previously designed TED SM model. How to use this overlap to construct better e^3value models is part of future work.

As part of follow-up research, we are planning a series of workshops to identify guidelines and a step-by-step way for deriving an e^3value model from the results of a TED workshop. Also, in upcoming research, we need to find out whether tangible modeling in general, and TED in particular, helps to lower the barriers for practitioners to engage in an e^3value modeling process.

Acknowledgments. We thank Daniel Krohmer for scientific feedback and Sonnhild Namingha for linguistic revision.

References

1. Boucharas, V., Jansen, S., Brinkkemper, S.: Formalizing software ecosystem modeling. In: Proceedings of the 1st International Workshop on Open Component Ecosystems, pp. 41–50. IWOCE 2009, Association for Computing Machinery, New York, NY, USA (2009). https://doi.org/10.1145/1595800.1595807
2. Brophy, C., et al.: Designing an open innovation orchestrator: the case of Australia's advanced robotics for manufacturing (arm) hub. CERN IdeaSquare J. Exp. Innov. **4**(1), 16–22 (2020). https://doi.org/10.23726/cij.2020.949
3. Dahalin, Z., Razak, R.A., Ibrahim, H., Yusop, N., Kasiran, M.: An enterprise architecture methodology for business-IT alignment: adopter and developer perspectives. Communications of the IBIMA, pp. 1–17 (2011). https://doi.org/10.5171/2011.222028
4. Gordijn, J., Akkermans, H.: Early requirements determination for networked value constellations: A business ontology approach. Technical report Vrije Universiteit (2006). https://dise-lab.nl/wp-content/uploads/2021/06/EarlyReqDet2006.pdf
5. Gordijn, J., Wieringa, R.: E3value User Guide - Designing Your Ecosystem in a Digital World. The Value Engineers, 1st edn. (2021)
6. Grosskopf, A., Edelman, J., Weske, M.: Tangible business process modeling – methodology and experiment design. In: Rinderle-Ma, S., Sadiq, S., Leymann, F. (eds.) BPM 2009. LNBIP, vol. 43, pp. 489–500. Springer, Heidelberg (2010). https://doi.org/10.1007/978-3-642-12186-9_46
7. Group, O.M.: Unified modeling language (2022). https://www.uml.org/
8. Guizzardi, G.: Ontological foundations for conceptual modeling with applications. In: Ralyté, J., Franch, X., Brinkkemper, S., Wrycza, S. (eds.) CAiSE 2012. LNCS, vol. 7328, pp. 695–696. Springer, Heidelberg (2012). https://doi.org/10.1007/978-3-642-31095-9_45
9. Hevner, A., March, S., Park, J., Ram, S.: Design science in information systems research. MIS Q. Manage. Inf. Syst. **28**(1), 75–105 (2004)
10. Huemer, C., Schmidt, A., Werthner, H., Zapletal, M.: A UML profile for the e 3-value e-business model ontology (2008)
11. Ionita, D.: Model-driven information security risk assessment of socio-technical systems. Ph.D. thesis, University of Twente, Netherlands (2018). https://doi.org/10.3990/1.9789036544832, iDS Ph.D. Thesis series No. 18-456 SIKS Dissertation Series No. 2018-06
12. Ionita, D., Nazareth, D., Vasenev, A., van der Velde, F., Wieringa, R.: The role of tangibility and iconicity in collaborative modelling tasks, pp. 1–14. CEUR (2017), eR Forum/Demos 2017, ER; Conference date: 06–11-2017
13. Ionita, D., Wieringa, R., Bullee, J.-W., Vasenev, A.: Tangible modelling to elicit domain knowledge: an experiment and focus group. In: Johannesson, P., Lee, M.L., Liddle, S.W., Opdahl, A.L., López, Ó.P. (eds.) ER 2015. LNCS, vol. 9381, pp. 558–565. Springer, Cham (2015). https://doi.org/10.1007/978-3-319-25264-3_42

14. Koch, M., Krohmer, D., Naab, M., Rost, D., Trapp, M.: A matter of definition: criteria for digital ecosystems. Digital Business **2**(2), 100027 (2022). https://doi.org/10.1016/j.digbus.2022.100027

15. Kostova, B., Gordijn, J., Regev, G., Wegmann, A.: Comparison of two value-modeling methods: e^3value and SEAM. In: 2019 13th International Conference on Research Challenges in Information Science (RCIS). IEEE (2019). https://doi.org/10.1109/rcis.2019.8876991

16. Moore, J.F.: The death of competition: leadership and strategy in the age of business ecosystems. Wiley (1996)

17. Nass, C., Trapp, M., Villela, K.: Tangible design for software ecosystem with playmobil. In: Proceedings of the 10th Nordic Conference on Human-Computer Interaction, pp. 856–861. Association for Computing Machinery, New York, NY, USA (2018). https://doi.org/10.1145/3240167.3240278

18. Nass Bauer, C., Trapp, M.: Tangible ecosystem design: developing disruptive services for digital ecosystems. In: Extended Abstracts of the 2019 CHI Conference on Human Factors in Computing Systems, pp. 1–5. Association for Computing Machinery, New York, NY, USA (2019). https://doi.org/10.1145/3290607.3298819

19. OMG, Parida, R., Mahapatra, S.: Business process model and notation (BPMN) version 2.0. Object Manage. Group **1**(4), 18 (2011)

20. Osterwalder, A., Pigneur, Y.: Business Model Generation: A Handbook for Visionaries, Game Changers, and Challengers. Wiley, The Strategyzer Series (2010)

21. Parker, G.G., Van Alstyne, M.W., Choudary, S.P.: Platform revolution: how networked markets are transforming the economy and how to make them work for you. WW Norton & Company (2016)

22. Rettig, M.: Prototyping for tiny fingers. Commun. ACM **37**(4), 21–27 (1994). https://doi.org/10.1145/175276.175288

23. H. Sadi, M., Yu, E.: Designing software ecosystems: how can modeling techniques help? In: Gaaloul, K., Schmidt, R., Nurcan, S., Guerreiro, S., Ma, Q. (eds.) CAISE 2015. LNBIP, vol. 214, pp. 360–375. Springer, Cham (2015). https://doi.org/10.1007/978-3-319-19237-6_23

24. Sadi, M.H., Yu, E.: Analyzing the evolution of software development: from creative chaos to software ecosystems. In: 2014 IEEE Eighth International Conference on Research Challenges in Information Science (RCIS). IEEE (2014). https://doi.org/10.1109/rcis.2014.6861055

25. da Silva Torres, I., Fantinato, M., Branco, G.M., Gordijn, J.: Design guidelines to derive an e^3value business model from a BPMN process model in the financial securities sector. In: Serral, E., Stirna, J., Ralyté, J., Grabis, J. (eds.) PoEM 2021. LNBIP, vol. 432, pp. 153–167. Springer, Cham (2021). https://doi.org/10.1007/978-3-030-91279-6_11

26. Tamanini, J.V., Koch, M., Nass, C.: Digitale Ökosysteme virtuell greifbar machen geht nicht? - doch! (2020). https://www.iese.fraunhofer.de/blog/digitale-oekosysteme-greifbar-machen/

27. Täuscher, K., Laudien, S.M.: Understanding platform business models: a mixed methods study of marketplaces. Eur. Manage. J. **36**(3), 319–329 (2018). https://doi.org/10.1016/j.emj.2017.06.005

28. Tsai, C.H., Zdravkovic, J., Stirna, J.: Modeling digital business ecosystems: a systematic literature review. Complex Syst. Inf. Model. Q. **30**, 1–30 (2022). https://doi.org/10.7250/csimq.2022-30.01

DSML and Meta-modeling

Dynamic Models – The MetaMorph Formalism and Model-Operations

Victoria Döller^(✉) and Dimitris Karagiannis

Research Group Knowledge Engineering, Faculty of Computer Science,
University of Vienna, Vienna, Austria
{victoria.doeller,dimitris.karagiannis}@univie.ac.at

Abstract. Models unfolding their full power are not static but dynamic, interactive artifacts. Mature modeling methods offer means to operationalize models, amplifying their value beyond mere visualizations. Nevertheless, operations on models are regularly not an integral part of the language specification, even less an object of formalization. In this approach, we demonstrate how to capture the core concepts of operations on models in our formalism MetaMorph to allow for an extension of the formal definition of a language's syntax with a precise but platform-independent specification of language functionality. We understand as a model a series of model states that flow into one another through the interaction of the modeler and provided operations. Thereby, we distinguish structural events for the basic changes and domain events for the semantic-aware operations on models, as well as model operations in the creation phase and the operationalization phase of a model. To examine our considerations on an example, we employ ProVis, a modeling method for stochastic education.

Keywords: Conceptual modeling · Metamodeling · Formalization · MetaMorph · Model operations · Dynamic models

1 Introduction

Models are an excellent tool for complexity management due to their abstraction and comprehensible visualization. Their value is even amplified through the operationalization of models, e.g., simulation, information translation, etc. Model functionality is a crucial point to amplify the value of models beyond mere pictures [1]. A prominent example is the firing mechanism on Petri Nets. Many domain-specific languages gain in value by the offered model operations. For example, in Model-Driven Software Engineering model-to-model transformations play an important role [2, Chap. 8]. Also the "Modelling for the Masses" movement [15] lists the *model processing dimension* as one of the guiding categorizations for prospective research in enterprise modeling and therefore explicitly names model operationalization as a declared research goal for the future.

© IFIP International Federation for Information Processing 2022
Published by Springer Nature Switzerland AG 2022
B. S. Barn and K. Sandkuhl (Eds.): PoEM 2022, LNBIP 456, pp. 151–166, 2022.
https://doi.org/10.1007/978-3-031-21488-2_10

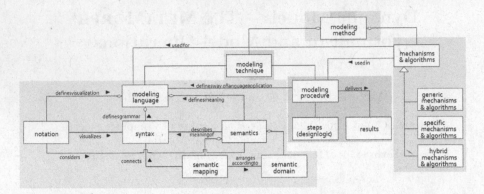

Fig. 1. Modeling Method Framework of Karagiannis and Kühn [10]

According to the Generic Modeling Method Framework of Karagiannis and Kühn [10] shown in Fig. 1 modeling methods consist not only of a modeling language but also comprise a functional part, i.e., mechanisms and algorithms, which amplify the value of a model. Still, mechanisms and algorithms are mostly treated as secondary in specifications and formalizations, and they are rather dependent on language external factors like the metamodeling technique [16] or the realization in an implementation. The result is a divergence of offered functionality in different tools. However, the functionality of a modeling language constitutes the operational value of models beyond mere pictures.

To overcome this problem and make mechanisms and algorithms an integral part of the language specification, our research objective is to examine a sound underlying formalism for dynamic, living models and utilize its power. To realize this, we intend to integrate model changing operations into the METAMORPH formalism presented in [3]. In the paper at hand, we concentrate on operations working on the model, changing the model state through time. This approach turns models into living, dynamic artifacts that have a creation phase, an operationalization phase and evolve over time. By doing this, we get rid of the static character of most model formalizations that ignore the practical employment of models as used by the modeler, i.e., as tools to be changed and worked on.

To demonstrate our considerations on a concrete case we employ the modeling method PROVIS [3] assisting stochastic education. This method contains only a few concepts, but each of them carries a lot of information in interdependencies and functionality. Therefore, PROVIS appears to be an appropriate candidate for the application of dynamic formalization.

In Sect. 2, we give a short recap of the background and related work on operations on models, including a short introduction to the METAMORPH formalism and PROVIS, the modeling method used as running example throughout this paper. Furthermore, we give a collection of foundational definitions in Sect. 3 and will examine the smallest possible building blocks of operations, the so-called structural events, in Sect. 4. Section 5 contains the exploration of domain events, i.e., language operations that use domain knowledge and produce semantically and syntactically valid models, also outlined in a short example of a model evolving over time. In the end, we will give a conclusion and outlook in Sect. 6.

2 Background

2.1 Related Work

Operations on models can be manifold. A taxonomy of transformations has been described in [11]. While there are many approaches dealing with the formal specification of model to model transformations between models conforming to different metamodels, e.g., QVT [12] – the exogenous transformations according to the taxonomy – there are not quite as many attempts to address the formal specifications of operations directly modifying a model, evolving it over time – the endogenous transformations according to the taxonomy. Much less approaches integrate model evolution in a sound formal foundation. None of the set-based formalisms, e.g., FDMM [6] or logic-based formalisms, e.g., FORMULA [8], known to the authors deal with the functional aspects of modeling languages. An exception is the theory of graph grammars and graph rewriting [7]. This approach is based on the principle of finding and replacing patterns in labeled graphs with other patterns. Nevertheless, graph grammars offer a powerful tool to describe model transformation but lack a suitable way of capturing other crucial concepts of modeling methods, e.g., attributes [3].

2.2 Systematization of Operations — Structural Events and Domain Events

A systematization of operations on models has been outlined by Olivé [13]. Olivé distinguishes structural events on models that form the core building blocks of an operation, and domain events, that introduce domain semantics.

A structural event is an elementary change in a model, i.e., an insertion or deletion of a concrete modeling element, object or relation. A domain event is a state change that is perceived as a valid change in the domain, i.e., a semantically and syntactically admissible operation on a model. Domain events are decomposed into the smallest possible changes in a model, resulting in a concatenation of structural events. They always map valid models to other valid models conforming to the language constraints, while structural events can invalidate a model and cause a violation of the postulates. According to Olivé, the concept of a domain event is akin to that of a transaction in the field of database systems, and they are treated as own entities. This is similar to the method of [14] supporting the modeling of functionality and events for the creation of model compilers.

2.3 ProVis – Probability Visualized

We use the modeling method ProVis to exemplify our considerations on model operationalization. ProVis is a method for modeling tree diagrams and unit squares for stochastic education in Austrian schools at the secondary level. For a detailed description of the language and the mathematical background, see [4]. In the following, we will recapitulate the most important aspects needed for the formalization of the functionality of the method.

The reduced metamodel of PROVIS is shown in Fig. 2 using the notation of CoChaCo [9]. For reasons of brevity, we omitted some concepts and attributes to keep the set of basic operations assessable.

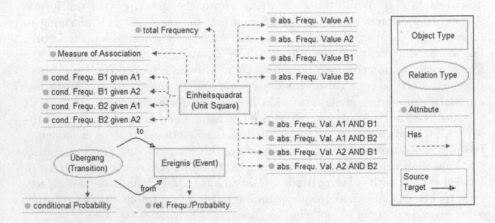

Fig. 2. The (reduced) metamodel of PROVIS

In Fig. 3, we see examples of a unit square on the left and a tree diagram in the middle. A unit square is an object on its own, whereas a tree diagram is a construct constituted from several events (rectangles) and transitions (arrows) between them. Unit squares visualize the amounts of two characteristics in a cohort, each of them with two possible values. An example for characteristics are A the number of submission and B the reviewers' decisions with values *A1: conference paper/A2: workshop paper* and *B1: accepted/B2: rejected*. The concrete numbers of submissions at the PoEM 2021 conference are depicted in Fig. 3 (counting full and short papers of the conference and papers from BES and EM4DT workshops as appeared in CEUR[1]). The frequencies of these values appear in the unit square as numbers and encoded in the size of the rectangles. Tree diagrams can be employed as probability trees to model processes, as well as frequency trees to model partitions, like the one depicted in Fig. 3.

Unit squares possess many attributes that are highly dependent on each other. The only free attributes are the four quantities of combinations A_iB_j. Also, in tree diagrams, the probabilities of an event (blue or green rectangle) depend on the probabilities of the preceding event and the intermediate transition (arrow). The rule for calculating this dependent value is called path multiplication rule (e.g., the percentage of the accepted conference submissions can be

---

[1] https://poem2021.rtu.lv/.

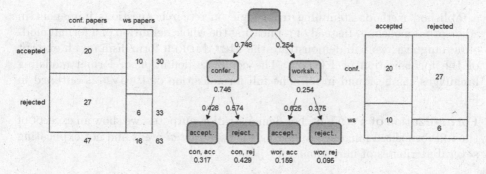

Fig. 3. A unit square and tree diagram depicting the paper submission numbers of PoEM 2021 (Color figure online)

derived from the conditional frequency of the acceptance rate (incoming transition) and the relative frequency of the conference papers under all submissions). All these dependencies and the compliance with the tree structure are captured in the constraints of the PROVIS language.

Besides the expressive strength of visualization of stochastic situations PROVIS additionally offers powerful mechanisms, e.g., the derivation of the transposed square given a unit square, see Fig. 3 right, or the creation of a tree diagram out of a unit square, to benefit from both visualization methods. Both the constraints and the offered functionality will be topics of interest in the considerations below to capture language functionality with METAMORPH.

2.4   METAMORPH

METAMORPH is a formalism based on sorted predicate logic and defines conceptual modeling languages as formal languages as explored in mathematical logic with a signature Σ and constraints **C**. The signature $\Sigma = \{\mathcal{S}, \mathcal{F}, \mathcal{R}, \mathcal{C}\}$ of the language $\mathcal{L}$ contains types partitioned in subgroups $\mathcal{S}_O$, $\mathcal{S}_R$, and $\mathcal{S}_D$ of $\mathcal{S}$ corresponding to the object types, the relation types, and the attribute domain types respectively. Furthermore, it contains function symbols in $\mathcal{F}$, relation symbols in $\mathcal{R}$, and constants in $\mathcal{C}$. Each relation type T comprises two function symbols $F_s^T : T \to T'$ and $F_t^T : T \to T''$ in $\mathcal{F}$ mapping a relation to its source and target modeling element. Also, attributes are realized as mappings $F_T^a : T \to D$ from an element of the attributed type T to the assigned value in the attribute domain D. Formal modeling languages are furthermore equipped with constraints written in first-order logic to ensure the proper behavior of instance models. A model of a formal modeling language $\mathcal{L}$ is defined as an $\mathcal{L}$-structure conforming to the language constraints **C**, i.e., a structure comprising a universe $\mathcal{U}_T$ of typed elements for each type T in $\mathcal{S}$ and interpretations of all function and relation symbols in $\mathcal{F}$ and $\mathcal{R}$ respectively and an interpretation of the constants in $\mathcal{C}$.

Treating modeling languages as a subgroup of formal languages allows for the investigation of common features of this subgroup and the application of established methods stemming from logic on research questions immanent in conceptual modeling. Instead of replicating the whole definition of a formal modeling language, we will demonstrate the METAMORPH formalism on an excerpt of the formalization of PROVIS. The complete definition of formal modeling languages can be found in [3]. The full formalization of PROVIS is outlined in [5].

Formalization of PROVIS. For demonstration purposes, we show an excerpt of the full formalized language (omitting the type *partial event* and not explicating several attributes of unit squares):

$$\Sigma = \{\mathcal{S}, \mathcal{F}, \mathcal{R}, \mathcal{C}\}, \mathcal{S} = \mathcal{S}_O \cup \mathcal{S}_R \cup \mathcal{S}_D$$

Object types and relation types:

$$\mathcal{S}_O = \{\mathbf{UnitSquare}, \mathbf{Event}\}, \mathcal{S}_R = \{\mathbf{Transition}\},$$

Domain types and a relation reflecting directed paths on trees:

$$\mathcal{S}_D = \{\mathbb{N}_0, \mathbb{R}, \mathbf{Percentage}\}, \mathcal{R} = \{Path \subset \mathbf{Event} \times \mathbf{Event}\},$$

Function symbols for source and target assignment of the relation *Transition* and attributes of Unit Squares and Events:

$$\mathcal{F} = \{F_s^{\mathrm{Tr}} : \mathbf{Transition} \to \mathbf{Event}, F_t^{\mathrm{Tr}} : \mathbf{Transition} \to \mathbf{Event},$$

$$F_{A_1B_1}^{abs} : \mathbf{US} \to \mathbb{N}_0, F_{A_2B_1}^{abs} : \mathbf{US} \to \mathbb{N}_0, F_{A_1B_2}^{abs} : \mathbf{US} \to \mathbb{N}_0, F_{A_2B_2}^{abs} : \mathbf{US} \to \mathbb{N}_0,$$

$$F_{A_1}^{abs} : \mathbf{US} \to \mathbb{N}_0, F_{A_2}^{abs} : \mathbf{US} \to \mathbb{N}_0, F_{B_1}^{abs} : \mathbf{US} \to \mathbb{N}_0, F_{B_2}^{abs} : \mathbf{US} \to \mathbb{N}_0,$$

$$F_{total}^{abs} : \mathbf{US} \to \mathbb{N}_0, F^{moA} : \mathbf{US} \to \mathbb{R},$$

$$F_E^{prob} : \mathbf{Event} \to \mathbf{Percentage}, F_{Tr}^{prob} : \mathbf{Transition} \to \mathbf{Percentage}\},$$

Constants for the attribute domains:

$$\mathcal{C} = \{0, 1, 2, ...\} \text{ of type } \mathbb{N}_0 \cup [0; 1] \text{ of type } \mathbf{Percentage} \cup (-\infty; \infty) \text{ of type } \mathbb{R}.$$

As an example of constraints, below we see the path multiplication rule (1), the calculation of the total frequency of the whole cohort in a unit square (2), and the transitive closure of the *Path* relation (3):

$$\forall x \in \mathbf{E}, t \in \mathbf{Tr} \ (f_t^{\mathrm{Tr}}(t) = x \implies f_E^{prob}(x) = f_{Tr}^{prob}(t) \cdot f_E^{prob}(f_s^{\mathrm{Tr}}(t))) \tag{1}$$

$$\forall x \in \mathbf{US} \ (f_{total}^{abs}(x) = f_{A_1B_1}^{abs}(x) + f_{A_1B_2}^{abs}(x) + f_{A_2B_1}^{abs}(x) + f_{A_2B_2}^{abs}(x)) \tag{2}$$

$$\forall x, y, z \in \mathbf{Event}(Path(x, y) \land Path(y, z) \implies Path(x, z)) \tag{3}$$

3   Dynamic Models Through Operations

When examining the dynamic aspects of models, we first have to adapt our notion and definition of a model. A model, as understood so far (defined in [3], Def. 2), is from now on considered as a model state at a concrete point in time. A model in the current conception comprises a whole set of model states, i.e., the row of states the concrete model runs through.

To make this conception concrete, we have to introduce some notation.

Definition 1. *Given a formal modeling language $\mathcal{L}$ with signature $\Sigma = \{\mathcal{S}, \mathcal{F}, \mathcal{R}, \mathcal{C}\}$ and set of constraints C we define:*

- *a **model state** $\mathcal{M}$ of a language $\mathcal{L}$ as an $\mathcal{L}$-structure conforming to the language constraints C, i.e. a structure comprising a universe $\mathcal{U}_T$ of typed elements for each type T in $\mathcal{S}$ and interpretations of all function and relation symbols in $\mathcal{F}$ and $\mathcal{R}$ respectively and an interpretation of the constants in $\mathcal{C}$ (see [3] for the detailed Definition).*
- *the **set of all model states** $\mathcal{M}$ as the set of all interpretations of the signature, where all universes $\mathcal{U}_T$ with T in $\mathcal{S}_O \cup \mathcal{S}_R$ are finite;*
- *the **set of valid model states** $\mathcal{M}^+$, that is the subset of all models $\mathcal{M}$ that fulfil the constraints in C;*
- *the set $\overline{\mathcal{U}}_T$ of all **object or relation elements of type** $T \in \mathcal{S}_O \cup \mathcal{S}_R$ appearing in any of the valid models in $\mathcal{M}^+$: $\overline{\mathcal{U}}_T - \bigcup_{m \in \mathcal{M}^+} \mathcal{U}_T^m$.*
- *the set $\overline{\mathcal{U}}$ of all **elements of any object or relation type** that is contained in any valid model, i.e. it is the sum over $\overline{\mathcal{U}}_T$ of all types $T \in \mathcal{S}_O \cup \mathcal{S}_R$: $\overline{\mathcal{U}} = \bigcup_{T \in \mathcal{S}_O \cup \mathcal{S}_R} \overline{\mathcal{U}}_T$.*
- *the **set $\mathcal{A}$ of operations** on a language $\mathcal{L}$ containing the functions mapping one model state m in the set $\mathcal{M}$ to another model state m' in $\mathcal{M}$.*

This notation now allows us to rework the definition of a model.

Definition 2. *A model is a row of valid model states $(m_1, m_2, \ldots)$, $m_i \in \mathcal{M}^+$, where for each pair (m_i, m_{i+1}) there exists an operation $a \in \mathcal{A}$ with $a(m_i) = m_{i+1}$.*

4   The Building Blocks of Domain-Specific Operations – Structural Events

Structural events are generic in the sense that their specification is independent of the domain semantics. The language-specific domain events can be built up by structural events. The set of structural events of each language contains an operation for the creation of each valid element, an operation for deleting each element, and operations for setting admissible attribute values to each possible element and each dedicated attribute.

Create

$$create[x] : \mathcal{M} \to \mathcal{M}; x \in \overline{\mathcal{U}}, \qquad create[x](m) = m'$$

$create[x]$ is an operation mapping a model state m that does not contain x to the model state m', which is almost identical to m besides the fact that it additionally contains the element x. Thereby, x is an object or relation element. The operation $create[x]$ does not change the model state if the element x is already contained in the model state m. The resulting model state need not be valid even if the initial model state was, e.g., a valid BPMN model becomes invalid when we add an additional start event. Note that $create[x]$ defines the creation of a fully determined element x stemming from the set $\overline{\mathcal{U}}$ with fully determined attribute values. For relation elements, this includes the determination of their source and target element. This differs from the idea of element creation in coding, where the most basic creation operators produce an element with possibly undetermined attributes, e.g., containing a null value. There are $|\overline{\mathcal{U}}|$ many $create[x]$ operations in the set $\mathcal{A}$ of all operators.

Create in PROVIS. Creation on the level of structural events does not ensure the fulfillment of constraints. This can be seen in PROVIS on the probability trees depicted in Fig. 3. When connecting the event of *conference papers* with the event of *accepted conference papers* (imagine that we deleted the existing connection before) with a transition assuming an acceptance rate of 20% the actual frequency value of the *accepted conference papers* event, 31,7%, would violate the multiplication rule: $0.746 \cdot 0.2 \neq 0.317$. Further incorrectness can arise when we introduce transitions causing cyclic connections in a model state. According to the constraints, only tree-like structures are admissible. Creating unit squares does not introduce incorrectness, as the attribute values are only dependent on other values of the same square. As the $create[x]$ operator only creates elements appearing in valid models, they will always conform to the constraints.

Delete

$$delete[x] : \mathcal{M} \to \mathcal{M}; x \in \overline{\mathcal{U}}, \qquad delete[x](m) = m'$$

$delete[x]$ is an operation mapping a model state m that contains x to the model state m', which is almost identical to m besides the fact that it does not contain the element x as well as all other elements with an attribute value equal to x. This includes relation objects with source or target object equal to x. The operation $delete[x]$ does not change the model state m if the element x is not contained in m. There are $|\overline{\mathcal{U}}|$ many $delete[x]$ operations in the set $\mathcal{A}$ of all operators.

Delete in PROVIS. In textscProVis, the deletion of unit squares is very simple, as unit squares are standalone objects not connected to any other object. When deleting events, there might be incoming or outgoing transitions that disappear with the deleted event, so it might happen that the deletion generates two trees out of one. In PROVIS, all attributes have values in $\mathbb{N}_0$, $\mathbb{R}$, or $[0; 1]$, and there are no attributes pointing to object or relation elements.

Set

$$set_v^a[x] : \mathcal{M} \to \mathcal{M}, x \in \overline{\mathcal{U}}_T, F_a : T \to T' \in \mathcal{S}, v \in \mathcal{U}_{T'}, \quad set_v^a[x](m) = m'$$

The set operation $set_v^a[x]$ maps a model state m to another mode state m' that is nearly identical besides that the attribute a of element x now points to the attribute value v, element of the attribute domain T' of a. The set operator might cause incorrectness, as we can set any value of the attribute domain type T' to any attribute a with domain type T'.

Notice that Olivé [13] considers attribute adaption as a concatenation of deletion and creation of the same object with a changed attribute value, but in our perception, this is a simplification with too many side effects. The main counterargument is that the deletion of an object might imply the disappearance of other elements, e.g., relations.

To calculate the number of existing *set* operations in $\mathcal{A}$ we have to define the set of all codomains of any function symbol $\mathcal{T} = \{T \in \mathcal{S} | \exists F \in \mathcal{F}$ that has T as codomain$\}$. The number of $set[x]$ operations is then smaller or equal to the sum over all universes of types T: $\sum_{T \in \mathcal{T}} |\overline{\mathcal{U}}_T|$. Notice that we need *smaller or equal* as there might be function symbols F not related to an attribute, e.g., a function for the usual addition + necessary for the definition of constraints.

Set in PROVIS. PROVIS is a language with a high interdependency of attribute values. Therefore, whenever an attribute value is changed, the model state may become invalid (dependent attributes, e.g., the total size of a cohort in a unit square), or a single attribute change causes a whole row of attribute adaptions according to the constructive constraints, e.g., the change of the amount of a concrete combination of characteristics in a unit square. If we rework the set operator to a concatenation of other operators, we already cross the border from structural events to domain events, as we use domain-specific semantics to ensure constraint satisfaction.

5 Language Specific Operations – Domain Events

Domain events e_d are language-specific and incorporate domain semantics and syntactic requirements. They are intended to produce model states that fulfill all the language constraints, i.e., they map a valid model state m to another valid model state m'.

$$e_d(m) = m'; m, m' \in \mathcal{M}^+$$

They use the semantics of the domain and are generic in a way that they can be defined on meta-level independent of a concrete model instance. Examples of domain events are the firing mechanism on Petri Nets or the deduction of a tree diagram from a unit square in the PROVIS modeling method.

5.1 Creation Phase vs. Operationalization Phase

When saying we operationalize a model, we usually talk about the functionality offered by a modeling method working on the model as a representation of a system under study. This operationalization usually does not include the phase of creating the model until it is a complete representation of the system under study. The phase of model creation, i.e., instantiating and connecting elements and specifying attributes, happens in general before the actual operationalization phase. It is furthermore questionable if, in the modeling phase, the model fulfills the constraints at each point in time. For example, if we start to create a BPMN model, we always begin with an empty model state not containing a start event even though it is required. Therefore, some languages might allow for the use of structural events in this phase and rely on the knowledge of the modeler to reach a valid state of the model.

Of course, this separation into a creation phase and an operationalization phase is not strict, and in many languages the creation, deletion, and adaption of single elements is a core functionality also when operating on the model. To back the creation of elements against decisive invalidations, we might enhance some structural events to respect the crucial constraints. A distinction between those constraints that might be temporarily violated and those which shall never be violated can roughly be made according to the systematization of restrictive and constructive constraints as described in [5].

Restrictive and Constructive Constraints. We distinguish two categories of constraints: restrictive ones that confine the creation, connection, and attribution of models and constructive ones that impose some dependencies between elements and values. Examples for the first type are cardinality constraints or the restrictions for tree-like structures without circles. Examples for the second type are rules for attribute values like the dependencies of frequencies in unit squares or the execution time of whole processes depending on the single tasks. Nevertheless, the delimitation is inconclusive. We can localize concrete constraints on both sides with different implications, e.g., the constraint on BPMN models to have exactly one start event. Employed as a restrictive constraint, each newly created model is invalid. Employed as a constructive constraint, then on model creation, the start event has to be created automatically.

In the light of operations on models, all the constructive constraints shall not be violated at any point in the model state flow. As the name already suggests this can be ensured by the automatization of construction, i.e., calculation of values and creation of elements using these constraints. Regularly structural events can be concatenated such that we result in basic operations for the creation or deletion of objects, still enriched with domain semantics ensuring that their application will not violate the constraints. In the following, we will use the naming convention of capitals for domain events and small initial letters for structural events.

Restrictive Constraints in ProVis. To ensure the fulfillment of restrictive constraints, we can employ the mechanism of preconditions that have to be fulfilled before a structural (turning into a domain) event can be applied. In ProVis tree diagrams have a tree-like structure, i.e., each element has at most one incoming transition, and we do not want to allow at any time any cyclic constellations. To do this we introduce a precondition on the operator $create[x]$, where x is a relation element of type *Transition* with source element a and target element b both of type *Event*. We lift the structural event $create[x]$ for x an element of type *Transition* to a domain event $Create_x^{Tr}$ and only admit the application to a model state m if m fulfils following preconditions:

$$\nexists y \in Tr(f_t^{Tr}(y) = b) \qquad \neg Path(a,b)$$

i.e., we do not allow two incoming transitions, and we only admit a connection between a and b if they do not already belong to the same tree. If m does not fulfil this requirement, the operator $Create^{Tr}[x]$ leaves m unchanged. Furthermore, the creation of a transition might cause an update of the probability value of the subsequent events due to the multiplication rule.

$$Create^{Tr}[x] = set_{val}^{ProbE}[c] \circ \ldots \circ set_{f_{Tr}^{prob}(x) \cdot f_E^{prob}(a)}^{ProbE}[b] \circ create[x]$$

Thereby, we have to update the probabilities of all event elements $c \in \overline{U}_E$ that are subsequently connected to b, $Path(b,c)$ with value $val = f_{Tr}^{prob}(z) \cdot f_E^{prob}(c')$ of the preceding transition z and event c'. The *set* operator for transition objects must include a similar procedure of updating all subsequent events.

Notice that this domain event cannot be completely defined on meta-level, as the concrete values that have to be set to the dependent attributes are dependent on attribute values of x, which are just determined on instance level. Therefore, we can only narrow down the set of $set_v^a[x]$ operators but not finally determine which $set_v^a[x]$ have to be concatenated.

Constructive Constraints in PROVIS. In the PROVIS method, the strong dependencies of attribute values in unit squares imply that for the creation of an element x, we only need to know the four main attribute values *Absolute Frequency* $A_i B_j$. This is similar to the practice in programming of a constructor having as input parameters the mandatory information of the object. When we want to lift the structural events of changing the four base values of a unit square to domain events guaranteeing the numerous constructive constraints, we add four "lifted" $Set_v^a[x]$ operators to the domain events. To make them operations of valid model states, we have to make this value adaption a concatenation of a couple of attribute value adaptions: When we change the absolute frequency of the combined characteristic $A_1 B_1$, this implies a change of the total frequency, the absolute frequency of characteristic A_1, of characteristic B_1, of the measure of association (moA) and the conditional frequencies $B_1|A_1$ and $B_2|A_1$. All the other absolute or conditional frequencies are not dependent on $A_1 B_1$, A_1, or B_1. Therefore the operation $Set_{val}^{A_1 B_1}[x]$ is made up of the structural events:

$$Set_{val}^{A_1 B_1}[x] = set_{v_6}^{moA}[x] \circ set_{v_5}^{B_2|A_1}[x] \circ set_{v_4}^{B_1|A_1}[x]$$

$$\circ set_{v_3}^{abstot}[x] \circ set_{v_2}^{B_1}[x] \circ set_{v_1}^{A_1}[x] \circ set_{val}^{A_1 B_1}[x]$$

where $v_1 = val + f_{A_1 B_2}^{abs}(x)$, $v_2 = val + f_{A_2 B_1}^{abs}(x)$, $v_3 = val + f_{A_1 B_2}^{abs}(x) + f_{A_2 B_1}^{abs}(x) + f_{A_2 B_2}^{abs}(x)$, $v_4 = f_{A_1 B_1}^{abs}(x)/f_{A_1}^{abs}(x)$, $v_5 = f_{A_1 B_2}^{abs}(x)/f_{A_1}^{abs}(x)$, and $v_6 = f_{B_1|A_1}^{cond}(x) -$

$f^{cond}_{B_1|A_2}(x)$. If we do not execute all these $set^a_v[x]$ operations, we end up with an invalid model because the constructive constraints are violated. This is similar to the practice in programming of a constructor having as input parameters the mandatory information of the object.

5.2 Lifted Structural Events and Domain Events for Operationalization

Until now, we mainly considered operations of PROVIS relevant in the *model creation phase*. The creation of unit squares and events is unproblematic regarding constraint satisfaction. To reach this also for the other creation events, we lifted those of creating a transition and simply directly employed the basic structural events for the rest: $Create^{US}[x] = create[x], Create^E[y] = create[y]$. When deleting an element, we cannot generate any violations of constraints, so also the $Delete^T$ operations of all types T simply coincide with the structural events. The $Set^{A_i B_j}_v[x]$ operation requires some adaption of other attributes in a unit square. This was exemplified in the operation $Set^{A_1 B_1}_v[x]$ in the previous section. The $Set^{ProbTr}_w[z]$ operation on transitions needs some post-processing in the form of attribute adaption of subsequent events similar to the creation of a transition. We do not allow for the change of event probabilities as their probability is either 1 (roots) or fully determined by the preceding transitions.

By adapting the structural events of PROVIS, we reached a couple of domain events for the model creation phase.

$$\mathbf{A}_{create} = \{Create^{US}[x], Create^E[y], Create^{Tr}[z],$$

$$Delete^{US}[x], Delete^E[y], Delete^{Tr}[z],$$

$$Set^{A_1 B_1}_v[x], Set^{A_1 B_2}_v[x], Set^{A_2 B_1}_v[x], Set^{A_2 B_2}_v[x], Set^{ProbTr}_w[z]\}$$

Thereby, x is an Element of type *Unit Square* in $\overline{\mathcal{U}}_{US}$, y is an Element of type *Event* in $\overline{\mathcal{U}}_E$, and z is an Element of type *Transition* in $\overline{\mathcal{U}}_{Tr}$. The values v are natural number in $\mathbb{N}$ and w are real numbers in $[0; 1]$. These elements form classes of operations, as for each $x \in \overline{\mathcal{U}}_{US}$ we do have one operation in $Delete^{US}[x]$, etc. Notice that we only include four set operations on unit squares, although there are 14 attributes in total. This is because of the dependency of all other attributes on the four main values $AbsoluteFrequencyA_iB_j$.

The main functions for *operating* on tree diagrams and unit squares are the following:

$$\mathbf{A}_{operate} = \{CreateTransposUnitSquare[x], CreateTreeFromUnitSquare[x]\}$$

For reasons of brevity, we will examine $CreateTransposedUnitSquare$ in detail and only give an outline of $CreateTreeFromUnitSquare$ as the latter one becomes a very extensive concatenation of seven creations of event elements and six creations of transition elements.

Transposing a unit square means changing the hierarchy of characteristics. In the example of PoEM submissions in 2021 from Fig. 3 left, the leading characteristic is the type of paper (conference or workshop). When we transpose it, we come to a unit square with quite a different appearance, see Fig. 3 right. When creating the transposed unit square of a given square x, we have to create an element y: $CreateTransposedUnitSquare[x] = create[y]$ where y is a unit square $y \in \overline{\mathcal{U}}_{US}$ and attribute values

$$f^{abs}_{A_1 B_1}(y) = f^{abs}_{A_1 B_1}(x), f^{abs}_{A_2 B_1}(y) = f^{abs}_{A_1 B_2}(x),$$

$$f^{abs}_{A_1 B_2}(y) = f^{abs}_{A_2 B_1}(x), f^{abs}_{A_2 B_2}(y) = f^{abs}_{A_2 B_2}(x).$$

Notice the switch of the values on the minor diagonal. The remaining attributes of y are dependent on these four frequencies and can be determined using the constructive constraints.

A possibility to define this operation in a manner more familiar to programmers is the following:

$$CreateTransposedUnitSquare[x]$$

$$= Set^{A_2 B_2}_{f^{abs}_{A_2 B_2}(x)}[y] \circ Set^{A_1 B_2}_{f^{abs}_{A_2 B_1}(x)}[y] \circ Set^{A_2 B_1}_{f^{abs}_{A_1 B_2}(x)}[y] \circ Set^{A_1 B_1}_{f^{abs}_{A_1 B_1}(x)}[y] \circ create[y]$$

for an arbitrary element $y \in \overline{\mathcal{U}}_{US}$. The initial attribute values of y are irrelevant as we overwrite them by applying the $Set^T_v[x]$ operations, and also, the dependent attributes are adapted due to the construction of these operations.

5.3 Case Study

We demonstrate the application of the previously defined operations of PROVIS on a concrete model starting with the empty model state m_0. We apply the lifted structural event of creating the unit square x depicted in Fig. 3 left (illustrating the creation phase of the model), and afterward, the domain event $CreateTransposedUnitSquare$ of this square (illustrating the operationalization phase). The graphical representation of the last model state contains exactly the two unit squares depicted in Fig. 3 (but not the tree diagram).

$$m_0 \xrightarrow{Create_{US}[x]} m_1 \xrightarrow{CreateTransposedUnitSquare[x]} m_2$$

To be exact, this concatenation of operations can be further decomposed into the lifted structural events:

$$CreateTransposedUnitSquare[x] \circ Create[x](m_0)$$

$$= Set^{A_2 B_2}_6[y] \circ Set^{A_1 B_2}_{10}[y] \circ Set^{A_2 B_1}_{27}[y] \circ Set^{A_1 B_1}_{20}[y] \circ Create[y] \circ Create[x](m_0) = m_2$$

Thereby x is the unit square with base attributes as depicted in Fig. 3 (see also below), and y is an arbitrary unit square. This concatenation could be further disassembled into simple structural events, which then can also be seen as a transition between (much more than two) possibly invalid model states in $\mathcal{M}$.

As there are no tree diagrams in these model states (no events and transitions), the corresponding universes are empty, and we have to consider only the attributes of unit squares:

$$m_0 : \mathcal{U}_{US} = \{\}, \mathcal{U}_E = \{\}, \mathcal{U}_{Tr} = \{\}$$

$$m_1 : \mathcal{U}_{US} = \{x\}, \mathcal{U}_E = \{\}, \mathcal{U}_{Tr} = \{\}$$

$$m_2 : \mathcal{U}_{US} = \{x, y\}, \mathcal{U}_E = \{\}, \mathcal{U}_{Tr} = \{\}.$$

The four base attribute values of the unit squares x and y look as follows:

$$f^{abs}_{A_1 B_1}(x) = 20, f^{abs}_{A_2 B_1}(x) = 10, f^{abs}_{A_1 B_2}(x) = 27, f^{abs}_{A_2 B_2}(x) = 6.$$

$$f^{abs}_{A_1 B_1}(y) = 20, f^{abs}_{A_2 B_1}(y) = 27, f^{abs}_{A_1 B_2}(y) = 10, f^{abs}_{A_2 B_2}(y) = 6.$$

With the constructive constraints of PROVIS, we derive automatically the frequencies of the different characteristics and the total frequency: $f^{abs}_{A_1}(x) = f^{abs}_{B_1}(y) = 20 + 27 = 47, f^{abs}_{A_2}(x) = f^{abs}_{B_2}(y) = 10 + 6 = 16, f^{abs}_{B_1}(x) = f^{abs}_{A_1}(y) = 20 + 10 = 30, f^{abs}_{B_2}(x) = f^{abs}_{A_2}(y) = 27 + 6 = 33, f^{abs}_{total}(x) = f^{abs}_{total}(y) = 63.$

For reasons of brevity, we skip the explication of conditional probabilities $B_i | A_j$ and the measure of association.

6   Conclusion and Outlook

In this paper, we presented an examination of the dynamic character of models. When we understand models as structures mutable through language functionality and interaction of the modeler we have to rethink the conception of a model as a concrete depiction of a system under study independent of time and come up with a notion of models integrating the changeable model states. Therefore, we adapt the definition of models being a row of model states that are interrelated by language-specific model operations.

We investigated the smallest possible building blocks of these operations, so-called structural events: the creation and deletion of objects and relations and the change of attribute values. The approach is based on the METAMORPH formalism that provides us with a concise notion and definition of modeling languages, model elements, and model states. We showed that structural events might cause a violation of language constraints, as they do not take into account domain semantics and showed that they might be "lifted" for constraint satisfaction.

Based on structural events, we can define domain events, which are language operations that use domain knowledge and produce semantically and syntactically valid models. We demonstrated the concrete constitution of both event types on the modeling method PROVIS from the area of stochastic education that comprises numerous constraints and powerful functionality.

To mature the presented approach, we intend to conduct a series of case studies to make notice of all the requirements on the specification of operations stemming from diverse domains. Also, a convenient, platform-independent syntax to specify algorithms on models is on our research agenda. Having available such a syntax, we may implement a prototype of platform-specific translators to turn platform-independent specifications into platform code. This is enabled by using structural events as basic building blocks of functionality and the fact that most common metamodeling platforms offer methods for element creation, deletion, and attribute adaption.

References

1. Bork, D., Buchmann, R.A., Karagiannis, D., Lee, M., Miron, E.T.: An open platform for modeling method conceptualization: the OMiLAB digital ecosystem. Commun. Assoc. Inf. Syst. **44**(1), 673–679 (2019)
2. Brambilla, M., Cabot, J., Wimmer, M.: Model-driven software engineering in practice: second edition. Synth. Lect. Softw. Eng. **3**(1), 1–207 (2017)
3. Döller, V.: Formalizing the four-layer metamodeling stack with MetaMorph: potential and benefits. Softw. Syst. Model. **21**(4), 1411–1435 (2022)
4. Döller, V., Götz, S.: Tree diagrams and unit squares 4.0: digitizing stochastic classes with the didactic modeling tool ProVis. In: Karagiannis, D., Lee, M., Hinkelmann, K., Utz, W. (eds.) Domain-Specific Conceptual Modeling: Concepts, Methods and ADOxx Tools, pp. 481–501. Springer, Cham (2022). https://doi.org/10.1007/978-3-030-93547-4_21
5. Döller, V., Karagiannis, D.: Formalizing conceptual modeling methods with METAMORPH. In: Augusto, A., Gill, A., Nurcan, S., Reinhartz-Berger, I., Schmidt, R., Zdravkovic, J. (eds.) BPMDS/EMMSAD 2021. LNBIP, vol. 421, pp. 245–261. Springer, Cham (2021). https://doi.org/10.1007/978-3-030-79186-5_16
6. Fill, H.G., Redmond, T., Karagiannis, D.: FDMM: a formalism for describing ADOxx meta models and models. In: ICEIS 2012 - Proceedings of the 14th International Conference on Enterprise Information Systems, vol. 3, pp. 133–144 (2012)
7. Heckel, R., Taentzer, G.: Graph Transformation for Software Engineers. Springer, Cham (2020). https://doi.org/10.1007/978-3-030-43916-3
8. Jackson, E., Sztipanovits, J.: Formalizing the structural semantics of domain-specific modeling languages. Softw. Syst. Model. **8**(4), 451–478 (2009)
9. Karagiannis, D., Burzynski, P., Utz, W., Buchmann, R.A.: A metamodeling approach to support the engineering of modeling method requirements. In: 27th IEEE International Requirements Engineering Conference, pp. 199–210 (2019)
10. Karagiannis, D., Kühn, H.: Metamodelling platforms. In: Bauknecht, K., Tjoa, A.M., Quirchmayr, G. (eds.) EC-Web 2002. LNCS, vol. 2455, p. 182. Springer, Heidelberg (2002). https://doi.org/10.1007/3-540-45705-4_19
11. Mens, T., Van Gorp, P.: A taxonomy of model transformation. Electron. Notes Theor. Comput. Sci. **152**(1–2), 125–142 (2006)
12. Object Management Group (OMG): MOF Query/View/Transformation - Version 1.3 (2016). https://www.omg.org/spec/QVT/1.3/PDF
13. Olivé, A.: Conceptual Modeling of Information Systems. Springer, Heidelberg (2007). https://doi.org/10.1007/978-3-540-39390-0
14. Pastor, O., Molina, J.C.: Model-Driven Architecture in Practice: A Software Production Environment Based on Conceptual Modeling. Springer, Heidelberg (2007). https://doi.org/10.1007/978-3-540-71868-0

15. Sandkuhl, K., et al.: Enterprise modelling for the masses – from elitist discipline to common practice. In: Horkoff, J., Jeusfeld, M.A., Persson, A. (eds.) PoEM 2016. LNBIP, vol. 267, pp. 225–240. Springer, Cham (2016). https://doi.org/10.1007/978-3-319-48393-1_16
16. Utz, W.: Design metamodels for domain-specific modelling methods using conceptual structures. In: Proceedings of the Doctoral Consortium Papers Presented at the 11th IFIP WG 8.1 Working Conference on the Practice of Enterprise Modelling, PoEM 2018, vol. 2234, pp. 47–60. CEUR-WS.org (2018)

Establishing Interoperability Between the EMF and the MSDKVS Metamodeling Platforms

Florian Cesal and Dominik Bork[✉][ID]

Business Informatics Group, TU Wien, Favoritenstrasse 9-11, 1040 Vienna, Austria
`dominik.bork@tuwien.ac.at`

Abstract. Many powerful metamodeling platforms exist, each with strengths, weaknesses, functionalities, programming language(s), and developer community. To exploit the mutual benefits of these platforms, it would be ideal to establish interoperability amongst them and the exchange of metamodels and models. This would enable language engineers to choose the metamodeling platform freely without risking a lock-in effect. Two well-documented and freely available metamodeling platforms are the Eclipse Modeling Framework (EMF) and Microsoft's Modeling SDK for Visual Studio (MSDKVS). This paper proposes the first achievements toward establishing interoperability between EMF and MSDKVS on an abstract syntax level and a graphical concrete syntax level. To develop such interoperability, we i) comprehensively analyze the two platforms, ii) present a conceptual mapping between them, and iii) eventually implement a bidirectional transformation bridge. The transformed results' validity, executability, and expressiveness are then quantitatively and qualitatively assessed by transforming a collection of publicly available metamodels.

Keywords: Metamodeling · Interoperability · EMF · Sirius · DSL · MSDKVS

1 Introduction

The definition and use of modeling languages offer many benefits in how software teams and language designers can efficiently cooperate on creating a model-based representation of the system under study. Metamodeling platforms offer means to define customized languages easily and many additional functionalities such as code generation, automatic validation, and graphically representing models. These platforms are widely used in enterprise modeling and model-driven software engineering (MDSE). However, once modellers work with one platform, switching to a different one is cumbersome, complex, and costly, especially because automated support for metamodeling platform interoperability is scarce.

This paper looks at the two well established and actively used metamodeling platforms Eclipse Modeling Framework (EMF) [23] and Modeling SDK for Visual Studio (MSDKVS) [22]. We propose a transformation bridge between EMF and MSDKVS related to bridges reported in [3, 15, 16, 18]. Such a bridging enables language designers to seamlessly switch between platforms by transforming already defined metamodels in one platform into syntactically and semantically equivalent metamodels in the

© IFIP International Federation for Information Processing 2022
Published by Springer Nature Switzerland AG 2022
B. S. Barn and K. Sandkuhl (Eds.): PoEM 2022, LNBIP 456, pp. 167–182, 2022.
https://doi.org/10.1007/978-3-031-21488-2_11

target platform. These bridges further enable reusability of existing metamodels in other platforms, decouple the developers of the underlying programming languages these platforms are built upon, and enable making use of specific platform capabilities employed elsewhere. The transformation bridges are based on a mapping between the meta-metamodel concepts of both platforms. This mapping is created by analyzing the similarities and identifying the differences between these platforms located at the M3 layer of the standardized metamodeling stack [6]. The previous approaches implemented transformation bridges targeting the platforms' abstract syntax elements (e.g., classes and relationships), mostly ignoring the platform's functionalities to graphically represent and manipulate the created models. This paper first extensively analyses the EMF and MSDKVS platforms and then proposes, implements, and evaluates a transformation bridge, thereby considerably advancing previous attempts (see Sect. 3.2).

In the remainder of this paper, Sect. 2 establishes the foundations. Section 3 then discusses related works. A comprehensive analysis of the platforms' concepts is presented in Sect. 4 which establishes the foundation for the bridging in Sect. 5. Section 6 then evaluates the bridge before conclusions are discussed in Sect. 7.

2   Metamodeling Foundations

Complete or partial representations of real-world objects, architectures, or software systems can be realized through the use of models. These models can then be shared and enable communication among stakeholders [6]. Concerning the validation and guidelines for defining said models, an abstraction hierarchy exists, divided into a stack of layers. An example of such a hierarchy stack, consisting of four layers, has been standardized by the OMG [6, 19]: **M0 Layer (runtime instances)** containing the application data or runtime instances; **M1 Layer (model layer)** describing the concrete user model based on the given metamodel (e.g. a UML model); **M2 Layer (metamodel layer)** defining the metamodel; **M3 Layer (meta-metamodel layer)** abstracting the definition for possible metamodels. In the OMG metamodeling hierarchy, the M3 layer is defined by the Meta-Object Facility (MOF) standard.

The M3 level also establishes the foundation for realizing interoperability of metamodeling platforms based on a common abstraction of their metamodels. Modeling languages consist of the following elements, which are taken into consideration when implementing the transformation bridge in the subsequent sections: **Abstract Syntax:** defines classes, their attributes, and associations required to represent the relevant parts of the modeled system, and constraints for restricting the set of valid models. Abstract syntaxes are most often specified via metamodels [5]. **Concrete Syntax:** defines the visual appearances for the abstract syntax elements (e.g., graphical and/or textual) [4].

In practice, language engineers and tool developers need to decide on the most appropriate metamodeling platform considering the requirements at hand. Metamodeling platforms provide IDEs to efficiently create the abstract and concrete syntax of modeling languages, generate editors to create models based on defined metamodels, define and execute code generators and model transformations. Two prominent exemplars of such platforms are introduced in the following.

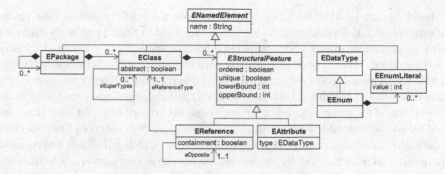

Fig. 1. Excerpt of the Ecore meta-metamodel [3]

2.1 EMF

The Eclipse Modeling Framework (EMF) is an open source metamodeling platform that provides a rich set of features for, e.g., defining metamodels, creating and validating models, transforming models, and serializing models into XMI format. EMF also allows runtime support to generate Java classes and programmatically manipulate the models through reflection. This section describes some of the core features of EMF and provides an overview of how metamodeling is realized with EMF.

Abstract Syntax in EMF. To realize metamodel support in EMF one needs to specify the metamodel by instantiating concepts from the EMF meta-metamodel. This meta-metamodel (see Fig. 1 for an excerpt) thus plays an essential role as it determines the expressiveness of all possible metamodels. An explicit definition of the Ecore meta-metamodel is given in various sources, e.g., in [3,6,18].

Concrete Syntax in EMF. The Eclipse website lists three frameworks that can be used for visualizing Ecore metamodels and models (i.e., Graphical Language Server Platform, Sirius, and Graphiti). For the matter of this paper, we only consider Sirius as it is the most commonly used framework and best resembles the possibilities of graphical viewpoint representations on the MSDKVS side. Sirius uses so called *Viewpoint Specification Projects (VSP)* containing descriptive model files ending with *.odesign* [24]. These files contain the specification of the graphical representation of a model and are comprised of layer definitions and tool sections containing toolbox operations with a structured dependency tree of further inner operation mappings, style mappings for model shapes, font layout properties, custom color definitions, and much more.

2.2 MSDKVS

MSDKVS supports the development of domain-specific languages by weaving abstract syntax and graphical concrete syntax (see [9,22] for a detailed introduction). MSDKVS offers a graphical user interface with an integrated editor to define metamodels (i.e., classes, relationships, and their properties) and a tree explorer, a property editor window, and several other features such as XML serialization of metamodels and models, code generators using a templating engine, and the possibility to build extensions to these features. The currently available MSDKVS NuGet Package[1] was released six months ago and still has an active community of language designers.

---

[1] https://www.nuget.org/packages/Microsoft.VisualStudio.Modeling.Sdk.

Abstract Syntax in MSDKVS. As MSDKVS does not publicly offer a view on the meta-metamodel, the transformation approach explained in Sect. 5 implicitly offers the ability to generate a MSDKVS meta-metamodel corresponding to the data of the serialized metamodel files. Figure 2 shows the core excerpt of the generalized version of the MSDKVS meta-metamodel as a UML class diagram, the full representation is provided here[2]. When creating a DSL in MSDKVS, one element always has to act as the root element of the metamodel and every subsequently created *DomainClass*, if not targeted by another embedded relationship, is referenced by this root class. The root class, by default, has the same name as the DSL itself, but can be changed after initial creation. The possible entities that can be created on the metamodeling canvas are available in the Dsl Designer Toolbox. These elements include *DomainClasses* and different types of *DomainRelationships*, like embedding relationships (i.e., containers) and reference relationships. Each element can further be attributed with various *DomainProperties*.

Regarding their XML serialization, the DslDefinition.dsl file, when opened in a text editor, contains all objects added on the DSL canvas and their mapping references to tool palettes, shapes (i.e., graphical concrete syntax), and other serialization properties needed for code generation. Every object on the canvas is given a *Moniker* description type to be able to be referenced in other parts of the DSL. Monikers are uniquely identifying names for elements. The XML content of the metamodel is grouped in different functional areas where only the entities' moniker types are used as references, e.g., *Source* and *Target* role types of a *DomainRelationship*.

Concrete Syntax in MSDKVS. Every class, relationship, and attribute can be visually enhanced with different shapes and decorators that are maintained within the editor's graphical interface adjoined to the abstract syntax definitions. Through mapping links between the concrete and abstract syntax definitions the language designer can customize the appearances and interaction possibilities like toolbox entries or graphically editing attributes in the Visual Studio runtime instances. MSDKVS does not offer the possibility to define concrete syntax on the metamodel layer.

3 Related Work

This section first offers an overview of existing works on metamodeling platform interoperability. It then takes a detailed look at related ambitions toward bridging EMF and MSDKVS and compares these works to this paper's approach.

3.1 Transformation Bridges

Interoperability deals with the exchange of information between two or more systems, and the ability to use that information in each system respectively [12]. As modeling languages for software development gained popularity in the early 2000s, a need for transforming the grammarware technical space (i.e., EBNF-based grammar tools) to the modelware technical space existed [25] to achieve interoperability between these sets of tools. When this interoperability was established, a plethora of metamodeling platforms followed, which in turn also raised the need for interoperability amongst them.

---

[2] Online supplementary material: https://tinyurl.com/EMF-MSDKVS

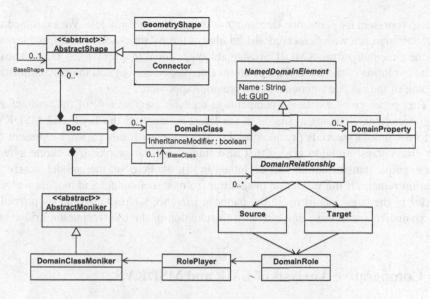

Fig. 2. Excerpt of the MSDKVS meta-metamodel

In the past several bridges between different metamodeling platforms have been proposed, including EMF and ARIS [16], EMF and MetaEdit+ [15], EMF and Visio [18], and EMF and Generic Modeling Environment [8]. Most recently, a transformation bridge between ADOxx and EMF has been proposed in [3]. These transformation bridges typically consist of one or several model transformations that are used for exchanging metamodels and models between the two platforms. These are so-called *horizontal exogenous transformations* [6,13], as the source and target of the transformation are situated on the same abstraction level but adhere to different meta-metamodels. Most of these works transform metamodels, i.e., do not consider interoperability at the model level which further requires a transformation between concrete syntaxes.

3.2 EMF and Microsoft DSL Tools

Research on bridging EMF and Microsoft DSL Tools has been proposed in the past [1, 7]. Differences regarding today's version of MSDKVS as opposed to the transformation approach in [7] are e.g., the serialized file formats (.dsldm compared to today's .dsl mentioned in [1]), the visualization of a meta-metamodel containing the *ValueProperty* entity compared to today's *DomainProperty*, and the representation of attributes for classes and relationships.

The previous approaches execute a chain of ATLAS transformation language transformations to generate the transformed metamodel using the *KM3 (Kernel MetaMeta-Model)*, a DSL for describing metamodels [14] as an intermediate representation of arbitrary metamodels. As a transformation already existed between KM3 and Ecore, the MS/DSL metamodels needed to be only transformed to this pivot KM3 metamodel. Thus, no direct transformation between EMF and MS/DSL tools existed, which introduces potential information loss as KM3 can be considered a generic platform-agnostic

DSL to represent the 'common denominator' of several metamodels. We examined the previous approach with preserved .dsldm files of the Atlantic-Zoo Github[3] and learned that the execution of the XML2DSL step always resulted in empty files. This is caused by the evolution of the MSDKVS platform (mentioned above) and the discontinuation of some of the used components in the previous approach.

This paper gives a detailed comparative analysis (see Sect. 4) of the abstract and concrete syntax elements available in the latest versions of the EMF and MSDKVS platforms that far exceeds previous works. Moreover, with this paper, we present the first direct transformation bridge that also transforms the graphical concrete syntax. One example transformation was explained in [7], the PetriNet metamodel, where the question remains if the validation of said transformed metamodel and models was successful in the target platform. In the paper at hand we address this gap by providing an exhaustive quantitative and qualitative evaluation of the transformation bridge (see Sect. 6).

4   Comparative Analysis of EMF and MSDKVS

This section comprehensively analyzes the two platforms regarding their abstract and concrete syntax capabilities. The list of relevant elements was adapted and extended from [3, 17] in terms of first-class concrete syntax concepts extracted through a detailed investigation of the platforms in question. A full list of the identified, analyzed, and mapped abstract and concrete syntax elements is provided in the online supplementary material[2]. In the following, we therefore concentrate the analysis on the core differences between EMF and MSDKVS as these differences establish the challenges and inform the design of a direct transformation bridge (see Sect. 5).

4.1   Abstract Syntax Features

EMF allows the definition of classes that inherit properties and possible relationship structures from multiple classes (i.e., **multiple inheritance**) whereas MSDKVS only allows entities to inherit from one referenced base object (i.e., **single inheritance**). MSDKVS, in contrast to EMF, allows **inheritance between relationships**. Furthermore, domain relationships in MSDKVS can also act as domain classes which can then be connected to other domain relationships as source or target role. One minor but challenging difference relates to the possibility of relationships between elements to have the **same name** in EMF, which leads to name clashes on the MSDKVS side where relationship names are required to be **unique**. On MSDKVS, domain classes are not directly referenced when creating a relationship. Instead, they are indirectly referenced through monikers, and a domain relationship is comprised of source and target **domain roles** also referencing these monikers. When implementing a transformation between MSDKVS and EMF, correctly resolving these indirect dependencies to achieve syntactical and semantical equivalence is very challenging.

---

[3] https://github.com/atlanmod/atlantic-zoo/tree/main/AtlanticDSLTools.

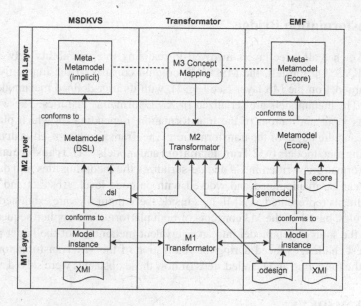

Fig. 3. Transformation bridge between EMF and MSDKVS

4.2 Graphical Concrete Syntax Features

MSDKVS offers the possibility to inherit properties among shapes (i.e., **shape inheritance**) while in EMF no inheritance between the graphical syntax specification is possible. Besides the support for widely used basic shapes like rectangles, circles, and icons, each platform offers *special shape types* that cannot be directly mapped to an equivalent one in the other platform. As metamodeling platforms often depend on an underlying programming language (e.g. EMF on Java, MSDKVS on C#), the available **coloring options**, **styles**, and **appearance attributes** are limited by the languages' libraries. As for MSDKVS, three different types of color palettes are available (system, web, and custom). EMF offers a selection of basic system colors per default. Metamodeling platforms also allow the use of custom **image files** to adapt the appearance of model elements. EMF and MSDKVS differ in their support of various file formats. Icons can be used to, for example, add custom appearances to tool palette items or composition shapes. Different types of **tools** have to be defined to create models in a runtime environment. The granularity of what types of tools can be created and customized varies greatly between EMF and MSDKVS. MSDKVS only allows the definition of essential **element creation tools** for domain classes and domain relationships. On the other hand, EMF offers the definition of a vast amount of additional tools containing, e.g., **edition tools**, **copy-paste tools**, or **reconnect edge tools**. This functionality is not customizable on MSDKVS, but some are automatically used when a creation tool is created. Thus, copying and pasting or deleting elements on the modeling canvas works out of the box.

5   Transformation Bridge

Figure 3 sketches all three layers involved in realizing interoperability between EMF and MSDKVS. On the left, the MSDKVS column consists of the implicitly defined meta-metamodel on the M3 layer (see Fig. 2), with its user-defined metamodel on the M2 layer. The metamodels are serialized in XML format as .dsl files. These .dsl files are used as input and output of the transformation, depending on which platform is the source and the target of the transformation. The Transformator itself is divided into transforming metamodels (**M2 Transformator**) and models (**M1 Transformator**). The M2 Transformator is written in C# and de-serializes the incoming files into data structures that can be manipulated and worked with on code level. Abstract and concrete syntax elements represented as XML tags inside these input files are examined, and the mapping rules, based on the M3 concepts of both platforms, are applied sequentially to transform the source metamodel into an equivalent metamodel of the target platform. The greatest challenges faced during the realization of the M2 Transformator are discussed in the following and detailed steps of how these obstacles were solved are given.

5.1   EMF2MSDKVS

Nested EPackage Flattening. We recognized different styles of EPackage definitions in publicly available EMF metamodels (see Table 1 in the Grouping row). Ecore metamodels can either have one or multiple EPackages defined, while EPackages may also have ESubPackages. Therefore, as MSDKVS usually only has one equivalent language definition, these EPackage contents are flattened and merged into one global EPackage before executing the transformation. Naming conventions and avoiding name clashes are transformed accordingly.

Entity Name Clashes. Detecting and resolving name clashes are essential when realizing metamodeling platform interoperability [3]. Different naming strategies to avoid possible name clashes, e.g., across multiple ESubPackages, are executed. For domain relationships, the MSDKVS names are changed as follows:

<sourceEClass.name>_<EReference.name>_<targetEClass.name>.

Name clashes on domain classes (if there are any), are resolved by mapping the EPackages' nsPrefix attribute to the DomainClass' Namespace attribute.

Multiple Inheritance. As EMF, in contrast to MSDKVS, supports multiple inheritance, a transformation of multiple inheritance structures into equivalent single inheritance structures is necessary. We adapted the *Expansion Strategy* pattern proposed by Crespo et al. [10] to translate the complex structures of multiple ESuperTypes in EMF into equivalent single BaseClass references in MSDKVS without information loss (see Fig. 4). Important to note is that also EReferences that target a super class have to be duplicated to the newly created domain classes as Domain Relationships in MSDKVS. In addition to the abstract syntax duplicates, this affects the transformation of all types of graphical concrete syntax mappings from Sirius as well, which results in more Shape classes on MSDKVS side and Creation Tools inside the modeling editor.

Root Element Pattern Matching. MSDKVS metamodels require a root element that is mapped to the diagram shape. This diagram shape provides the modeling canvas

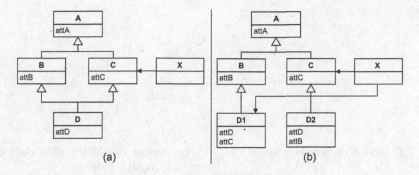

Fig. 4. Adapted *Expansion Strategy* [10]: (a) multiple inheritance in EMF; (b) transformed single inheritance in MSDKVS

in the runtime instances of a domain model. As per API requirement, this selected root element has to be the source domain role of domain relationships marked as containment relationships, where the targets are all domain classes that are neither part of an existing containment relationship (e.g., children of compartments) nor should target any base classes they would inherit from. When transforming an Ecore metamodel into MSDKVS, existing EClasses are matched against these criteria. If such an EClass can be found, this EClass is transformed to be the root diagram element in MSDKVS. If no EClass is suitable, then an additional default domain class is generated that acts as the diagram's root element.

Icon Mapping. Sirius supports the definition of icon styles on different node mappings, referencing workspace images in various image file formats. For MSDKVS, a requirement to attribute a model entity with icons is that the images have to be in the Bitmap (BMP) format. Therefore, library calls to convert these files to the required format on the target platform are employed in the M2 transformation.

5.2   MSDKVS2EMF

Relationship Roles. Domain Relationships in MSDKVS differ from their required representation on the target EMF side in so far, that the source and the target entities of said relationships are referencing the corresponding domain classes through monikers. Source and target domain roles can have different names attributed to them compared to their actual classes used for creating the domain relationship. This construct has to be considered when transforming from EMF to MSDKVS too, as for every EReference at least one role has to be created in MSDKVS. Domain classes are then referenced through moniker types by their unique names. When transforming from MSDKVS to EMF, the transformator has to look up the source and the target domain classes and transform these DomainClasses into the EReferences' eTypes and eOpposites accordingly.

Attributable Relationships. In MSDKVS not only classes but also relationships can have attributes. As already mentioned in [7], this behavior can be implemented similarly, meaning that domain relationships with attributes attached to them are mapped

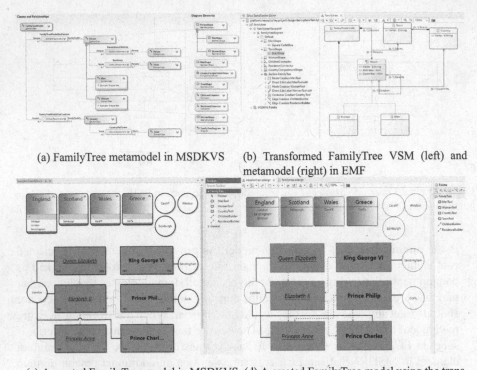

(a) FamilyTree metamodel in MSDKVS   (b) Transformed FamilyTree VSM (left) and metamodel (right) in EMF

(c) A created FamilyTree model in MSDKVS (d) A created FamilyTree model using the transformed metamodel in EMF

Fig. 5. FamilyTree metamodel and model in MSDKVS and transformed into EMF. (Color figure online)

to classes that are referenced from both transformed domain classes, leading to additional EClass and EReference entities on the target EMF side. Multiplicities are transformed accordingly to maintain the original behavior.

Shape Inheritance. MSDKVS allows inheritance on the graphical representation of classes and relationships. Therefore, the M2 Transformator has to check possible inherited shape classes and transform them accordingly.

Implicit Modeling Tool Capabilities. MSDKVS supports only the explicit definition of element creation tools on domain classes and domain relationships, while other tooling capabilities that can be explicitly defined in Sirius are inherently available on MSDKVS' modeling canvas. To achieve an equivalent experience, the number of tools on EMF is thus typically higher because the M2 Transformator generates these additional tools for every Node or Edge Creation Tool defined in MSDKVS.

Color Naming. MSDKVS supports a variety of colors for graphical properties (e.g., FillColor, TextColor, and BackgroundColor). Sirius only supports a small subset of these named colors, e.g., standardized system colors like white, black, and green. To be able to transform said colors from MSDKVS into equivalent colors in EMF, the M2 Transformator looks up the composing red, green, and blue color values for MSDKVS' named colors and transforms them to Custom User Palettes used by Sirius which can be named by the designer.

5.3   MSDKVS2EMF Transformation Example

For showcasing the transformation bridge, we will, in the following, refer to a small example of a family tree metamodel which we created in MSDKVS and subsequently transformed, using our transformation bridge (see Sect. 5) to a valid EMF metamodel. The example, adapted from the tutorial of Sirius[4], comes also with a graphical concrete syntax specification on MSDKVS' side, which enables to exemplify feasibility of the transformation bridge. The goal of this example case is thus to show (and illustrate) the feasibility of realizing syntactic and semantic equivalence between the two platforms involving the abstract and the graphical concrete syntax. Full images can be found here[2].

Figure 5a shows the source metamodel inside the Visual Studio IDE. In this example, a basic family tree metamodel with graphical concrete syntax descriptions has been created that contains a compartment relationship between *Country* and *Town* and an inheritance structure between the *Person* domain class as the base class of *Man* and *Woman*. Figure 5c shows a manually created model of an excerpt of the family tree of the British House of Windsor based on the previously defined metamodel in MSDKVS.

The result of executing the M2 Transformator on the source MSDKVS metamodel is shown in Fig. 5b, displaying the resulting Ecore metamodel both graphically and in a tree structure. Eventually, Fig. 5d shows a model created manually within a run-time instance that uses the transformed Ecore metamodel and the Sirius .odesign specification. The original model created previously in MSDKVS was used as a reference to show how both appear visually to the modeler, respectively.

6   Evaluation

This section reports on the results of experimenting with the M2 Transformator. The transformation is implemented as two uni-directional transformations which means that either MSDKVS metamodels (*.dsl files) or EMF metamodels (*.ecore files) with optional .genmodel and .odesign files for graphical concrete syntax mappings and code editor generation settings can be used as input.

We searched and selected a representative set of metamodels of both platforms from publicly available collections and also through dedicated metamodel search engines [21]. A collection of 44 metamodels from MSDKVS and 75 randomly selected metamodels from the AtlanMod Atlantic Zoo[5] with additional 22 metamodels referencing and containing Sirius VSMs and 18 metamodels (some of which overlapping with VSM available metamodels) containing EMF specific features like multiple inheritance or nested EPackages was composed. Thus, the metamodels have been selected mostly at random, all manual additions were motivated by the goal to have a representative set of metamodels (i.e., a set that differs in size, contained metamodeling concepts, and are equipped with a graphical concrete syntax specification).

---

[4] https://wiki.eclipse.org/Sirius/Tutorials/StarterTutorial.
[5] https://github.com/atlanmod/atlantic-zoo.

6.1 Research Questions

The aim of the experiments was to evaluate the transformation bridge's overall validity and the success rate, i.e., whether the transformed metamodels are syntactically and semantically equivalent and whether it is possible to transform all source metamodels, respectively. To help with the analysis, additional methods were implemented to create informative output files in addition to the resulting metamodels to list the steps the M2 Transformator has executed and the entities it has created on the target side. After traversing through every metamodel and transforming it, the summarized statistics provide insights on different criteria (see Table 1).

Table 1. Source metamodels abstract (left) and transformation success rate (right)

	EMF			MSDKVS		
	Min	Med	Max	Min	Med	Max
Grouping	1	2	20	1	1	1
Classes	1	14	673	2	8	39
Abstract Classes	0	2	83	0	1	9
Inherited Classes	0	7	679	0	3	34
Multiple Inheritances	0	0	134	-	-	-
Relationships	0	12	437	0	9	40
Attributes	0	10	124	1	15	103
Enumerations	0	0	15	0	1	21

Direction	Abstract Syntax			Concrete Syntax		
	Cases	Errors	Rate	Cases	Errors	Rate
MSDKVS → EMF	44	1	97.73%	44	3	93.18%
EMF → MSDKVS	75	0	100%	22	2	90.91%

The derived statistics were analyzed and described based on quantitative metrics reported in the literature [2,11,17,20]. Afterwards, a qualitative analysis is concerned with the validation of the transformed metamodels on the target platform by investigating the equivalence of execution functionality (i.e., the modeling support by create, delete, redo/undo tools etc.) of the source and the transformed metamodels in their respective metamodeling platforms.

With the evaluation, we thus aim to respond to the following research questions: *RQ1: Are the transformed metamodels valid when opened in the target platform?*, and *RQ2: Are the transformed metamodels executable, i.e. can editor code be generated and runtime instances successfully started?*

6.2 Experimental Setup

In the following, we dive deeper into the analytical aspects of the metamodel transformation approach. First, quantitative aspects are listed and compared. Table 1 shows statistical information about the experiment's source metamodels' abstract syntax, the statistics of the conrete syntax is provided in the online supplementary material (see Footnote 2). To analyse the qualitative aspects, the transformed metamodels are opened with the target platform. Both platforms offer automatic validation, meaning that when the project files are opened, their internal structure is validated. Validation errors, if present, are listed accordingly. As the MSDKVS diagram editor on the M2 layer offers the ability to define concrete syntax elements upon the abstract syntax entities, the validation step checks both areas for errors. On EMF side, the transformed .odesign files containing the definitions for graphical concrete syntax mapping required separate, manual validation. If the validation yielded no errors, the platforms' functionalities upon creating models were tested (i.e., starting of runtime instances and creating/editing models).

6.3   Results

RQ1: Validity of Transformed Metamodels. For the transformation validity we not only concern the abstract syntax but also the constraints on the concrete graphical syntax. We encountered only one erroneous case (out of 44) in the direction MSDKVS → EMF considering the abstract syntax. This error resulted from the fact that one of the metamodels from MSDKVS did not use the Dsl root tag in its XML serialization. Instead, DslLibrary was observed to be the root element. If changed to Dsl, the transformation executed successfully. The M2 Transformator though has to be extended to also allow DslLibrary as a root XML tag for loading MSDKVS metamodels. Regarding the concrete graphical syntax, two erroneous cases have been identified. One case was caused by the fact that the mapping rule for mapping port shapes to inner mappings in bordered nodes in EMF had not been implemented yet. The second error occurred because of a missing transformation of icon decorator styles for domain properties of compartments.

The direction EMF → MSDKVS yielding a 100% success rate (based on 75 cases) considering the abstract syntax. The additional Sirius validation considered the 22 metamodels which contained a graphical concrete syntax specification. In the runs that followed, two out of 22 were faulty, stemming from the fact that multiple Ecore metamodels were referenced from within the .odesign file, therefore creating shapes for not available entities. In the next steps regarding the M2 Transformator implementation, these errors will be looked at accordingly.

As the M2 Transformator is implemented as a bridge between two XML serialization formats, most of the initial problems that occurred originated from de-serializing the input metamodel files to data structures. XML namespace errors were among the most common types of exceptions because of limitations the default C# library provides when de-serializing Ecore metamodel files, as they contain numerous classes using the same typed attributes (e.g., firstModelOperations and subModelOperations in tool sections). These errors could be eliminated eventually by changing the content of the metamodel files before the de-serialization.

RQ2: Executability of Transformed Metamodels. The executability assumes a valid metamodel in order to run the code generators for creating and executing modeling runtime instances in the platforms. When the code generation throws errors or the modeling canvas cannot be initialized, the transformed metamodel files are deemed faulty with regards to their executability and semantic evaluation. All transformed metamodels, that threw no errors during their validation phase, could be used to generate model code on the target platforms and thus initialize runtime editor instances for modeling purposes. As a final step, a small subset of metamodels on each side and their transformed results were selected for manually evaluating and comparing their interaction on the modeling layer, similarly to how the example in Sect. 5.3 was conducted. Regarding e.g., their tool palette functionalities, their interaction on the modeling canvas, and their entity styling no major inequalities were observed.

6.4 Limitations

A few limitations adhere to the transformation approach based on the M2 layer. The M2 transformator is specific to the EMF and MSDKVS metamodels. Each additional platform requires a mapping according to the identified rule sets and each rule requires an implementation in C#. For serializing the new metamodel representations, the XML schema has to be analyzed and corresponding data structures for (de-)serialization have to be added. Existing transformations can afterwards be reused, thus creating M3 level bridges spanning multiple metamodels. Another limitation is the realization of the transformator on the current platform versions. Core updates to these platform metamodels therefore require similar updates of the transformator.

Regarding the involved metamodel entities and unique features of each platform, some limitations in the tranformation's current state are present as well. Many of the advanced model operations supported by Sirius (e.g., filtering using query languages, flow control operations like *Begin*, *For* and *If*, Dialog, and Model Representations operations) cannot be mapped directly to available operations in MSDKVS. As mentioned in Sect. 4, only element creation tools are supported, which target specific metamodel entities. These features are correctly mapped to and from Sirius' model operations *Change Context*, *Create Instance*, and *Set*.

7   Conclusion

We established interoperability between the EMF and MSDKVS platforms by conceptualizing and implementing a bidirectional transformation bridge able to transform metamodels defined within both platforms. The evaluation was conducted by choosing a representative set of publicly available metamodels[2]. By providing mapping rules also for the graphical notations available in both metamodeling platforms, we showed that it is possible to transform means of graphically representing these elements of transformed metamodels to achieve not only syntactic but also visual interoperability.

Future research concentrates on the realization of the M1 Transformator to transform models between EMF and MSDKVS. Furthermore, the realization of roundtrip transformations based on defined mapping tables and an additional transformation log file is on our agenda. Eventually, we will release the bridge's code and metamodels open source and deploy the transformation bridge as a service at: http://me.big.tuwien. ac.at/.

Acknowledgements. This research has been partly funded by the Austrian Research Promotion Agency (FFG) via the Austrian Competence Center for Digital Production (CDP) under the contract number 854187.

References

1. Bézivin, J., Hillairet, G., Jouault, F., Piers, W., Kurtev, I.: Bridging the MS/DSL tools and the eclipse modeling framework. In: International Workshop on Software Factories at OOPSLA (2005)
2. Bork, D.: Metamodel-based analysis of domain-specific conceptual modeling methods. In: Buchmann, R.A., Karagiannis, D., Kirikova, M. (eds.) PoEM 2018. LNBIP, vol. 335, pp. 172–187. Springer, Cham (2018). https://doi.org/10.1007/978-3-030-02302-7_11
3. Bork, D., Anagnostou, K., Wimmer, M.: Towards interoperable metamodeling platforms: the case of bridging ADOxx and EMF. In: Franch, X., Poels, G., Gailly, F., Snoeck, M. (eds.) CAiSE 2022. LNCS, vol. 13295, pp. 479–497. Springer, Cham (2022). https://doi.org/10.1007/978-3-031-07472-1_28
4. Bork, D., Karagiannis, D., Pittl, B.: Systematic analysis and evaluation of visual conceptual modeling language notations. In: 12th International Conference on Research Challenges in Information Science, pp. 1–11. IEEE (2018). https://doi.org/10.1109/RCIS.2018.8406652
5. Bork, D., Karagiannis, D., Pittl, B.: A survey of modeling language specification techniques. Inf. Syst. **87** (2020). https://doi.org/10.1016/j.is.2019.101425
6. Brambilla, M., Cabot, J., Wimmer, M.: Model-Driven Software Engineering in Practice. Synthesis Lectures on Software Engineering, 2nd edn. Morgan & Claypool, San Rafael (2017)
7. Brunelière, H., Cabot, J., Clasen, C., Jouault, F., Bézivin, J.: Towards model driven tool interoperability: bridging eclipse and microsoft modeling tools. In: Kühne, T., Selic, B., Gervais, M.-P., Terrier, F. (eds.) ECMFA 2010. LNCS, vol. 6138, pp. 32–47. Springer, Heidelberg (2010). https://doi.org/10.1007/978-3-642-13595-8_5
8. Bézivin, J., Brunette, C., Chevrel, R., Jouault, F., Kurtev, I.: Bridging the generic modeling environment (GME) and the eclipse modeling framework, January 2005
9. Cook, S., Jones, G., Kent, S., Wills, A.: Domain-specific development with visual studio DSL tools, May 2007
10. Crespo, Y., Marqués, J., Rodríguez, J.: On the translation of multiple inheritance hierarchies into single inheritance hierarchies, pp. 30–37, January 2002
11. Di Rocco, J., Di Ruscio, D., Iovino, L., Pierantonio, A.: Mining metrics for understanding metamodel characteristics. In: Modeling in Software Engineering. ACM (2014)
12. Geraci, A., et al.: IEEE Standard Computer Dictionary: Compilation of IEEE Standard Computer Glossaries. IEEE Press (1991)
13. Hebig, R., Seidl, C., Berger, T., Pedersen, J.K., Wasowski, A.: Model transformation languages under a magnifying glass: a controlled experiment with Xtend, ATL, and QVT. In: ACM Joint Meeting on European Software Engineering Conference and Symposium on the Foundations of Software Engineering, pp. 445–455. ACM (2018)
14. Jouault, F., Bézivin, J.: KM3: a DSL for metamodel specification. In: Gorrieri, R., Wehrheim, H. (eds.) FMOODS 2006. LNCS, vol. 4037, pp. 171–185. Springer, Heidelberg (2006). https://doi.org/10.1007/11768869_14
15. Kern, H.: The interchange of (meta)models between MetaEdit+ and eclipse EMF using M3-level-based bridges. In: 8th Workshop on Domain-Specific Modeling, pp. 14–19 (2008)
16. Kern, H.: Modellaustausch zwischen ARIS und Eclipse EMF durch Verwendung einer M3-Level-basierten Brücke, pp. 123–137, September 2008
17. Kern, H., Hummel, A., Kühne, S.: Towards a comparative analysis of meta-metamodels. In: Lopes, C.V. (ed.) SPLASH 2011 Workshops, pp. 7–12. ACM (2011)
18. Kern, H., Kühne, S.: Integration of Microsoft Visio and Eclipse modeling framework using M3-level-based bridges. In: Workshop on Model-Driven Tool and Process Integration (2009)
19. Kühne, T.: Matters of (meta-)modeling. Softw. Syst. Model. **5**(4), 369–385 (2006)

20. Langer, P., Mayerhofer, T., Wimmer, M., Kappel, G.: On the usage of UML. In: Fill, H.G., Karagiannis, D., Reimer, U. (eds.) Modellierung 2014, pp. 289–304. GI (2014)
21. López, J.A.H., Cuadrado, J.S.: MAR: a structure-based search engine for models. In: 23rd International Conference on Model Driven Engineering Languages and Systems, pp. 57–67. ACM (2020)
22. Microsoft: Official online documentation of the modeling SDK for visual studio (2022). https://docs.microsoft.com/en-us/visualstudio/modeling/modeling-sdk-for-visual-studio-domain-specific-languages, last accessed on 08.05.2022
23. Steinberg, D., Budinsky, F., Paternostro, M., Merks, E.: EMF: Eclipse Modeling Framework 2.0, 2nd edn. Addison-Wesley Professional, London (2009)
24. Viyović, V., Maksimović, M., Perisić, B.: Sirius: a rapid development of DSM graphical editor. In: Intelligent Engineering Systems, INES 2014, pp. 233–238. IEEE (2014)
25. Wimmer, M., Kramler, G.: Bridging grammarware and modelware. In: Bruel, J.-M. (ed.) MODELS 2005. LNCS, vol. 3844, pp. 159–168. Springer, Heidelberg (2006). https://doi.org/10.1007/11663430_17

Beyond Business Development: Regulatory Assessment of Energy Sector Projects with Contextual Requirements Engineering

Sybren de Kinderen[1]([⊠]), Qin Ma[2], Monika Kaczmarek-Heß[3], and Rik Eshuis[1]

[1] Information Systems Group IE&IS, Eindhoven University of Technology, Eindhoven, The Netherlands
{s.d.kinderen,h.eshuis}@tue.nl
[2] University of Luxembourg, 2 Avenue de l'Université, 4365 Esch-sur-Alzette, Luxembourg
qin.ma@uni.lu
[3] University of Duisburg-Essen, Universitätstrasse 9, D-45141 Essen, Germany
monika.kaczmarek-hess@uni-due.de

Abstract. The energy sector is characterized by considerable regulatory variation. Thus, for developing a new energy sector project, typical early phase business development activities need to be supplemented with a careful regulatory assessment. In this paper, we investigate to what extent contextual requirements engineering can be useful to support regulatory analyses in the energy sector. To this end, we first derive a set of requirements, and then show both the potentials and shortcomings of contextual requirements engineering for regulatory analysis. A demand side flexibility scenario, focusing on assessing the rights and obligations imposed by the European Clean Energy Package, is used for motivation and illustration purposes. Finally, we provide a discussion on working towards a modeling method, which intertwines business development and regulatory assessment.

Keywords: Energy sector · Regulatory analysis · Contextual requirements engineering · Goal modeling

1 Introduction

Fostered by (recent) developments such as digital transformation, decentralized production and consumption of energy, and transition towards renewable energy sources, the energy sector increasingly forms a breeding ground of new projects [22,23,30]. Such projects range from virtual currencies to promote the trade of green energy [21], to the use of blockchain technology for managing electric vehicles [5]. Although the potential benefits on an economical, social and

B. S. Barn and K. Sandkuhl (Eds.): PoEM 2022, LNBIP 456, pp. 183–198, 2022.
https://doi.org/10.1007/978-3-031-21488-2_12

environmental level are promising [22], several challenges still remain [24]. This is especially visible in the development phase of new energy sector projects, where intertwined with typical business development activities, such as business model assessment or cost-benefit analyses, a careful assessment of rights and responsibilities associated with existing *regulations* must also be made [10,17,23,33].

For example, consider the de-carbonization of the European Union's energy system. The EU overhauled its energy policy framework in 2019 and approved the Clean Energy Package (CEP) [25] aiming at: (1) enhancing and promoting market competition, (2) strengthening energy security, and (3) protecting the environment, e.g., through renewable energy sources [20,25,36]. Specifically, the 2019 CEP recognizes the central role of energy consumers "in achieving the flexibility necessary to adapt the electricity system to variable and distributed renewable electricity generation" [25]. As such, it supports the change towards decentralized production of electricity using renewable sources, by (1) reinforcing the right of consumers to produce, store, consume, and sell their own energy, (2) offering them the possibility to reap financial benefits by adjusting consumption behavior, and (3) engaging them in balancing responsibilities [20,25].

Please note that all activities in the EU member states must respect the EU directives in terms of results to be achieved. However, the EU directives provide member states flexibility in how they implement directives into national laws. As a result, the regional energy market regulation can vary from one country to another, cf. [17], taking into consideration stakeholders and their appeals, and regional peculiarities. Such regional variation in energy sector's regulation influences, among others, the allowed configuration of value networks, and thus shape the distribution of costs and benefits across a network of actors, cf. [23, p. 43], [14, p. 14], and consequently, investment decisions [9].

There exist several candidate conceptual modeling approaches for regulatory assessment, see [1]. Moreover, conceptual modeling has already been used as an instrument to support business development analyses in the energy sector [15, 18,35]. The objective of this paper is to capitalize on the potentials of conceptual modeling in both regards, i.e., to systematically analyze the effect of regulation on the business development of new projects in the energy sector. Doing so, existing model-based business development instruments for the energy sector can be complemented with regulatory analysis, as it is highly relevant for and inextricably intertwined with business development activities as stated earlier. Yet, as we will also see in this paper, specifically in Sect. 4, current regulatory support for the early business development phase is not fully researched, with the focus on a regulatory assessment aiming more at the operational side, like on business process compliance, or the compliance of a software product, see [1].

Therefore, in this paper we select an existing contextual requirements engineering technique and apply it for regulatory assessment during business development. The selected goal modeling approach [2] proposes to represent varying environment around a software system as contexts and attach the contexts to variation points in goal models, so as to enable reasoning about variants the software system can adopt in order to adapt to its local surroundings. In the same vein, we exploit the contextual goal modeling approach to represent the varying regulatory environment surrounding energy sector projects, and systematically incorporate and reason about the influence of: (1) regulation on the configuration of goals of actors participating in a project, as well as (2) the relations among goals. The use of the existing modeling approach in a new application context allows us to gain important insights regarding both potentials and shortcomings of such an approach, and to define next steps towards a fully-fledged modeling method, which intertwines business development and regulatory assessment.

To reach our goal, inline with the design science [40] research approach followed, we first make use of a motivating scenario in Sect. 2 to reach problem awareness. We then derive a set of requirements towards an analysis tool supporting the targeted assessment in Sect. 3, and discuss existing modeling approaches. We select a contextual requirements engineering approach and apply it to the motivating scenario in Sect. 4. We critically reflect on the requirements fulfillment of the selected approach in Sect. 5, and sketch a research outlook. As such, we report on the coverage of one engineering cycle [40].

2 Motivating Scenario

Our motivating scenario is inspired by [8, pp. 134–139], and has been extended with ideas from [32,41], as well as the already mentioned EU Clean Energy Package (CEP) [25], especially when it comes to the implication of the CEP for actors other than households.

The scenario considers the influence of the CEP on a household wishing to use their electric vehicle (EV) to offer *demand side flexibility* services to independent aggregators. Demand side flexibility concerns "the ability of a customer (Prosumer) to deviate from its normal electricity consumption (production) profile, in response to price signals or market incentives" [11]. In the scenario, it means that the household can offer storage capacity of their EV to store the surplus electricity in the grid, or respectively, offer the electricity stored in their EV back to the grid when there is a shortage.

According to Art. 15 (2c) of the CEP [25], households have the right to offer such demand side flexibility services. And if they do so, they act as an *active customer*, meaning "a final customer [...] who consumes or stores electricity generated within its premises [...] or who sells self-generated electricity or participates in flexibility or energy efficiency schemes" (Art. 2(8)). Active customers, in parallel to the right to offer demand side flexibility services, have also several obligations. The most prominent of these is, according to Art. 15 (2f) of the CEP, a *balance responsibility*. In this scenario, a balance responsibility means that the household offering demand side flexibility services via its EV is equally obliged to keep electricity supply and demand in balance, so as not to burden the grid infrastructure with over- or under-supply of electricity.

The household offers demand side flexibility services to an *independent aggregator*, meaning, "a market participant engaged in aggregation who is not affiliated to the customer's supplier" ([41] citing the CEP [25]). The Art. 17 (1) of CEP grants independent aggregators the right to offer demand side flexibility services themselves, too. They do so by aggregating demand side flexibility services from multiple smaller parties, such as the household from the scenario. Moreover, consistent with the obligations of active customers, according to the Art. 17 (3d) of CEP, the right of independent aggregators to offer demand side flexibility services is also accompanied by a balancing responsibility obligation.

Independent aggregators use the aggregated demand side flexibility to offer balancing services to a Transmission Systems Operator (TSO). A TSO operates the national electricity grid and relies on the balancing services to maintain an overall balance between supply and demand on the electricity grid. Every TSO of an EU member state has to act in accordance with the EU directive 2017/1485, which stipulates that a TSO is responsible for restoring any grid imbalance within 15 min [39]. To restore imbalance, the TSO negotiates with parties offering balancing services (in our scenario the independent aggregators) via an electronic bidding system, the aFRR (automatic Frequency Restoration Reserve [39]), about the balance required.

3   Requirements and Existing Modeling Approaches

In this section, first, considering the motivating scenario, we derive a set of requirements, and then discuss suitability of existing approaches to fulfill those.

3.1   Requirements

We argue that to support both business development and regulatory assessment of energy sector projects, a satisfactory model-based instrument needs to:

Requirement 1. Account for multiple energy sector stakeholders assuming different roles.

Rationale: Energy sector projects require cooperation of multiple stakeholders involved in a value network to operate properly [15], such as a household, an electric utility company, a grid operator, a regulatory institution, and a government department. In addition to that, some stakeholders assume different roles during a project. What stakeholders are part of the project, what roles are required, which stakeholders may assume which roles, and what constellation of stakeholders and roles in general is required or possible, these aspects are mostly imposed by existing regulation, hence constitute an important perspective to capture during regulatory assessment of energy sector projects.

Example: The motivating scenario refers to three stakeholders: a household, an independent aggregator, and a transmission system operator. Among them, the household can take on the role of both a prosumer, in the sense of being an energy consumer and producer, and an active consumer in the sense of the CEP, if the household offers demand side flexibility services via its EV.

Requirement 2. Account for different types of goals and corresponding relations between goals.

Rationale: The regulatory changes mentioned in the introduction lead to a transformation of the EU's energy system into a "decentralized system composed of heterogeneous social and technological actors motivated by different interests and agendas" [20, p. 142]. We use the notion of goals as an abstraction to cover a stakeholder's broad interests and agendas. Each actor pursues different goals of a different nature. Some of the goals can be intrinsic in nature, some economically motivated, while other goals may take a form of obligations and be assigned in line with the existing regulation to a specific role played by the stakeholder. Therefore, when conducting business development analysis and regulatory assessment of an energy sector project, it is of utmost importance to be able to (1) differentiate between different types of goals (e.g., intrinsically motivated, or obligatory) and sources of those, and (2) capture different relations among goals, e.g., the achievement of one goal can impact (positively or negatively) the achievement of another goal, or the fulfillment of a goal of a stakeholder can be delegated to another stakeholder/role by fulfilling another goal of the latter.

Example: In the context of motivating scenario, each stakeholder pursues their own goals. The household wants to contribute to transition towards green energy out of its social responsibility, and at the same time, to earn extra income for economic reasons. The active consumer (a role played by the household) has a balancing responsibility obligation as defined by the CEP. The fulfillment of this obligation can be delegated to an independent aggregator, whose original goal is to offer balance services.

Requirement 3. Explicitly account for the varying regulatory environment surrounding energy sector projects and its influence.

Rationale: Regulatory variability considerably influences the constellation of stakeholders, their investment decisions, and/or valuation of an energy sector project, cf. e.g., [14,17], and in that way influences also the goals pursued by stakeholders, as well as possible ways to fulfill those goals. Regulatory variability can be observed in legal definitions, applicable frameworks (influencing the way the stakeholders cooperate as well as goals they pursue), and incentive policies introduced (e.g., remuneration schemes for prosumers to offer surplus of generated electricity to the grid, for example with net-metering[1]). If relevant for business development purposes such regulatory variability should be explicitly captured within the model in relation to the stakeholder goals and the means to fulfill these goals. In the following, we elaborate further on three dimensions of regulatory variability: (1) traceability to source of differences, (2) the consequences of regulation, and (3) the specific impact on a specific object of analysis.

Firstly, normative legislation coming from different sources and the corresponding goals imposed by them should be accounted for. Indeed, regulatory context(s) in which the project is to be realized has a strong influence on the goals of stakeholders, for it not only shapes the current goals of a stakeholder,

---

[1] Net metering is an electricity billing mechanism that allows prosumers to use the grid to "store" electricity generated from solar panels and use that electricity anytime.

but also frames the possible ways to satisfy them. Some regulations are high-level and strategic, and apply to all initiatives, hence their influence on energy sector projects is universal and no variability is allowed. In contrast, other regulations are rather low-level and region-specific, hence may differ from one region to another [17]. Therefore, when capturing the regulatory origin of a goal of a stakeholder, i.e., the piece of regulation that influences the existence and/or nature of this goal, we not only need traceability from the goal back to the regulation source, but also need to reflect upon how the transition from high-level universal regulation to regional specific regulation influences the refinement from high-level goals into low-level goals, (or in the opposite direction the contribution of low-level goals to the achievement of high-level goals), and further from low-level goals to their respective means of implementations.

Secondly, we need to consider the consequences of regulation in terms of (a) enabling/disabling a certain business model, (b) constraining the shaping of the underlying value network IT infrastructure, (c) inducing different cost efficiency [19], (d) bringing about financial consequences, e.g., in terms of fines in case of not compliance, and (e) allow the project to make the most or least of regional peculiarities (where an example of regional peculiarity can be either abundance or scarcity in other source of energy).

Thirdly, the specific impact on a specific object of analysis needs to be accounted for. On the one hand, we need to identify what is influenced, i.e., the object of influence, it can be either a single goal, a single dependency relation, a single actor, or a composition of those of any complexity. On the other hand, the exact way in which the object is influenced, i.e., the influence itself, can also vary. In some cases, the object is enabled or required by a piece of regulation. Such an influence can be sufficiently captured by attaching the relevant regulation to the concerned object to indicate the corresponding authorization or obligation relation. However, in other cases, the influence may involve elaborating on more information from another perspective beyond stakeholder goals. For example, a regulation obliges the fulfillment of a goal, but allows different ways to achieve it. To capture such an influence and allow for conducting analysis thereof, we need to not only attach the regulation to the concerned goal, but also elaborate on, e.g., what (financial) consequences we need to face, if the goal will not be satisfied, and different costs and benefits implied by each way of fulfilling the goal, as allowed by the regulation.

Example: The CEP influences the decisions and goals pursued by stakeholders, e.g., by giving the right to households to offer demand side flexibility services, hence become active customers and consequently making them responsible for balancing. This is might be different in non-EU countries.

3.2 Selecting a Modeling Approach

Contextualization has been studied in requirements engineering [2,3], business process management [31], software engineering [34], as well as in business capability engineering [37]. Since we require an approach that supports modeling of multiple actors and their goals, cf. Requirement 1 and 2, we focus on approaches originating in the field of requirements engineering, more specifically goal modeling techniques, representing users, (different types of) goals, possible ways to satisfy those, and analysis thereof. There exist a variety of Goal-Oriented Requirements Analysis (GORE) modeling techniques, such as i-star [42], the Goal-oriented Requirements Language (GRL) [4] or TROPOS [7], see also [16].

With their focus on modeling (short/medium/long)-term goals, these techniques form a useful point of departure for goal analysis and have also been used to that extent to support analysis of various initiatives, also in the energy sector [26]. Nevertheless, in order to select a candidate approach for our purposes, namely to represent varying regulation of energy sector projects and to systematically analyze its influence, we need to still consider two aspects. Firstly, the goal modeling approach should be suitable for analyzing regulation. Secondly, it should account for the three dimensions of regulatory variability discussed in Requirement 3, i.e., briefly, being able (a) to trace intentional elements back to their regulatory origin, (b) to reflect different types of influence, and (c) to elaborate on necessary details of influence when needed.

When it comes to the first consideration, goal-oriented modeling techniques have indeed already been applied for legal and regulatory compliance analysis [1, 13], or for modeling regulations [27].

When it comes to the second consideration, goal modeling techniques have also been extended to explicitly model the notion of context, and the influence thereof on goal models, e.g., [2,3]. For instance, contextual goal modeling has been applied in a case study on medicinal product development to manage regulatory traceability specifically [43]. As a consequence, such an extension serves as a promising starting point towards the second consideration, namely to account for regulatory variability, being one type of context. However, the structure employed by contextual goal modeling techniques to represent contexts is "flat". Namely, contexts are expressed in terms of propositional logic formulae of facts, whose truth value can be checked against a surrounding context [2].

Alternatively, the idea of variability is used for expressing regulatory goal models, such as in [27]. Variability, a notion originating from software product line engineering [6,28], allows to specify commonalities and differences in family of software products in terms of conceptual models, of which feature models are a prominent exemplar. When used for regulation specifically, variability is visible in, e.g., that different articles are applicable to different types of organizations. As such goal models need to be extended with variability mechanisms, to deal with such (local) adaptations.

For one, [27] propose to use feature models to define (multiple dimensions of) features and the cross-cutting constrains among features, in parallel to the goal family model representing the regulation, and annotate the intentional elements in the goal family model with features defined in the feature model.

To summarize, goal modeling has proven to be suitable for analyzing regulation, and in the meantime has also been extended with context or augmented with feature models to account for variability. We choose the contextual goal

Table 1. Regulation as variation points for the contextual goal model

C0	Art. 15(2c) of the CEP, the right of the active customer to offer demand side flexibility services
C1	Art. 15(2f) of the CEP, the balance responsibility for the active customer
C2	Art. 17(1) of the CEP, the right for the independent aggregator to offer flexibility services
C3	Art. 17(3d) of the CEP, the balance responsibility for the independent aggregator
C4	EU directive 2017/1485, a EU member TSO is responsible for restoring any grid imbalance within 15 min
C5	Art. 2(8) of the CEP, a household offering demand side flexibility becomes an active customer

modeling approach proposed in [2] mainly out of two considerations. First and foremost, the contextual goal modeling approach in [2] extends TROPOS goal models by defining six types of locations in the goal models, namely goals, AND and OR decomposition links, means-end links, contribution links, and dependency links, as variation points. A variation point may be annotated with a context to reflect its influence. For example, one can annotate a goal with a context to indicate that the goal is activated, if and only if, the annotating context holds, or annotate a dependency link from a goal to an actor with a context to indicate that the fulfillment of the goal can be delegated to the actor, if and only if, the annotating context holds. In contrast, [27] only allows to annotating goals with features defined in the companion feature model that captures the variability. In addition, the authors of the selected contextual goal modeling technique also enable context analysis, its verification, as well as reasoning techniques to derive requirements from an annotated contextual goal model to a subset of goal model elements that should be fulfilled given the current context(s).

Secondly, we select the approach from [2] because only one dimension is exhibited in the regulation aspect exemplified by the motivation scenario, which mainly consists of extracts (e.g., articles and paragraphs) from two legal documents, namely CEP and EU directive 2017/1485, without touching upon any cross-regulation relations or constraints, contextual goal modeling suffices in this regard. Of course, we are aware that regulatory environment can get more complicated and would eventually require additional models to capture regulation variability itself, such as using feature models as in [27].

4   Modeling the Motivating Scenario

Figure 1 shows a contextual goal model of the scenario described in Sect. 2. It is accompanied by Table 1, which shows six regulation extracts acting as contexts influencing variation points in the goal model.

The goal model shows that a household can perform the task T0: *offer demand side flexibility* (T0) as a means to the end of fulfilling the goal G1: *earn additional income*. A context C0 annotates the means-end link from T0 to

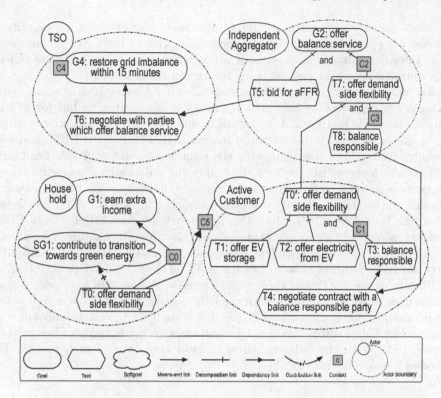

Fig. 1. Contextual goal model for the EV demand side response scenario

G1, because this means-end link represents a variation point in the goal model and it holds only under the regulation represented by C0, namely Art. 15(2c) of the CEP. In the meantime, execution of T0 also positively contributes to the soft goal SG1: *contribute to a transition towards green energy* of the household.

Additionally, we can see how, for task T0, there is a dependency to the actor active customer, which is annotated by context C5. In the used contextual requirements engineering technique, such an annotated dependency indicates also a variation point, meaning that the execution of a task (or fulfillment of a goal) can be delegated to another actor, if the context annotating the variation point holds. In our scenario, as per Table 1, we can see that context C5 entails the CEP Art. 2(8) of the definition of an active customer. As such, the delegation of T0 can only take place if this article of CEP is in force.

On the side of the active customer, we can see that the delegated task T0' has an AND decomposition into the tasks T1: *offer EV storage capacity*, T2: *offer electricity from EV*, and T3: *balance responsible*. We observe here another variation point: the AND decomposition link from T0' to T3 is annotated with context C1, namely Art. 15(2f) of the CEP. This article explicitly requires an active customer to be financially responsible for any imbalance s/he causes in the electricity system. In the context of C1, the only possible means to T3 is T4:

negotiate contract with a balance responsible party. Note that in the described use case [8, pp. 134–139], under the regulation prior to the CEP, a household could offer flexibility services without an accompanying balance responsibility. This option is no longer possible with the enactment of the CEP.

An independent aggregator has a goal G2: *offer balance service* as its main business. Achievement of this goal requires the aggregator to bid for aFFR requests from TSO (T4), and in the meantime have access to electricity storage or stored electricity to match the request. Art. 17(1) of the CEP, modeled as context C2, grants the aggregator the right to offer demand side flexibility (T7) to match the aFFR requests. But since the independent aggregator does not possess its own electricity storage capacity, it realizes T7 by aggregating demand side flexibility offered by active customers (through the AND decomposition link from T7 to T0'). Moreover, as enforced by Art. 17(3d) of the CEP, modeled as context C3, an aggregator should also take the balance responsibility (T8). Doing so, an independent aggregator becomes a balance responsibility party, and constitutes a means of realizing T4 on the side of active customer.

Finally, on the TSO's side there exists a goal G4: *restore grid imbalance within* 15 min in order to be compliant with the EU directive 2017/1485, which dictates the maximum time span for an EU member state TSO to restore imbalance is 15 min. The TSO realizes this goal by *negotiate with parties which offer balance service* (T6). With the independent aggregator being one of such parties, T5 becomes a means of realizing T6.

5   Discussion

Now that we have used the selected approach to model our scenario, here we first reflect on the lessons learned, and then provide an outlook on future work.

5.1   Lessons Learned

The Contexts and Variation Points Provide Added Value for Including Regulation During Early Phase Business Development. We have found that the idea of contexts and variation points offer us a suitable means to, for a given scenario, express how regulation influences both the rights and obligations of the involved actors. For example, it has allowed us to model that a household, under the CEP, has the right to offer demand side flexibility services through its electric vehicle, but that equally, this right is accompanied by a balance responsibility obligation. Related to that, the idea of adding contexts to *relations* between motivational elements has proven to be helpful. For example, adding contexts to relations has allowed us to express that, when a household offers flexibility services, under the CEP it is regarded as an active customer with all its inherent responsibilities. In this sense, next to a satisfaction of Requirements 1 and 2, we also found that the used contextual requirements engineering technique satisfies well Requirement 3 regarding the expression of contexts and different variation points, at least for the modeled scenario. As such, in terms of flexibility the used technique stands out positively.

Additional Expressiveness Is Needed to Express Regulatory Considerations. While the contexts and variation points have certainly been helpful for our purposes, we have experienced that the used contextual requirements engineering technique has its shortcomings. In particular, this concerns (1) *a lacking distinction between actor and role*. In our scenario, we experienced that regulation often applies to predefined roles. For example, we experienced this when modeling the notion of an active customer. As we have discussed, as soon as a private actor (the household in our case) starts offering flexible demand response services to the grid, they are treated as an active customer, and naturally, a household then has to act according to all rights and obligations granted to an active customer. Nevertheless, while using the selected modeling technique, we did not have the expressive power at our disposal to model this. Instead, as a workaround, we had to model the active customer as yet another actor. Note here that original TROPOS meta model does have the concept of an role, which is also associated to an actor [38, p. 403]. Nevertheless, this role concept appears to be insufficiently reflected in the contextual adaptation of TROPOS we used. So, while this original TROPOS role concept forms a nice point of departure, for future work it needs to be taken more explicitly into consideration, especially in treating roles in a differentiated manner when it comes to regulation. (2) *The dependency relation from the used technique does not naturally mirror the modeling of legal scenarios.* We find that the modeling of legal considerations at times is not fully natural with the constructs offered by the used contextual requirements engineering technique. In particular, this concerns the idea of a dependency, which we can only model between a task or goal on the one hand, and an actor on the other, meaning that the full set of motivational elements of the dependent actor is implied, if the dependency holds. This actor-centric dependency is logical given the agent-oriented background of TROPOS. Also, for our simple scenario, this dependency largely works: we mostly use it to model the active customer, who has relatively straightforward responsibilities. Yet, we speculate that for more complex scenarios, such actor-centric dependencies may not offer the desired modeling flexibility. As such, for future work, we may capitalize on the notion of contexts and variation points, but use it in conjunction with modeling techniques that do not necessarily have an agent-oriented background. Note that one could argue that, if a dependency towards an actor exists, this implies per definition that actor is acting in a role, notably a role "triggered" by the execution of a task or goal. At the same time, the notion of a role is not mentioned in the work of [2], so even if it is there, it is there implicitly at best.

5.2   Towards Intertwining Regulation and Business Development

Building on the above lessons learned, and considering our overall aim, we formulate the following actions going forward.

Capitalizing on Complementary Strengths of Modeling Techniques.
As we discussed, the used contextual requirements engineering technique proved
especially valuable in its ability to add contexts to both (1) motivational elements
(e.g., goals) and (2) relations between those (e.g., dependency, means-end), and
make them variation points in goal models. Nevertheless, we also observed deficiencies, as mentioned in the lessons learned. Compounding these, we observed
a lack of mature software tool support for contexts and variation points.

To remedy this we envision capitalizing on a combination of the strengths of
different modeling techniques. Especially, we consider to additionally account for
the work of [27], which adapts GRL goal models and combines them with feature
models for regulatory modeling (as per Sect. 4). While offering less flexibility for
expressing variation points, using feature models in tandem holds the promise
to capture regulatory environment in multiple dimensions as well as constraints
cross-cutting dimensions. Moreover, GRL comes with a mature software tool
(i.e., the jUCMNav tool), and additionally, because it is agent-oriented, GRL
offers more flexibility in expressing dependencies than TROPOS.

When it comes to contexts and variation points generally, we find it is also an
opportunity to enrich the modeling of regulatory environment of energy sector
projects with existing enterprise modeling techniques, e.g., to explicitly account
for the consequence of a regulation in terms of configuration of value network.

For instance, in the case study used in our previous work [29], regulation
influenced the configuration of a value constellation requiring additional value
exchanges and actors. In [29], we expressed this regulatory influence on top of
the e^3value model [15], nevertheless in an informal manner only, namely, by
highlighting the influence with color and traceability links.

Accounting for Regulation More Extensively. In addition to capitalizing
on feature models to express regulations in multiple dimensions and to address
cross-dimensional constraints among them as in [27], we also aim at taking on
board the characteristics of regulation specifically. Especially, following [1] there
exist several goal-oriented approaches that can aid to this end. Here approaches
are said to either focus on intent, i.e., on gaining an understanding of the law by
itself, or to focus on structure, i.e., on gaining an understanding of the intended
relation between different structural elements of the law (so not so much on the
semantics of the law itself [1]). For example, consider legal URN [12, pp. 87–90]
[13], a goal modeling approach with a focus on modeling the structure of law.
During the modeling of regulation, legal URN among others capitalizes on the
idea of Hohfeldian squares, which basically refer to an inter dependency between
rights of different persons, such as a right from one person implying a right for
an another (a correlative right) [12, pp. 16–18]. Together with other concepts,
which help to identify modeling elements in a law text (e.g., clauses, subjects,
and actors), and with the help of a framework, legal URN is one example of a
(structural) approach which can aid in the translation of regulation.

**Re-using Models Capturing Varying Regulatory Environments and
Their Influence on Business Development.** Despite the varying characteristic of regulation over time and/or across regions, energy sector projects

from the same region and time are regulated under the same regime. As such, a model capturing the regulation and its influence on the business development of a project can be re-used in the context of different projects and for different purposes. Just like in support of model-driven compliance tasks, an invariant regulatory model is re-used for, among others, compliance checking and compliance analysis [1]. For future work, we aim to capitalize on the invariant nature of models that intertwine regulatory assessment and business development of energy sector projects, and re-use (part of) them across projects. Moreover, by observing and defining patterns in these models, we can also provide aid in decision making during early phase business development activities, e.g., (1) to decide on the regulatory suitability of several (ideal type) business model scenarios for deploying an energy sector project, or (2) to decide on the distribution of costs and benefits over actors according to the obligations and right granted by a regulation (e.g., an active customer is financially responsible for any imbalance caused by it under the CEP), and more.

In the longer run, as stated, we envision working towards a modeling method wherein the modeling of business case development and regulation are closely intertwined. Here we build upon existing modeling methods to support business case development, also with a focus on the energy sector [15,18]. While the exact shape of such a method is open for further work, we do intent to take the above considerations as our point of departure.

6   Concluding Outlook

In this paper, we propose to use a contextual requirements engineering technique for modeling the effect of regulation during the early, business development, phase of new energy sector projects. We find the idea of contexts and variation points valuable, especially the possibility to annotate both motivational elements and relations, and make them variation points. Nevertheless, we did experience limitations, e.g., regarding the (agent-oriented) modeling of dependencies.

As a response, for future work we consider moving forward with a "best-of-breed" modeling approach. Also, we consider to enrich other business development modeling techniques with variation points, notably $e^3 value$. Finally, as stated, in the longer run we aim at a modeling method, which intertwines business development and regulatory analysis. To achieve this, a first step is to take regulation more systematically into account during modeling, whereby we can take inspiration from existing work like [1].

References

1. Akhigbe, O., Amyot, D., Richards, G.: A systematic literature mapping of goal and non-goal modelling methods for legal and regulatory compliance. RE **24**(4), 459–481 (2019)
2. Ali, R., Dalpiaz, F., Giorgini, P.: A goal-based framework for contextual requirements modeling and analysis. RE **15**(4), 439–458 (2010)

3. Ali, R., Dalpiaz, F., Giorgini, P.: Reasoning with contextual requirements: detecting inconsistency and conflicts. Inf. Softw. Technol. **55**(1), 35–57 (2013)
4. Amyot, D., Ghanavati, S., Horkoff, J., Mussbacher, G., Peyton, L., Yu, E.: Evaluating goal models within the goal-oriented requirement language. Int. J. Intell. Syst. **25**(8), 841–877 (2010)
5. Andoni, M., Robu, V., Flynn, D., Abram, S., Geach, D., Jenkins, D., McCallum, P., Peacock, A.: Blockchain technology in the energy sector: a systematic review of challenges and opportunities. Renew. Sust. Energ. Rev. **100**, 143–174 (2019)
6. Apel, S., Batory, D.S., Kästner, C., Saake, G.: Feature-Oriented Software Product Lines - Concepts and Implementation. Springer, Heidelberg (2013). https://doi.org/10.1007/978-3-642-37521-7
7. Bresciani, P., Perini, A., Giorgini, P., Giunchiglia, F., Mylopoulos, J.: Tropos: an agent-oriented software development methodology. Auton. Agents Multi-Agent Syst. **8**(3), 203–236 (2004). https://doi.org/10.1023/B:AGNT.0000018806.20944. ef
8. Buijze, A., et al.: Power to the people - een onderzoek naar alternatieven voor de huidige balans-onverantwoordelijkheid van kleinverbruikers. Technical report, Utrecht Unversity, in cooperation with TNO (2021)
9. Cambini, C., Meletiou, A., Bompard, E., Masera, M.: Market and regulatory factors influencing smart-grid investment in Europe: evidence from pilot projects and implications for reform. Util. Policy **40**, 36–47 (2016)
10. de A. Dantas, G., et al.: Public policies for smart grids in Brazil. Renew. Sustain. Energy Rev. **92**, 501–512 (2018)
11. European Smart Grids Task Force Expert Group 3: Demand side flexibility perceived barriers and proposed recommendations. Technical report (2019)
12. Ghanavati, S.: Legal-URN framework for legal compliance of business processes. Ph.D. thesis, University of Ottawa (2013)
13. Ghanavati, S., Rifaut, A., Dubois, E., Amyot, D.: Goal-oriented compliance with multiple regulations. In: Gorschek, T., Lutz, R.R. (eds.) 22nd International Requirements Engineering Conference, pp. 73–82. IEEE (2014)
14. Giordano, V., Onyeji, I., Fulli, G., Jimenez, M.S., Filiou, C.: Guidelines for conducting a cost-benefit analysis of smart grid projects. Technical report (2012). https://ses.jrc.ec.europa.eu/publications/reports/guidelines-conducting-cost-benefit-analysis-smart-grid-projects. Accessed 06 Aug 2021
15. Gordijn, J., Akkermans, H.: Business models for distributed generation in a liberalized market environment. Electr. Power Syst. Res. **77**(9), 1178–1188 (2007)
16. Horkoff, J., et al.: Goal-oriented requirements engineering: an extended systematic mapping study. RE **24**(2), 133–160 (2019)
17. Inês, C., Guilherme, P.L., Esther, M.G., Swantje, G., Stephen, H., Lars, H.: Regulatory challenges and opportunities for collective renewable energy prosumers in the EU. Energy Policy **138**, 111212 (2020)
18. de Kinderen, S., Kaczmarek-Heß, M., Ma, Q., Razo-Zapata, I.: A modeling method in support of strategic analysis in the realm of enterprise modeling: on the example of blockchain-based initiatives for the electricity sector. EMISAJ **16**(2), 1–36 (2021). https://doi.org/10.18417/emisa.16.2
19. Meletiou, A., Cambini, C., Masera, M.: Regulatory and ownership determinants of unbundling regime choice for European electricity transmission utilities. Util. Policy **50**, 13–25 (2018)

20. Mengolini, A., Masera, M.: EU energy policy: a socio-energy perspective for an inclusive energy transition. In: Weijnen, M.P.C., Lukszo, Z., Farahani, S. (eds.) Shaping an Inclusive Energy Transition, pp. 141–161. Springer, Cham (2021). https://doi.org/10.1007/978-3-030-74586-8_7

21. Mihaylov, M., Jurado, S., Van Moffaert, K., Avellana, N., Nowe, A.: NRG-X-Change: a novel mechanism for trading of renewable energy in smart grids. In: Helfert, M., Krempels, K.H., Donnellan, B. (eds.) 3rd International Conference on Smart Grids and Green IT Systems, pp. 101–106. Scitepress (2014)

22. Moretti, M., Djomo, S.N., Azadi, H., May, K., De Vos, K., Van Passel, S., Witters, N.: A systematic review of environmental and economic impacts of smart grids. Renew. Sustain. Energy Rev. **68**, 888–898 (2017)

23. Nordling, A., Pädam, S., af Burén, C., Jörgensen, P.: Social costs and benefits of smart grid technologies. Technical report, Power Transmission & Distribution Systems, ISGAN Annex (2018)

24. Norouzi, F., Hoppe, T., Elizondo, L.R., Bauer, P.: A review of socio-technical barriers to smart microgrid development. Renew. Sust. Energ. Rev. **167**, 112674 (2022)

25. OJL: Directive (EU) 2019/944 of the European Parliament and of the Council of 5 June 2019 on Common Rules for the Internal Market for Electricity and Amending Directive 2012/27/EU (2019)

26. Orellana, M.A., Silva, J.R., Pellini, E.L.: A model-based and goal-oriented approach for the conceptual design of smart grid services. Machines **9**(12), 370 (2021)

27. Palmieri, A., Collet, P., Amyot, D.: Handling regulatory goal model families as software product lines. In: Zdravkovic, J., Kirikova, M., Johannesson, P. (eds.) CAiSE 2015. LNCS, vol. 9097, pp. 181–196. Springer, Cham (2015). https://doi.org/10.1007/978-3-319-19069-3_12

28. Pohl, K., Böckle, G., van der Linden, F.: Software Product Line Engineering - Foundations, Principles, and Techniques. Springer, Heidelberg (2005). https://doi.org/10.1007/3-540-28901-1

29. Razo-Zapata, I.S., Ma, Q., Kaczmarek-Heß, M., de Kinderen, S.: The conjoint modeling of value networks and regulations of smart grid platforms: a Luxembourg case study. In: 2017 IEEE CBI, vol. 02, pp. 83–88 (2017)

30. Reis, I.F., Gonçalves, I., Lopes, M.A., Antunes, C.H.: Business models for energy communities: a review of key issues and trends. Renew. Sust. Energ. Rev. **144**, 111013 (2021)

31. Rosemann, M., Recker, J., Flender, C.: Contextualisation of business processes. Int. J. Bus. Process. Integr. Manag. **3**(1), 47–60 (2008)

32. Schittekatte, T., Deschamps, V., Meeus, L.: The regulatory framework for independent aggregators. Electr. J. **34**(6), 106971 (2021)

33. Simões, M.G., et al.: A comparison of smart grid technologies and progresses in Europe and the US. IEEE Trans. Ind. Appl. **48**(4), 1154–1162 (2012)

34. Simons, C., Wirtz, G.: Modeling context in mobile distributed systems with the UML. J. Vis. Lang. Comput. **18**(4), 420–439 (2007)

35. Smart Grid Coordination Group: Smart grid reference architecture. Technical report, CEN-CENELEC-ETSI (2012)

36. Sokolowski, M.: Regulations in the European Electricity Sector. Routledge Studies in Energy Law and Regulations, Routledge, London (2016)

37. Stirna, J., Grabis, J., Henkel, M., Zdravkovic, J.: Capability driven development – an approach to support evolving organizations. In: Sandkuhl, K., Seigerroth, U., Stirna, J. (eds.) PoEM 2012. LNBIP, vol. 134, pp. 117–131. Springer, Heidelberg (2012). https://doi.org/10.1007/978-3-642-34549-4_9

38. Susi, A., Perini, A., Mylopoulos, J., Gi, P.: The Tropos metamodel and its use. Informatica **29**(4), 401–408 (2005)
39. TenneT: Manual aFRR for BSPs. Technical report, TenneT TSO B.V (2022)
40. Wieringa, R.J.: Design Science Methodology for Information Systems and Software Engineering. Springer, Heidelberg (2014). https://doi.org/10.1007/978-3-662-43839-8
41. Willems, B., Zhou, J.: The clean energy package and demand response: setting correct incentives. Energies **13**(21), 5672 (2020)
42. Yu, E., Giorgini, P., Maiden, N., Mylopoulos, J.: Social Modeling for Requirements Engineering. MIT Press, Cambridge (2011)
43. Ozturk Yurt, Z., Eshuis, R., Wilbik, A., Vanderfeesten, I.: Context-aware process modelling for medicinal product development. In: Serral, E., Stirna, J., Ralyté, J., Grabis, J. (eds.) PoEM 2021. LNBIP, vol. 432, pp. 168–183. Springer, Cham (2021). https://doi.org/10.1007/978-3-030-91279-6_12

Participatory Modeling

A Methodology for DSML-Assisted Participatory Agent-Based Enterprise Modelling

Thomas Godfrey[1]([✉])[iD], Rahul Batra[2], Sam Douthwaite[2][iD],
Jonathan Edgeworth[2], Simon Miles[1][iD], and Steffen Zschaler[1][iD]

[1] Department of Informatics, King's College London, Bush House, Strand Campus,
30, Aldwych, London WC2B 4BG, UK
{thomas.1.godfrey,simon.miles,steffen.zschaler}@kcl.ac.uk
[2] Guy's and St Thomas' NHS Foundation Trust, Westminster Bridge Rd,
London SE1 7EH, UK
{cidr.correspondence,Sam.Douthwaite,jonathan.edgeworth}@gstt.nhs.uk

Abstract. Participatory agent-based modelling (ABM) can help bring
the benefits of simulation to domain users by actively involving stakeholders in the development process. Collaboration in enterprise modelling can improve the model developer's understanding of the domain
and therefore improve the effectiveness of domain analysis. Where many
agent-oriented methodologies focus on the development of one-off models, domain-specific modelling languages (DSML) can improve the re-use
of concepts identified in domain analysis across multiple case studies
and expose modelling concepts in domain-appropriate terms, increasing model accessibility. To realise the benefits of DSMLs we need to
understand how DSML development can be incorporated into typical
agent-based modelling. In this paper we discuss existing methodologies
for ABM development and DSML development, and we discuss the benefits merging the two can bring. We present a methodology for DSML-
assisted participatory agent-based modelling, and support the methodology with a case study—a modelling exercise conducted in collaboration
with a hospital emergency department on the topic of infection control
for COVID-19 and Influenza.

Keywords: Agent-based modelling · Participatory modelling ·
Domain-specific modelling

1 Introduction

Agent-based modelling (ABM) can be an attractive option for enterprise modelling due to the capacity of agent-based models to capture: high levels of het-
erogeneity, organic interactions between model entities, and organic emergent

T. Godfrey—Supported by the KCL funded Centre for Doctoral Training (CDT) in
Data-Driven Health.

behaviours [7]. To develop effective agent-based models, it is important that model developers have a strong understanding of the domain. Developers need to identify the actors involved in a process, their behaviours, and how they interact between themselves and the environment. These behaviours need to be translated into a set of rules to model but determining *which* actors and actions should be captured and *how* they should be modelled can be a complex process. Participatory modelling [28] encourages close collaboration between domain stakeholders and model developers, improving the quality of domain analysis. However, existing approaches to participatory modelling typically depend on general-purpose, or agent-oriented, languages that require the model developer to translate design concepts into a technical implementation. This abstraction process is manual, is prone to error and ambiguities, and presents a lack of re-use.

Domain-specific modelling languages (DSMLs) [9] are an attractive tool for supporting participatory modelling. DSMLs consist of a concrete syntax (the language grammar), an abstract syntax (a meta-model of the language structure), and semantics (the 'meaning' of the language concepts). DSMLs expose domain-appropriate concepts in the concrete syntax, allowing the user to utilise these high-level terms to implement models. This can allow domain stakeholders to collaborate on the model implementation directly, reducing the risk of abstraction errors. Models written in a DSML are typically automatically generated into computer-readable code, allowing for traceability of the model, and efficiency of development. In developing a DSML, the developer performs domain engineering [23] by identifying the common and variable properties of the domain and formalising them in the language syntax. The DSML can then be used to generate specific model instances by expressing the particulars of the model using the language concepts (known as application engineering). The meta-model of the DSML effectively provides an (evolving) domain model for future modelling exercises, improving the re-use of concepts for specific applications.

Existing approaches to DSML-assisted modelling methodologies place the abstraction level of the DSML at the ABM platform level (such as easyABMS [11], and the work of Stark and Barn [2]) or use technically complex languages [14]. Other approaches exist that use high domain-level concepts such as MAIA [12] and INGENIAS [22] for developing social science simulations. However, these works provide a generic language that developers need to learn how to instantiate correctly. In this paper we present a methodology for creating DSMLs for ABM development in a domain-agnostic way such that developers can adapt a language for their particular domain. We refer to these languages as 'high-level DSMLs'. We take inspiration from the vision of DSMLs for ABM development outlined by Zschaler and Polack [30], and the principles of effective participatory modelling detailed in the CoSMoS project [27]. We make the following contributions:

1. A novel methodology for DSML-assisted participatory agent-based modelling
2. A review of current approaches to participatory ABM and DSML development

3. An ABM case study on infection control in a hospital emergency department to motivate and illustrate our methodology

In Sect. 2, we introduce a participatory modelling case study conducted in collaboration with St Thomas' Hospital Emergency Department in London. We use this case study to motivate the need for a methodology for DSML-assisted participatory modelling. We discuss some existing methodologies for participatory agent-based modelling and domain-specific modelling languages in Sects. 3 and 4. In Sect. 5, we use the case study to motivate our methodology for DSML-assisted agent-based modelling.

2 Case Study

In this section we detail the case study for our methodology—a modelling case study conducted in the Spring of 2022 in collaboration with St. Thomas' Hospital emergency department (ED) and infection control teams. The intention of the study was to analyse the infection control measures for COVID-19 and Influenza introduced in the hospital emergency department during the Winter of 2021. An ABM was developed for this study, using a healthcare-focused DSML. Below we provide background information to the case study, and the motivation for developing a participatory modelling methodology.

At St. Thomas' Hospital, the infection control team are in regular contact with the ED to help anticipate, and mitigate, infection control problems. The product of these meetings is typically a policy-revision for hospital staff. New policies define how staff should manage patient care such as what tests they should perform on patients, how to interpret test results, and where patients should be admitted to according to their infection status [19]. In St. Thomas' Hospital, these policies are communicated to staff through 'action cards' which are flowchart-like process descriptions that are available on the trust intranet. As new policies are introduced, these action cards will be updated and replaced. An example of an action card used during a peak of COVID-19 prevalence in 2020 can be found in Fig. 1.

During the Winter of 2021, infection control were cautious about the potential return of Influenza as well as the already expected COVID-19. This would introduce further complications for infection control as staff would need to mitigate the risk of cross-infection between patients with different infectious diseases. This required new rules on patient isolation, and triggered the introduction of new rapid tests for Influenza and COVID-19. As part of this planning, a series of new action cards were developed using our DSML and discussed between the infection control and ED teams. In the spring of 2022, we modelled the processes defined in these action cards and evaluated directional changes in infection control metrics between the different action cards including: infection risk (measured by the number of infected patients admitted to a non-infectious cohort) and resource usage (measured as number of tests used within a particular time-frame).

To be used for ALL Majors A/B & and Pt's being admitted from Majors C/UCC

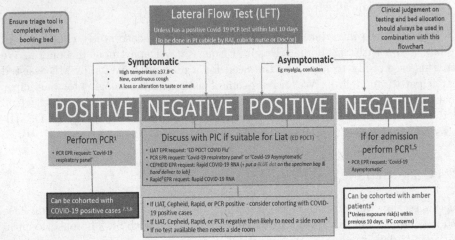

Fig. 1. Action card example.

During the study, we identified some key areas where typical agent-oriented methodologies are not suitable for the healthcare domain. In a hospital environment, staff need to make decisions quickly to keep up with the rapid needs of patient care. Restrictions on time can often make typical ABM development infeasible due to their time and resource requirements. Strong domain analysis often requires the developer to spend considerable time within, and learning about, the domain. Typical agent-oriented methodologies do not formalise the findings of domain analysis into re-usable concepts, instead focusing on application-engineering for a particular case study. This results in poor re-use of domain concepts in the modelling process and additional development overheads for subsequent modelling exercises. Every time a domain process changes and every time a new model is developed, the developers need to restart the model conceptualisation and design steps. With a DSML, we expected domain analysis to contribute additively to the language meta-model. As more models are developed, we expected the scope and specificity of the language to improve for the target domain. When specific models are developed in the future, there should be less requirement to complete any further domain analysis, and instead the DSML will already provide the necessary concepts to instantiate. This subsequently makes the model development process less cumbersome on stakeholders and developers over time.

Hospital EDs are continually evolving to keep up with demands. In our example above, the series of action card iterations introduced both variations on existing domain processes, as well as the introduction of entirely new processes. In a typical agent-based modelling approach, making changes such as these to the model can be complex and unwieldy. The definition of high-level domain processes is distributed across individual agent and environment definitions,

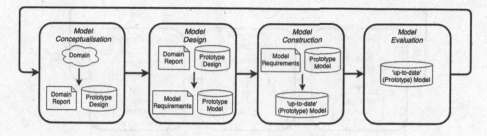

Fig. 2. The ABM development cycle.

making it challenging to identify and refactor the model implementation. The model developer (in collaboration with domain stakeholders) would need to decompose each action card into distinct agent definitions, where each agent has their own list of behaviours representing part of the overall action card process. If an alternative action card is to be tested, the model developer would need to repeat this decomposition process again or attempt to refactor the existing agent implementations. This activity is manual, time-consuming, and error-prone. Using a DSML, we expected to largely avoid these issues by capturing high-level domain processes explicitly in the modelling language. With a high-level DSML, action cards can be modelled in one central viewpoint (with orthogonal high-level concerns captured in alternative modelling viewpoints). The decomposition of the global domain process into individual agents and their behaviours is completed automatically during code generation, making changes to domain processes easier and quicker to facilitate.

We have identified the potential for using DSMLs in model development, and how they can benefit collaboration with domain stakeholders and improve re-use in domain analysis. In the next sections, we discuss methodologies for how to develop DSMLs, and how DSML development can be incorporated into typical ABM methodologies. We start with a description of typical ABM methodologies.

3   Agent-Based Modelling Methodologies

Ramanath and Gilbert [24] present a literature review on the topic of participatory ABM development and identify patterns in previous work on social simulations to develop a methodology for participatory modelling. They describe the participatory design process as consisting of 4 key phases which we present in Fig. 2 and discuss below:

The first phase is **model conceptualisation** in which the model developers consult domain stakeholders to learn about domain processes, the relevant domain problems, and the stakeholders' expectations for model outputs. This phase is conducted through the use of different example scenarios developed informally by the model developers. The model developers may conduct their own independent research in the relevant literature prior to this stage in order to form foundational knowledge of the domain.

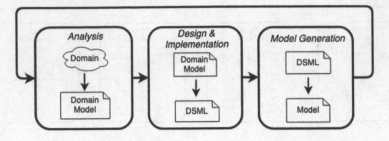

Fig. 3. The DSML development cycle.

The next phase is **model design**. This step involves taking the results of scenario analysis into a workshop setting with groups of domain stakeholders. The intention is to conceptualise and design the model with the end-users, sharing informal model prototypes and discussing model structure requirements. The aim of this process is to identify the main entities involved in domain processes (whether active or passive) and to identify their key attributes, behaviours, and interactions. Ideally, a diverse group of stakeholders should be present in these activities in order to contribute their respective background knowledge on domain processes to be implemented in the model.

The output of the model design phase is formalised during **model construction**. During this phase, a basic agent-based simulation is developed by the model developers with input from the domain stakeholders. The developers will translate the entities identified during model design into agents with their respective properties and behaviours. The simulation is not intended to be complete, but instead should provide a concrete software artifact for analysis in the next phase.

The **evaluation** phase is conducted with the stakeholders in the form of a user panel. This involves the model developers demonstrating the simulation to the stakeholders and discussing any ambiguities that remained during its implementation. For example, the model developers should clarify any issues related to agent behavioural rules, data availability, etc. that were not resolved during model construction. The user panel will provide an opportunity for the domain stakeholders to experience first-hand a version of the model and to provide feedback. Lee et al. [17], and Klügl [16] provide excellent resources on ABM output analysis and validation techniques. The feedback produced from these user panels can be used to inform changes to the model design for further iterations of development, starting again from **model conceptualisation**. Once the model is deemed fit for purpose, it can be used to conduct experiments to provide meaningful outputs to stakeholders.

4   DSML Methodologies

In this section, we discuss existing approaches to DSML development.

Mernik et al. [18] review a range of DSML-related papers and identify patterns in the development processes. They distil these patterns into a methodology covering all aspects of development from 'decision' of when to develop a DSML to 'deployment' of the language. For the scope of this paper we will focus on the intermediary steps of domain analysis, design and implementation, which we present in Fig. 3 and discuss below:

Analysis involves gathering knowledge about the domain and the scope of the problem(s) the users wish to address. The intention of this phase is to establish the terminology used in the domain problem, and the semantics of different domain concepts. These concepts will then be formalised in the next phase.

Next, the **design and implementation** phase then involves converting the domain model generated in the analysis phase into a DSML definition. This will include identifying which domain concepts are constant and which are variable. We refer to Voelter [29], or Fowler [9] for fundamental concepts of DSML design.

Once the DSML has been developed, it can then be used in application engineering to generate specific model instances. We refer to this phase as **model generation**, which involves identifying which DSML concepts are needed for a particular model case study, and creating instantiations of those concepts.

5   A Methodology for DSML-Assisted Participatory Agent-Based Modelling

In this section, we propose a methodology for DSML-assisted participatory agent-based modelling influenced by Mernik et al. [18] for the DSML-side, and Ramanath and Gilbert [24] for the ABM-side. We adopt the terminology of the CoSMoS approach [27] to describe the abstraction level of different models developed in the process. The *domain model* refers to a description of a domain problem as understood from observations etc. The *platform model* refers to the formal specification of the domain model including technical requirements for it's implementation. Finally, the *simulation model* is the concrete model implementation itself.

The methodology follows an iterative cycle of steps from system analysis to evaluation. A diagram of the methodology is shown in Fig. 4. The steps are divided into those that constitute domain engineering and those that constitute application engineering via the dotted lines. The large boxes named system analysis, model formalisation, implementation, and model evaluation represent the ABM development steps. Inside the large boxes, we represent the DSML-related processes involved. For example, in system analysis, the domain is translated into a high-level DSML specification. In model formalisation, generation rules are added to the high-level DSML such that it can be translated into an agent-oriented DSML. Implementation then constitutes the application engineering process in which the DSML is instantiated for specific modelling case studies. At this stage, either the implementation step is repeated to represent development of multiple models, or if the DSML is not sufficient to specify a particular

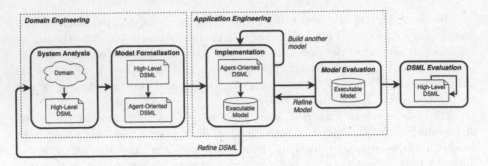

Fig. 4. The methodology cycle.

model, then there is a feedback loop to system analysis to show repetition of the domain engineering steps. The model(s) generated during implementation will then be validated [16]. At this stage, if the model is not fit for purpose, then there is a loop back to implementation such that the model (i.e. the DSML instantiation) can be refined. A final (optional) step is to evaluate the high-level DSML using comprehension and usability exercises. We discuss each step below:

5.1   System Analysis

During system analysis, the developer will seek to understand the domain to be modelled. This involves establishing what domain problems are to be addressed and what the criticality of those problems are. The criticality will depend on what the domain stakeholders wish to learn from the model [13]: Will the model be used to encourage *learning* between stakeholders? Will it be used to *explain* domain behaviours? Or will it be used to make *predictions* about future behaviours? Once the domain problem has been established, the problem should be decomposed into it's related domain processes and the stakeholders involved in those processes. These stakeholders should be consulted so that they can contribute their domain knowledge about the process from their respective backgrounds, viewpoints and vocabularies.

In a typical ABM methodology, this step involves the production of informal design artefacts to form a domain model. This domain model is constructed on a model-by-model basis with an application-engineering approach—focusing on identifying and recording domain processes for a particular domain problem. Using DSMLs introduces a shift towards a domain engineering approach. The DSML is not intended to be a single-use product, and instead should be used to construct a variety of models in the same domain. The DSML meta-model will need to be constructed as an ontology of re-usable, generic, domain concepts that can be instantiated for specific models as and when they are developed. The repeated exercise of domain engineering conducted during this step allows the DSML to mature and reduces the need for further domain analysis in future case studies.

For a brand-new DSML, domain analysis will involve *construction* of the language meta-model. The language developer will take the findings of the domain analysis step described above to identify the scope and nature of domain concepts. These concepts will provide the basis for the language abstract syntax, and the vocabulary used by the stakeholders to describe those concepts will provide the basis for the language concrete syntax. For a more mature DSML, domain analysis should involve *maintenance* of the meta-model. The developer should supplement the DSML with new concepts, or refactor existing concepts, where appropriate.

Case Study Experience. In our healthcare case study, we identified that action cards (such as the one shown in Fig. 1) are a familiar notation for describing healthcare processes in our target hospital domain. While healthcare professionals may not think of action card development as 'modelling', action cards can be seen as informal 'grass-roots' models [25]. We took these pre-existing models as the basis for our own DSML design. An example of an action card written in our DSML is shown in Fig. 5.

For simpler processes, the action card DSML offered sufficient scope to model the domain processes our domain stakeholders were interested in. For example, to model the rapid COVID-19 test described in Sect. 2, we simply used the DSML to define an *action* in an *action card* that made reference to the rapid *test*, which included a property for time *duration*. The tests are conducted at the bedside and results are available within a very short time period. However, we later needed to make additions to the language for more complex processes—for example, the introduction of a point-of-care test called a LIAT [4]. The LIAT requires staff to swab the patient, and then transport the sample to an analyser machine which can process the sample and return a result within 30 min. Because of the longer execution time, and the more complex testing process, our DSML did not expose a suitable level of granularity to accurately model this type of test.

In identifying this gap, we needed to update our DSML design. We added a new language concept to represent a *testing process*—effectively a sub-process that can be defined for each type of test in the DSML which can be referenced by the existing action card concept. The DSML generator automatically weaves the testing process definition into the action card where appropriate. While these processes are inter-dependent, they can be captured in their own distinct viewpoint and vocabulary in the DSML allowing for a multi-view modelling approach to model development [5].

5.2 Model Formalisation

From the previous step, a domain problem has been identified and represented using a high-level DSML. In typical participatory ABM methodologies, the next step would be to translate the domain model into a platform model (i.e. translate the informal design artefacts into an agent-oriented formalisation). However, rather than creating a domain model for a singular problem, we have developed

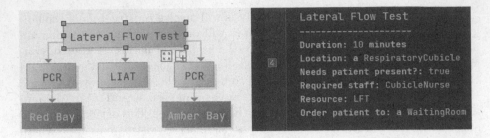

Fig. 5. Action card concrete syntax.

a DSML suitable for capturing a variety of domain problems. The next stage, therefore, is to establish how these DSML concepts can be translated into an executable model. Primarily, this will involve implementing generation rules for each domain concept added to the DSML during the system analysis step. The developer will need to consider how these new generation rules will interact with each other, and with the concepts that already exist in the language from previous development cycles, if any.

In line with [30], we do not translate domain-level concepts directly into a platform model written in a general-purpose language, but instead develop an internal agent-oriented DSML to sub-divide the code generation process. Either existing agent-oriented language can be adopted (such as DSL4ABMS [26], ReLogo [21], or ESL [6]) or the language developer can implement their own. The developer, in collaboration with domain stakeholders, will then determine how the high-level DSML concepts should translate into ABM concepts in the agent-oriented language. In collaborating on developing these generation rules, the developers explicitly encode knowledge about the domain that may otherwise remain implicit. As the DSMLs mature and less language refactoring is required, this step should become simpler and quicker to complete.

The benefits of dividing the DSML generation in this way include: improving model traceability, reducing the risk of abstraction errors, and allowing for modularity in the implementation technique of the model. For example, while in the current work we focus on agent-based modelling, it is possible (and sometimes desirable [8]) to use alternative modelling techniques such as system dynamics, Monte Carlo modelling etc. [15] either alongside, or in place of, agent-based modelling. Alternative internal DSMLs can be developed and 'swapped-in' to provide the specific implementation details.

Case Study Experience. From our own experience, we identified action cards as an important concept during system analysis and so designed our DSML such that action cards could be encoded explicitly in the language, using graphical language elements. This high-level DSML is then automatically generated into an agent-oriented internal DSML as discussed above. This allowed for a separation of concerns, simplifying the generators for the DSML by splitting the generation process in two. The structure of the DSML is shown in Fig. 6.

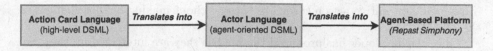

Fig. 6. The DSML structure.

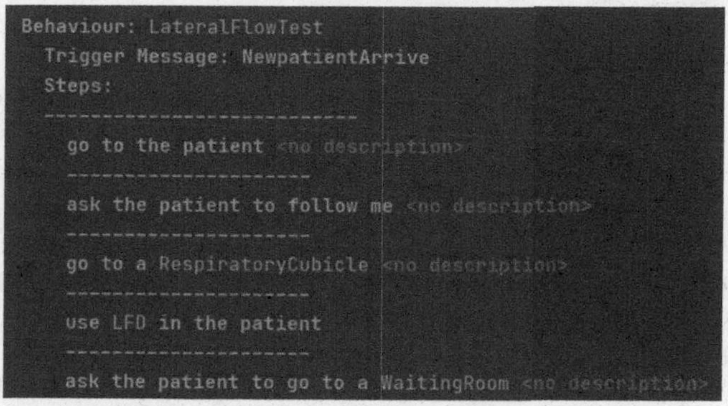

```
Behaviour: LateralFlowTest
  Trigger Message: NewpatientArrive
  Steps:
  ------------------------------
    go to the patient <no description>
  ----------------------
    ask the patient to follow me <no description>
  ----------------------
    go to a RespiratoryCubicle <no description>
  ----------------------
    use LFD in the patient
  ----------------------
    ask the patient to go to a WaitingRoom <no description>
```

Fig. 7. Actor language concrete syntax.

Figure 7 shows a sample of the generated actor language code. Specifically shown is the actor rules for the 'lateral flow test' action, detailing how an agent should administer a lateral flow COVID-19 test (LFD) on a patient. Shown is the trigger for this behaviour (in this case, the patient arriving in the department), and the sub-steps for the action including taking the patient to a respiratory cubicle, using the LFD on the patient, and asking the patient to go back to the waiting room.

5.3 Implementation

During implementation, the DSML will then be used to specify a specific model instance. The language concepts will be used to construct the model which will get automatically generated into computer-readable code according to the generation rules implemented in the previous step. If the DSML is not sufficient to express a particular model, then the development cycle should be restarted from the 'system analysis' step (see feedback loop 'refine DSML' in Fig. 4).

Case Study Experience. We include another feedback loop for 'build another model'. For example, as discussed in our case study, we wished to model not just a single action card but to compare a series of different action cards. For example, during our case study one alternative action card we wished to model involved adding a test for whether the patient has had a recent contact with a COVID-19 infectious person, and a workflow for deciding whether the patient should be admitted to a side room or not. By this stage of development, we were able to implement alternative action cards like these without making further changes to the DSML.

Once the developer has produced the models they are interested in, they can be automatically generated into code and then evaluated in the next step.

5.4   Evaluation

Model Evaluation. The generated model can now be calibrated and evaluated. Calibration involves testing the model under different parameter values and updating these parameter values until model outputs are representative of real-world data [17]. Evaluation then involves using the calibrated parameter values to check that the model behaviour matches real-world observations and data under different concrete scenarios [16]. We note that the level of detail required during evaluation should depend on the criticality of the domain problem as established during system analysis. If the model is to be used for prediction, then it is especially important that the model is evaluated to a high standard. There is less requirement for detailed evaluation if the model is to be used for explanation, and less so again for learning. There should be an appropriate balance between a well-evaluated model and a model that can produce results more quickly. If the model is deemed unfit for purpose then the developer should return to the implementation step to check that the model has been implemented correctly in the DSML.

DSML Evaluation (Optional). Primarily, the DSML will be evaluated naturally via completion of the development cycle, specifically during the 'refine DSML' feedback loop and via repeated modelling exercises. The system analysis step will highlight any issues in language coverage via missing concepts in the DSML syntax which can be added where appropriate. However, if time permits, the DSML can be evaluated more formally according to the language comprehensibility and usability. To evaluate the comprehensibility of the DSML, we refer to Moody's 'cognitive framework' [20] metrics, and for usability evaluation, we refer to Barišić et al. [3] and Alaca et al. [1].

Case Study Experience. As part of our healthcare case study we found that the DSML aided parts of the evaluation steps. Because the model design artefacts were explicitly and formally encoded in the language, we were able to more easily conduct face validity with the domain stakeholders. We could refer directly to the model definition in the DSML during model execution, rather than using more informal design documents. For example, we were able to discuss the definition of an action card in our DSML with staff from the ED and infection control teams at St. Thomas' Hospital. Even before executing the model, we were able to discuss and resolve any ambiguities in the modelling requirements. The staff were able to identify errors in the action card definition, but were also able to identify potential practical issues with the action card in vivo and were able to suggest real-world changes to the action card that could be investigated. Our interaction indicated that the healthcare staff were able to understand the action card DSML without significant previous experience, and they were able to use the model to identify and discuss issues with real-world clinical practise even before execution.

Upon executing the model, the stakeholders could then observe the different staff and patient agents moving through a representation of the hospital wards in a graphical interface. Simultaneously, we displayed the action card definition implemented using our high-level DSML. This allowed us to directly relate properties of the model execution to the related concepts in the DSML, encouraging discussion with the stakeholders about potential errors. Of any errors, either the model definition was wrong and so the model should be updated in the DSML, or the model had not been implemented correctly and so the DSML itself should be inspected (see feedback loops for 'refine model' and 'refine DSML' in Fig. 4).

It should be noted, however, that using DSMLs did not significantly impact model calibration. This is a process that relies on statistical comparison of model outputs with real-world data and is typically conducted through the use of statistical software packages (such as RRepast [10]). These tools usually require the developer to define scripts for data analysis, and for model inputs and outputs to be in particular formats. The only benefit of our DSML was that it could generate the relevant scripts and fulfil the relevant formatting requirements during model generation.

6   Conclusions

We motivated our work by a participatory modelling exercise conducted in the domain of infection control in emergency care. We intend for our methodology to reflect the practical demands of participatory modelling, including the limited capacity for stakeholder involvement and the need for rapid model results. While we initially assumed that the benefit of DSMLs would be the ability for domain stakeholders to directly interact with model implementation, we found that the primary benefits were the promotion of communication between stakeholders on domain problems, and the re-use of domain concepts for improving the pace of system analysis. Our future work will focus on evaluating the methodology through further modelling case studies. Open research topics include investigating the use of bi-directional feedback of model execution to DSML design as discussed by Zschaler and Polack [30] and the full integration of model and domain through a digital twin as discussed by Barat et al. [2].

References

1. Alaca, O.F., Tezel, B.T., Challenger, M., Goulão, M., Amaral, V., Kardas, G.: AgentDSM-Eval: a framework for the evaluation of domain-specific modeling languages for multi-agent systems. Comput. Stand. Interfaces **76**, 103513 (2021). https://doi.org/10.1016/j.csi.2021.103513. https://www.sciencedirect.com/science/article/pii/S0920548921000088

2. Barat, S., Kulkarni, V., Clark, T., Barn, B.: An actor based simulation driven digital twin for analyzing complex business systems. In: 2019 Winter Simulation Conference (WSC), pp. 157–168 (2019). https://doi.org/10.1109/WSC40007.2019.9004694

3. Barišić, A., Amaral, V., Goulao, M., Barroca, B.: Quality in use of domain-specific languages: a case study. In: Proceedings of the 3rd ACM SIGPLAN Workshop on Evaluation and Usability of Programming Languages and Tools, pp. 65–72 (2011)

4. Blackall, D., Moreno, R., Jin, J., Plotinsky, R., Dworkin, R., Oethinger, M.: Performance characteristics of the roche diagnostics cobas Liat PCR system as a COVID-19 screening tool for hospital admissions in a regional health care delivery system. J. Clin. Microbiol. **59**(10), e01278-21 (2021)

5. Bork, D., Sinz, E.J.: Bridging the gap from a multi-view modelling method to the design of a multi-view modelling tool. Enterp. Model. Inf. Syst. Archit. (EMISAJ) **8**(2), 25–41 (2013)

6. Clark, T., Kulkarni, V., Barat, S., Barn, B.: ESL: an actor-based platform for developing emergent behaviour organisation simulations. In: Demazeau, Y., Davidsson, P., Bajo, J., Vale, Z. (eds.) PAAMS 2017. LNCS (LNAI), vol. 10349, pp. 311–315. Springer, Cham (2017). https://doi.org/10.1007/978-3-319-59930-4_27

7. Crooks, A.T., Heppenstall, A.J.: Introduction to agent-based modelling. In: Heppenstall, A., Crooks, A., See, L., Batty, M. (eds.) Agent-Based Models of Geographical Systems, pp. 85–105. Springer, Dordrecht (2012). https://doi.org/10.1007/978-90-481-8927-4_5

8. Fakhimi, M., Anagnostou, A., Stergioulas, L., Taylor, S.J.E.: A hybrid agent-based and discrete event simulation approach for sustainable strategic planning and simulation analytics. In: Proceedings of the Winter Simulation Conference 2014, pp. 1573–1584 (2014). https://doi.org/10.1109/WSC.2014.7020009

9. Fowler, M.: Domain Specific Languages, 1st edn. Addison-Wesley Professional (2010)

10. García, A.P., Rodríguez-Patón, A.: Analyzing repast symphony models in R with RRepast package. bioRxiv, p. 047985 (2016)

11. Garro, A., Russo, W.: EasyABMS: a domain-expert oriented methodology for agent-based modeling and simulation. Simul. Model. Pract. Theory **18**(10), 1453–1467 (2010)

12. Ghorbani, A., Bots, P., Dignum, V., Dijkema, G.: MAIA: a framework for developing agent-based social simulations. J. Artif. Soc. Soc. Simul. **16**(2), 9 (2013)

13. Heldal, R., Pelliccione, P., Eliasson, U., Lantz, J., Derehag, J., Whittle, J.: Descriptive vs prescriptive models in industry. In: Proceedings of the ACM/IEEE 19th International Conference on Model Driven Engineering Languages and Systems, MODELS 2016, pp. 216–226. Association for Computing Machinery, New York (2016). https://doi.org/10.1145/2976767.2976808

14. Iba, T., Matsuzawa, Y., Aoyama, N.: From conceptual models to simulation models: model driven development of agent-based simulations. In: 9th Workshop on Economics and Heterogeneous Interacting Agents, vol. 28, p. 149. Citeseer (2004)

15. Katsaliaki, K., Mustafee, N.: Applications of simulation within the healthcare context. J. Oper. Res. Soc. **62**(8), 1431–1451 (2011)

16. Klügl, F.: A validation methodology for agent-based simulations. In: Proceedings of the 2008 ACM Symposium on Applied Computing, pp. 39–43 (2008)

17. Lee, J.S., et al.: The complexities of agent-based modeling output analysis. J. Artif. Soc. Soc. Simul. **18**(4) (2015)

18. Mernik, M., Heering, J., Sloane, A.M.: When and how to develop domain-specific languages. ACM Comput. Surv. (CSUR) **37**(4), 316–344 (2005)

19. Merrick, B., et al.: Real-world deployment of lateral flow SARS-CoV-2 antigen detection in the emergency department to provide rapid, accurate and safe diagnosis of COVID-19. Infect. Prev. Pract. **3**(4), 100186 (2021). https://doi.org/10.1016/J.INFPIP.2021.100186. https://linkinghub.elsevier.com/retrieve/pii/S2590088921000755
20. Moody, D.: The "physics" of notations: toward a scientific basis for constructing visual notations in software engineering. IEEE Trans. Softw. Eng. **35**(6), 756–779 (2009)
21. Ozik, J., Collier, N.T., Murphy, J.T., North, M.J.: The ReLogo agent-based modeling language. In: 2013 Winter Simulations Conference (WSC), pp. 1560–1568. IEEE (2013)
22. Pavón, J., Gómez-Sanz, J.J., Fuentes, R.: The INGENIAS methodology and tools. In: Agent-Oriented Methodologies, pp. 236–276. IGI Global (2005)
23. Pohl, K., Böckle, G., Van Der Linden, F.: Software Product Line Engineering, vol. 10. Springer, Heidelberg (2005). https://doi.org/10.1007/3-540-28901-1
24. Ramanath, A.M., Gilbert, N.: The design of participatory agent-based social simulations. J. Artif. Soc. Soc. Simul. **7**(4) (2004)
25. Sandkuhl, K., et al.: Enterprise modelling for the masses – from elitist discipline to common practice. In: Horkoff, J., Jeusfeld, M.A., Persson, A. (eds.) PoEM 2016. LNBIP, vol. 267, pp. 225–240. Springer, Cham (2016). https://doi.org/10.1007/978-3-319-48393-1_16
26. Santos, F., Nunes, I., Bazzan, A.L.: Model-driven agent-based simulation development: a modeling language and empirical evaluation in the adaptive traffic signal control domain. Simul. Model. Pract. Theory **83**, 162–187 (2018)
27. Stepney, S., Polack, F.: Engineering Simulations as Scientific Instruments: A Pattern Language: With Kieran Alden, Paul S. Andrews, James L. Bown, Alastair Droop, Richard B. Greaves, Mark Read, Adam T. Sampson, Jon Timmis, Alan F.T. Winfield. Springer, Cham (2018). https://doi.org/10.1007/978-3-030-01938-9
28. Voinov, A., Bousquet, F.: Modelling with stakeholders. Environ. Model. Softw. **25**(11), 1268–1281 (2010). https://doi.org/10.1016/j.envsoft.2010.03.007. https://www.sciencedirect.com/science/article/pii/S1364815210000538. Thematic Issue - Modelling with Stakeholders
29. Völter, M., et al.: DSL Engineering - Designing, Implementing and Using Domain-Specific Languages. dslbook.org (2013). http://www.dslbook.org
30. Zschaler, S., Polack, F.A.C.: A family of languages for trustworthy agent-based simulation. In: Proceedings of the 13th ACM SIGPLAN International Conference on Software Language Engineering, SLE 2020, pp. 16–21. Association for Computing Machinery, New York (2020). https://doi.org/10.1145/3426425.3426929

Advantages and Limitations of Experiments for Researching Participatory Enterprise Modeling and Recommendations for Their Implementation

Anne Gutschmidt[✉]

University of Rostock, 18059 Rostock, Germany
anne.gutschmidt@uni-rostock.de

Abstract. Participatory enterprise modeling (PEM) means that stakeholders become directly involved in the process of creating enterprise models. Based on their different perspectives, they discuss and exchange knowledge and ideas in joint meetings and, with the support of modeling experts, they collaboratively create the models. Although there is a lot of empirical and theoretical work on group work and collaboration that we can build on, there are still many aspects of PEM that we should research. The participatory approach is claimed to lead to higher model quality and commitment, empirical evidence is, however, still scarce. Moreover, there are many factors that might influence productivity and the outcome of participatory modeling projects, such as facilitation methods or the tools used for modeling. In this paper, I will discuss the special value, but also methodical challenges and limitations of experimental studies on PEM compared to surveys and case studies. I will give methodical recommendations on how to design and implement experiments on PEM and discuss how they can eventually add to case studies carried out in companies.

Keywords: Participatory enterprise modeling · Experiment · Research methods · Empirical studies

1 Introduction

Participatory enterprise modeling (PEM) means that stakeholders become directly involved in the process of creating enterprise models [24]. It is a form of knowledge elicitation beside traditional approaches such as interviews, observation or viewing documents. It is an essential part of modeling methods such as the 4EM method [23]. In PEM, stakeholders represent the experts of the organization that directly contribute their domain knowledge and their ideas in collaborative modeling sessions while so-called method experts support them with their knowledge of the modeling method including modeling notation and tools.

B. S. Barn and K. Sandkuhl (Eds.): PoEM 2022, LNBIP 456, pp. 216–231, 2022.
https://doi.org/10.1007/978-3-031-21488-2_14

The crucial part of PEM is the collaboration of several domain experts holding different perspectives on the issue to be modeled. The discussion and exchange between the domain experts is said to lead to more commitment [1,23], higher model quality and acceptance of the models [16] and less iterations for revising models [24]. To empirically investigate how to best implement PEM sessions and to examine the effects of PEM on outcome and the participants' perception is very difficult. Above all, we benefit from case studies (e.g. [22,25]) that describe how PEM projects have been carried out in real companies including the particular circumstances and outcomes. From these case studies, practitioners may learn for which organizations PEM is suitable and what is required of method experts.

In this paper, I would like to encourage PEM researchers to add to these case studies by engaging in experiments. Experiments, especially when carried out in a controlled laboratory surrounding, allow the investigation of the influence of one or more independent variables on one or several dependent variables. Only the independent variables are changed by the researchers, further boundary conditions should be controlled and at best be held constant. Thus, in an experiment, we could, for example, directly examine the influence of a participatory setting on variables such as model quality by comparing it to a conventional setting. Case studies, however, consider different organizations with different people which makes them comparable only to a certain extent. Considering a case in the real world makes the capturing and controlling of all boundary conditions impossible. However, experiments often include an artificial setting which limits their external validity, i.e. we must be careful when we want to generalize the outcome of an experiment with regard to the real world. That is why I suggest experiments not as an alternative, but as a supplement to non-experimental research designs, such as surveys and case studies, for examining PEM.

This paper deals with the questions: 1) What are the major challenges when researching PEM? 2) Which options do we have concerning a research design for PEM? 3) How can we handle possible weaknesses of experiments in the field of PEM?

In the second section of the paper, I will give a brief overview of PEM and its challenges for research, followed by a description of options for research desins in Sect. 3. Section 4 will deal with examples of existing empirical studies on PEM. In Sect. 5, I will discuss the suitability of experiments for researching PEM in comparison with surveys and case studies, followed by a list of recommendations for designing and implementing PEM experiments in Sect. 6 that are based on experiences from experiments that I have been involved in. The paper ends with a conclusion.

2   Participatory Enterprise Modeling

Participatory enterprise modeling (PEM) may be defined by a list of main characteristics. On the one hand, these characteristics show how different PEM is compared to other modeling tasks, e.g. collaborative modeling among modeling experts. Thus, PEM represents an object of research in itself. On the other hand, some of these characteristics give hint on factors influencing the success of modeling projects that should be systematically investigated.

PEM Involves Two Basic Roles: So-called Method Experts and Domain Experts. Domain experts represent the stakeholders that hold the knowledge about the domain, i.e. the company. The method experts master the modeling method, including modeling notation and tools, and support the domain experts in creating useful and formally correct models [23,24]. This makes the group of participants heterogeneous concerning their motivation and purpose and the knowledge they contribute to the overall results. Their knowledge should complement each other such that with their joint effort they will reach the goals of the modeling project.

Stakeholders Become Directly Involved in the Process of Creating Enterprise Models. PEM is to be seen as a form of knowledge elicitation beside traditional approaches such as interviews, observation or viewing documents [23,24]. Modeling methods such as 4EM specifically emphasize a participatory approach with the direct involvement of stakeholders for knowledge elicitation [23]. Thus, the domain experts are no longer passive, but witness the modeling process while giving input at the same time.

Domain Experts are Usually Modeling Novices. As mentioned above, it is the method experts' task to create formally correct models. Moreover, to ensure that the domain experts can participate at full extent, it is important that modeling notation and tools do not cause any barriers. Consequently, the modeling notation should be easy to understand and the tools should be easy to handle [23,24].

For PEM, There Exist a Variety of Tools. With the domain experts being modeling novices, they should not be burdened with complex modeling tools. Often, paper and pen in combination with a whiteboard or plastic wall are used [23,24]. Digital tools are preferably handled by method experts, the so-called tool operator. Some authors even claim that digital tools may distract the participants from their original task [24].

Domain Experts Contribute Different Perspectives on the Subject to Be Modeled. That means that the exchange of knowledge and the discussion of possibly opposing ideas is an essential part of PEM [22]. The domain experts do not contribute in an isolated way to the creation of the models, they have to collaborate.

Method Experts May Take on the Roles of Facilitator, Tool Operator and Minute Taker. The facilitator leads the discussion and is thus responsible for everybody being heard. The other two roles are optional. A tool operator usually handles the modeling tool (e.g. a modeling software) while a minute taker documents additional relevant information [23,24].

The Outcome of PEM Usually are Formal Models that Can be Used by the Company. Enterprise modeling generally serves the purpose of capturing and documenting processes, organization and product structures, IT systems and further relevant perspectives in the form of graphical representations [22,28]. The created models can be used for simulation and deployment, e.g. business process models. In many cases, however, their special use lies in sense-making, communication and improvements within the organization [16].

These special characteristics pose special challenges when one wants to implement a successful PEM project. That is why it is interesting not only for researchers, but also for practitioners to learn more about PEM, and factors having a positive or negative influence on outcome and perception of the modeling process.

Similarly to the challenges of implementing PEM projects, there exist a variety of challenges when researching PEM. Firstly, we struggle with the same problems as any other researcher dealing with teamwork: teams consist of several individuals, thus, there exist an infinite number of combinations of individuals with different personality, skills, rank etc. Consequently, **team composition** is a serious confounding factor. Moreover, it is challenging to differentiate which of the above-mentioned factors, such as structure of modeling session, facilitation methods, modeling notation, modeling tools etc., have what kind of influence on which variables. PEM is therefore a very complex field of research with a **large number of influencing variables** that must be taken into account.

This can be overcome at least in part with large sample sizes. Which leads us to another challenge when researching PEM. PEM is a very special form of teamwork with a very special constellation of participants including method experts trained in a modeling method and domain experts that may be considered as modeling novices. PEM is not yet so common that researchers can easily obtain large sample sizes. Moreover, the people and companies involved in PEM projects may not be willing to share information for research purposes for different reasons. That is why **we often deal with rather small sample sizes** which results in a lower external validity, i.e., it is difficult to generalize results to the general population.

The next section will give a rough overview of basic decisions that have to be made about the research design when studying PEM.

3   Research Design Options for Examining PEM

Besides the decision of whether to choose an experimental or a non-experimental design, further characteristics of the research design have to be taken into consideration. Research designs could be distinguished based on the data collected and analyzed, i.e. quantitative, qualitative or mixed, and the general purpose, e.g. descriptive, exploratory (looking for special phenomena and generating hypotheses) and explanatory (testing hypotheses) [4,29].

The distinction that is most important for this paper contrasts experimental from non-experimental design. An experiment is the only research method allowing the examination of causal relationships [4]. One or more independent variables are arbitrarily manipulated by researchers such that the effects on one or more dependent variables can be analyzed. This is, however, possible only when so-called confounding factors that may also influence the dependent variable are controlled by the researcher. Another important aspect of experiments is that at least two groups or treatments, respectively, are compared. Each treatment is connected with a different value of the independent variable, e.g. one group could be modeling in a participatory way while a second one works in a non-participatory way. If the participants are randomly assigned to the treatment, we consider it to be a "real" experiment, otherwise it is a quasi-experiment. Moreover, experiments must be repeatable [4,29].

In non-experimental studies, researchers usually have less control. They do not manipulate independent variables, that means, there is also no (random) assignment to any treatment [4]. Wohlin et al. distinguish between surveys and case studies [29]. Surveys are typically used in retrospective. That means we would, for example, ask persons about their experience in a PEM project in the past. Usually, a representative sample is drawn to make conclusions with regard to the population. Surveys may assess both quantitative and qualitative data depending on the research agenda which may be descriptive, exploratory or explanatory. In contrast to this, a case study may refer to e.g. an individual, a group, a company or a project that is investigated in depth. Phenomena are not considered in retrospective, but while they are happening [29]. Although case studies are often associated with exploratory designs they may also be descriptive or explanatory [30]. Section 4.1 will demonstrate this method's popularity in PEM research.

4   Example Studies on Participatory Enterprise Modeling

This section will present some examples of experimental and non-experimental studies in the field of PEM. Surveys do not seem to play an important role for researching PEM. There exists some empirical work on participatory modeling in the context of environmental planning and management where few survey studies can be found. E.g., Veisi et al. [27] used interviews and questionnaires to study the degree of congruence of expectations of a modeling project among the different participants that could be stakeholders and scientists. Even in the context of environmental planning, case studies seem to be dominating, e.g. [3]. In the next sections, I will therefore concentrate on exemplary case studies and experiments in the context of PEM.

4.1   Case Studies

As mentioned above, there have been empirical studies on PEM, most of them being case studies, mostly descriptive or exploratory. In this context, with case studies, we often refer to a study based on one example [4] of a modeling project within a real world company or organization. Some researchers try to draw conclusions or give recommendations relying on experiences they made in PEM projects in real companies, others evaluate suggested approaches or tools.

Stirna et al. present several cases in a descriptive way. Based on their experiences in these modeling projects and companies, they give recommendations how to carry out a PEM project including preparation activities such as assessing organization and problem and role assignment. They also give recommendations how to implement a modeling session itself [25]. Fellmann et al. suggest a process model describing the course of a modeling session based on several PEM cases carried out in different companies [5].

Nolte and Herrmann present an evaluation of their approach for participatory process modeling [18]. The approach especially considers the involvement of lay modelers by giving them the opportunity to add annotations to the model on their own between modeling sessions. Their evaluation is based on a study with several trials including different processes to be modeled and different group sizes. It gives hint on further improvements for the method, e.g. how to encourage lay modelers to make annotations.

Sandkuhl and Seigerroth present a list of criteria that should help to assess whether a modeling project is suited for a participatory approach. Their analysis is based on a literature review on the one hand and the exploration of real projects on the other hand, carried out either in a participatory or a conventional way [22]. Thus, they actually compare the participatory approach with what they call a conventional approach. E.g. they found that participatory and conventional approach are very similar concerning the adhering of time limits and budget, but PEM was better with regard to meeting the goals of the modeling project.

Koç et al. examined goal modeling according to the 4EM method as a design thinking method based on an exploratory study with several modeling projects within one company. Their exploration also involves questionnaires and interviews to collect quantitative and qualitative data to answer their research questions [15].

Gjersvik et al. present a method called modeling conference where they describe how process models can be created in a participatory way, changing between working in small groups and in a plenum [8]. They tested their method in a case company where they measured acceptance and ownership with regard to the model two times, i.e. after the first model was created and after the final revised version was shown. They found that acceptance increased between the two measurements, but not ownership feelings, whereas acceptance and ownership was rated higher by those who had actually participated in the modeling conferences than those who had not participated.

4.2 Experimental Studies

Experiments on PEM may refer to how modeling projects or sessions are implemented or they even try to evaluate the efficacy of PEM. To do so, it is always necessary to compare several treatment groups. E.g. in an experimental study, we investigated the suitability of a tabletop compared to a whiteboard in participatory modeling sessions. We found that, for small goal models, both tools were equally accepted by the users [10] and equally suited, while tabletops seemed to encourage parallel working and whiteboard users seemed less aware of what their collaegues where doing [11].

Another experiment that we conducted at the University of Rostock dealt with the influence of being able to draw oneself on the feeling of ownership and identification with the model [14]. We used a tabletop in participatory sessions, but in some teams we had only the method expert handle the tool while in the other teams the participants were allowed to handle the modeling software themselves. We found that identification with the model increased when only the method expert handled the tool. We also evaluated different tools for different kinds of models, i.e. goal models and process models in a small experiment [12].

In order to find some more empirical support for PEM's acclaimed benefits, we conducted an experiment for investigating the influence of a participatory approach in process modeling on ownership feelings and perceived model quality [13]. We compared teams of domain experts working collaboratively, supported by a facilitator, with a setting where a domain expert and a method expert were creating an individual model. The individual models of a designated group were merged to a joint model. Ownership feelings did not show differences between both treatments while model quality was perceived as higher by those participants who had worked alone with the modeling expert. Moreover, model quality was perceived as higher by all participants after the model had been revised and/or merged by the method experts. We took Luebbe et al. as an example, who compared interviews with modeling sessions where in the latter one, an individual domain expert witnessed the creation of the model [17]. They did not, however, consider the collaboration of domain experts involving more than one person in a modeling session beside the method expert.

Experimental research on PEM seems generally hard to find. That is why all of the above-presented PEM studies are own studies. To underline this, in 2018, Fischer et al. presented a systematic review of experimental studies on conceptual modeling [7] which takes a more general perspective than just considering PEM. The review shows that even in the broad field of conceptual modeling, experimental studies involving collaboration among the participants are scarce. There is no hint in this review on experiments involving modeling in groups or teams, but on studies with individuals modeling on their own or assisted by a method expert.

To sum up, both non-experimental studies in real world surroundings and experiments in more controlled surroundings bring more insight into the workings of PEM. The list of research issues in this context seems to be endless starting from questioning the efficacy of PEM itself and continuing with questions on how to design PEM projects and participatory modeling sessions.

The next section will further scrutinize the advantages and limits of experiments compared to non-experimental studies in the context of PEM.

5   Why Experiments on Participatory Modeling?

As mentioned above, PEM is a research field with many issues to be studied, starting with fundamental questions like whether PEM really increases model quality and commitment, leading to questions referring to selected aspects of PEM such as the influence of tools or facilitation methods on the extent of participation in modeling sessions. Most of these questions eventually seek for uncovering and examining causal relationships, but not all research designs are suitable for this purpose.

As stated in Sect. 3, surveys are well-suited when a representative overview is needed. They are used in real-life context and a sufficiently large sample allows us to draw conclusions on the population. Wohlin et al. recommend to limit the amount of questions contained in a survey to not scare off participants and receive complete answers [29]. However, PEM is connected with such a great number of influencing factors that they cannot all be accommodated in a survey. Moreover, surveys are retrospective [29] which makes them prone to selective recall and thus a recall bias [2]. Consequently, surveys are not suitable for examining causal relationships in the PEM context.

In contrast to surveys, case studies are less representative as they concentrate on just one case. That means their external validity is low. Nevertheless, the aim of case studies is not to draw conclusions on the general population but to increase knowledge and understanding of certain phenomena [21,29]. Authenticity is the particular strength of case studies, i.e., real-life cases are examined. This, however, also means that the researcher has little control over confounding factors, thus, internal validity is also low [29,30].

Many of the research questions that we have with regard to PEM, especially when we seek causal relationships, can best be answered when we compare different settings, e.g. participatory versus non-participatory setting, tool A versus tool B etc. We could deal with these research questions with so-called comparative case studies where purposefully selected cases are contrasted with each other [9]. It is, however, to be questioned whether it is feasible for researchers to "collect" several cases. Moreover, not all participants in real-life PEM projects might be willing to be interrogated or recorded during the project. Furthermore, the data that is collected over all cases should be consistent to a certain extent. So, while comparative case studies appear to be an interesting approach to studying PEM and causal relationships within this context, they are connected with some difficulties in the context of PEM.

An experiment is the only research method allowing the examination of causal relationships [4,29]. Consequently, compared to non-experimental studies including case studies, the advantage of experiments is that we are able to directly observe causal relationships.

Thus, experiments are connected with a high internal validity. This is, however, given only if we control all possible confounding variables. These are variables that could also have an influence on the dependent variables. As was already indicated in Sect. 2, this is not easy to ensure in the context of PEM. Still, we can try to control as many variables as possible, e.g. by determining the modeling task, notation etc. In Sect. 6 I will present more details on how to deal with this special challenge posed by the PEM context.

Experiments, especially when conducted in a laboratory environment, offer only limited external validity. Controlling so many possibly confounding variables often produces a situation that is rather artificial. A key remedy is to create a situation that is very close to real life, e.g. by choosing a context for the modeling task that is close to the participants' life and interests. Based on our previous studies, I have listed some experiences and recommendations in Sect. 6. Yet, it becomes clear that it is a major challenge to keep external and internal validity in balance. Increasing the one will almost always mean a decrease in the other.

To sum up, every research approach – survey, case study and experiment – have their own advantages and disadvantages while at the same time, PEM causes very complex and challenging situations that researchers have to handle. It important to acknowledge that these approaches, especially case study and experiment, may complement each other when examining PEM. One method may compensate the weaknesses of the other method. Empirical findings obtained by one method may be supported by findings from another study that used a different research method. E.g., a PEM case study may lead to hypotheses that could be tested in a more extensive experiment. Case studies could again test findings from experiments and/or evaluate recommendations that have been suggested based on the findings from experiments.

That is why I suggest that we need a multitude of research methods supplementing each other to learn more about PEM. Experiments on PEM still seem underrepresented, probably because of the high amount of effort with regard to their implementation.

We have learned that even in a laboratory, it is very hard to control possible confounding factors. To support future experimental research and help other researchers in designing experiments in the context of PEM, experiences from our former experiments will be presented in the next section, leading to recommendations for implementing experiments.

6   Lessons Learned and Recommendations for Future Experiments

6.1   The Kind of Model

In one of our studies, we made the participants create a process model [12]. The task was to capture the process of registering a bachelor thesis or a seminar paper of a similar extent. We found that elicitation of this as-is process did not cause any contradicting positions, arguments, or discussions. In fact, we found that this kind of task did not profit from a participatory setting. Consensus did not have to be sought, it was already there. This is in accordance with what Sandkuhl and Seigerroth found: PEM is suitable for e.g. goal modeling rather than for modeling technical aspects. That is why experiments on PEM should deal with modeling tasks that require that the participants coordinate their different views and opinions. Goal modeling tasks, where the participants have to gather and discuss their different ideas in a certain domain context in terms of goals and problems, appear to be particularly suited.

6.2   Time Limits

Modeling needs time. Moreover, the participants involved have to be welcomed and informed about the upcoming process. Sometimes, a brief warm-up is advisable, especially when the participants have not met each other before. In some cases, we have also given a quick introduction to the modeling notation. In addition to that, filling out questionnaires and interviewing the participants cost further time.

Our experience has shown that, unfortunately, only a few people are willing to spend a lot of time in an experiment about enterprise modeling. So, we have always set a time limit for the modeling task which was usually about 30 min. (A whole meeting could take 90 min including, beside the modeling task, all the above mentioned activities such as welcome, introduction etc.) Some of our first participants complained that the time was not enough. They seemed unsatisfied with the unfinished models. So, in the next studies, we decided to tell the participants they should not expect to create a perfect model in time and that we were interested in their first spontaneous ideas. Still, this might influence the participants' assessment of the final model. Here are some ideas that might help to handle the lack of time and to save time for the benefit of the actual modeling task:

First, dispense with any details on the modeling notation. The domain experts should concentrate on the content while the modeling experts make sure that the right concepts and modeling elements are used as is also claimed by other authors, e.g. [23,24].

Second, we rule out that questionnaires can be filled out later, after the meeting. The questionnaires should capture the participants' perceptions and feelings at this exact point in time. This can be guaranteed only if the participants fill out the questionnaire right away.

Third, use different time limits when comparing a participatory setting with conventional settings. Participatory sessions take more time, since several persons are involved that have to agree on the modeling content. This extra time should be reflected in the experimental design such that in individual sessions, participants should take less time.

6.3   Modeling Task and Participatory Culture

If we want to engage the participants in the modeling task, they should have the feeling that the outcome will be of relevance and used in some way. In addition, the participants should have the feeling that they have the power to change something or that at least they will be heard. So, we must also choose a context where the participants' ideas are of interest to the persons responsible. In our first studies, we set tasks in a fictitious context [11] which potentially decreases external validity. In the last studies, we chose a context that had more to do with the life of the participants which included students and university staff, e.g. describing the process of applying to a university to increase their involvement and motivation [12]. We must also ensure that there is generally an organizational culture allowing participation. If the study was, for example, set in the context of organizations with an authoritarian leadership style, the participants might believe less that their contributions are of any value and, thus, be less motivated. This would consequently again decrease external validity.

6.4   Who is Modeling?

We noticed that some participants are more willing to model themselves, i.e. handle a modeling tool, than others. To keep conditions similar for all participants, it is advisable that basically the modeling experts handle the modeling tool. The participants should however be provided with an opportunity to add contributions in a simple way, like, in a non-digital setting, they would write down e.g. goals and problems on cards and hand them to the modeling experts. This is more time-efficient than letting the participants dictate their ideas to the modeling experts [20]. Moreover, that way, the participants make sure that their exact wording is kept. A tool operator would take on the task to arrange all the contributions in a model.

6.5   The Challenges of Online Participatory Modeling

During the Covid-19 pandemic, we had to come up with strategies of how to enable modeling sessions in online mode. We were seeking a setting that comes as close as possible to a physical face-to-face meeting. That is why we chose a combination of video conference software and online modeling tool (e.g. in [12]). Ideally, all the participants use a web camera, audio is mandatory. For the modeling, it is important to have a suitable tool. We found that the following characteristics should be fulfilled: First, the tool should allow that participants of a participatory modeling session can work separately in a personal workspace during brainwriting phases and they should be able to easily move the content they have produced to a joint workspace. It should also be possible that the tool operator can move or copy elements from individual workspaces to the joint workspace. Second, the workspace provided by the tool must be big enough and allow zooming in and out to accommodate extensive models. Third, the software should allow collaborative use. Parallel working must be possible such that there will be no productivity blocking.

When participants are able to take part in the trials from every place it is hard to control the conditions in the surroundings. What we can do is to ask the participants to use a screen as big as possible, because otherwise it will be hard for them to view the model to be created. They should not use a mobile phone. As we cannot stipulate a certain equipment (not everyone has a big computer screen at home) we must at least assess the equipment in a questionnaire.

6.6   Assessing Subjective Perceptions as Dependent Variables

Some dependent variables reflect the perceptions of the participants of a modeling session. E.g. we assessed psychological ownership, the feeling that one owns the model, in a study [14]. When aiming for an explanatory study where hypotheses should be tested, it is important to consult the respective theories about the constructs of interest, e.g. theories from cognitive or social psychology. That makes research on PEM particularly interdisciplinary. Furthermore, if possible, one should use metrics that have already been developed and tested to assess these constructs. Usually, a set of statements to be rated by the participants is used to assess a construct, see for example [26]. If the construct comprises several facets, e.g. model quality with empirical quality, semantic quality etc. [16], these facets use different sets of statements. For each facet, the average value of the ratings per person reflects the final value of the respective variable for the respective individual, e.g. empirical quality. To test the suitability of the metrics in one's own study, a factor analysis for testing the construct validity (are we measuring what we want to measure?) and a reliability analysis to rule out errors in the measurement are recommended [6].

6.7   Dealing with Small Sample Sizes

When aiming for a statistical analysis of quantitative data, t-tests or an analysis of variance are the most common method. As mentioned before, it is, however, often difficult to obtain a large sample size for PEM experiments. As a consequence, necessary prerequisites of these statistical methods cannot be fulfilled, e.g. normal distribution and homogeneity of variance. In this case, nonparametric tests such as Kruskal-Wallis test or Mann-Whitney-U test must be used. For more details see [6].

6.8   Modeling Experts Might Be Seen as Co-owners

In one of our former studies [13], the participants who did not collaborate with other domain experts, but worked with only one method expert perceived a higher collective psychological ownership than individual psychological ownership [19]. That means the feeling that they owned the model jointly with other persons was stronger than the feeling "the model is mine". We also interviewed the participants about their ownership feelings. The interviews give hint that the participants perceive the modeling experts as co-owners since they draw the model. When talking alone to a modeling expert, there is probably more intense exchange as the modeling expert concentrates on only one person. The participants also seem to have trust in the modeling experts as they perceive model quality as higher after the modeling experts have revised the model. In the future, we have to elaborate the true role of the modeling expert. Therefore, it is important to assess how much the participants think they themselves, the other participants and the method expert each contributed to the overall result.

6.9   Be Prepared, but Do Not Expect to Be Able to Foresee Everything

When performing an experiment, it is important to control as many surrounding conditions as possible [29]. This includes the words with which we welcome participants and give them instructions, and the way the whole procedure is implemented and the modeling session is facilitated. For each study, we usually prepare a script and "behavior rules" for the study leader/facilitator and other third persons involved. All persons involved should get some practical experience in pre-tests before the real experiment takes place. It might be advisable to train some situations even before the pre-tests. For a study where we wanted to test the opportunity of drawing oneself on a tabletop versus letting a tool operator draw everything on the tabletop [14], the team of researchers tried to explore situations that might occur. We practiced how the tool operator should react to situations such as when a participant utters something but does not give an exact order of what to draw, or when several participants speak at the same time. If it is generally difficult to recruit participants, such "pre-pre-tests" might be run through within the group of researchers. This allows the researchers to see the study setting from the perspective of a participant and may lead to its further improvement.

7   Conclusion

Experimental studies for researching PEM are very hard to implement. Major challenges include the limited willingness of participants to spent the time that is needed to create a useful model, and the effort and sometimes even the impossibility of controlling all surrounding factors. Nevertheless, laboratory experiments enable a more controlled environment than most case studies. Therefore, they allow us, on the one hand, to observe the direct influence of independent variables on dependent variables. On the other hand, in contrast to studies of real world cases, the generalizability is limited. This paper contains some practical recommendations on what to consider when planning an experiment in the context of PEM based on experiences from former experimental studies. In this paper, it was also suggested to consider experiments as a supplement to other research designs, particularly case studies. The different research methods can add to each other and lead to richer findings. For example, in experiments, we noticed that method experts might be considered as co-owners of the models. In the future, case studies should elaborate this further: During real-life PEM projects, one should repeatedly ask all participants about their feelings of ownership and about possible co-owners both quantitatively, to have some metric assessment, and qualitatively to understand this assessment better. This could support and underline our findings from the experiments and it would give hint on what influences the emergence of ownership feelings in the course of a PEM project and what effects it might have in a real-life setting. Finally, the option of field experiments should also be considered. That means, we should aim for studies including comparable cases in the real world. Here, it is important that the treatments (values of the independent) variables can actually be implemented without being disadvantageous in any form for the parties involved. Still, it might be an even greater challenge to find a way to standardize as much of the implementation and evaluation of all cases as possible.

References

1. Barjis, J.: CPI modeling: collaborative, participative, interactive modeling. In: Proceedings of the 2011 Winter Simulation Conference (WSC), pp. 3094–3103 (2011). https://doi.org/10.1109/WSC.2011.6148009
2. Bowling, A., Ebrahim, S.: Quantitative social science: the survey. In: Handbook of Health Research Methods: Investigation, Measurement and Analysis, pp. 190–214 (2005)
3. Deith, M.C., et al.: Lessons learned for collaborative approaches to management when faced with diverse stakeholder groups in a rebuilding fishery. Mar. Policy **130**, 104555 (2021). https://doi.org/10.1016/j.marpol.2021.104555. https://www.sciencedirect.com/science/article/pii/S0308597X21001664
4. Döring, N., Bortz, J.: Forschungsmethoden und Evaluation in den Sozial- und Humanwissenschaften, 5th edn. Springer, Heidelberg (2016). https://doi.org/10.1007/978-3-642-41089-5
5. Fellmann, M., Sandkuhl, K., Gutschmidt, A., Poppe, M.: Structuring participatory enterprise modelling sessions. In: Grabis, J., Bork, D. (eds.) PoEM 2020. LNBIP, vol. 400, pp. 58–72. Springer, Cham (2020). https://doi.org/10.1007/978-3-030-63479-7_5
6. Field, A.: Discovering Statistics Using IBM SPSS Statistics. Sage, Thousand Oaks (2013)
7. Fischer, M., Rosenthal, K., Strecker, S.: Experimentation in conceptual modeling research: a systematic review. In: AMCIS (2019)
8. Gjersvik, R., Krogstie, J., Folstad, A.: Participatory development of enterprise process models. In: Information Modeling Methods and Methodologies, pp. 195–215 (2005). https://doi.org/10.4018/978-1-59140-375-3.ch010
9. Goodrick, D.: Comparative Case Studies. SAGE Publications Limited, Thousand Oaks (2020)
10. Gutschmidt, A.: Empirical insights into the appraisal of tool support for participative enterprise modeling. In: EMISA Forum, vol. 38, no. 1. De Gruyter (2018)
11. Gutschmidt, A.: On the influence of tools on collaboration in participative enterprise modeling—an experimental comparison between whiteboard and multi-touch table. In: Andersson, B., Johansson, B., Barry, C., Lang, M., Linger, H., Schneider, C. (eds.) Advances in Information Systems Development. LNISO, vol. 34, pp. 151–168. Springer, Cham (2019). https://doi.org/10.1007/978-3-030-22993-1_9
12. Gutschmidt, A.: An exploratory comparison of tools for remote collaborative and participatory enterprise modeling. In: ECIS 2021 Research-in-Progress Papers (2021)
13. Gutschmidt, A., Lantow, B., Hellmanzik, B., Ramforth, B., Wiese, M., Martins, E.: Participatory modeling from a stakeholder perspective: on the influence of collaboration and revisions on psychological ownership and perceived model quality. Softw. Syst. Model. 1–17 (2022). https://doi.org/10.1007/s10270-022-01036-7

14. Gutschmidt, A., Sauer, V., Schönwälder, M., Szilagyi, T.: Researching partici-
    patory modeling sessions: an experimental study on the influence of evaluation
    potential and the opportunity to draw oneself. In: Pańkowska, M., Sandkuhl, K.
    (eds.) BIR 2019. LNBIP, vol. 365, pp. 44–58. Springer, Cham (2019). https://doi.
    org/10.1007/978-3-030-31143-8_4
15. Koç, H., Sandkuhl, K., Stirna, J.: Design thinking and enterprise modeling: an
    investigation of eight enterprise architecture management projects. In: Augusto,
    A., Gill, A., Nurcan, S., Reinhartz-Berger, I., Schmidt, R., Zdravkovic, J. (eds.)
    BPMDS/EMMSAD -2021. LNBIP, vol. 421, pp. 228–242. Springer, Cham (2021).
    https://doi.org/10.1007/978-3-030-79186-5_15
16. Krogstie, J.: Model-Based Development and Evolution of Information Systems: A
    Quality Approach. Springer, London (2012). https://doi.org/10.1007/978-1-4471-
    2936-3
17. Luebbe, A., Weske, M.: Tangible media in process modeling – a controlled exper-
    iment. In: Mouratidis, H., Rolland, C. (eds.) CAiSE 2011. LNCS, vol. 6741, pp.
    283–298. Springer, Heidelberg (2011). https://doi.org/10.1007/978-3-642-21640-
    4_22
18. Nolte, A., Herrmann, T.: Facilitating participation of stakeholders during process
    analysis and design. In: De Angeli, A., Bannon, L., Marti, P., Bordin, S. (eds.)
    COOP 2016: Proceedings of the 12th International Conference on the Design of
    Cooperative Systems, 23-27 May 2016, Trento, Italy, pp. 225–241. Springer, Cham
    (2016). https://doi.org/10.1007/978-3-319-33464-6_14
19. Pierce, J.L., Jussila, I.: Collective psychological ownership within the work and
    organizational context: construct introduction and elaboration. J. Organ. Behav.
    31(6), 810–834 (2010)
20. Rittgen, P.: Collaborative modeling of business processes: a comparative case study.
    In: Proceedings of the 2009 ACM Symposium on Applied Computing, SAC 2009,
    pp. 225–230. Association for Computing Machinery, New York (2009). https://doi.
    org/10.1145/1529282.1529333
21. Runeson, P., Höst, M.: Guidelines for conducting and reporting case study research
    in software engineering. Empir. Softw. Eng. **14**(2), 131–164 (2009). https://doi.
    org/10.1007/s10664-008-9102-8
22. Sandkuhl, K., Seigerroth, U.: Participative or conventional enterprise modelling?
    Multiple-case analysis on decision criteria. In: Rowe, F., et al. (eds.) 28th Euro-
    pean Conference on Information Systems - Liberty, Equality, and Fraternity in a
    Digitizing World, ECIS 2020, Marrakech, Morocco, 15–17 June 2020 (2020)
23. Sandkuhl, K., Stirna, J., Persson, A., Wißotzki, M.: Enterprise Modeling: Tackling
    Business Challenges with the 4EM Method. The Enterprise Engineering Series,
    Springer, Heidelberg (2014). https://doi.org/10.1007/978-3-662-43725-4
24. Stirna, J., Persson, A.: Enterprise Modeling - Facilitating the Process and the
    People. Springer, Cham (2018). https://doi.org/10.1007/978-3-319-94857-7
25. Stirna, J., Persson, A., Sandkuhl, K.: Participative enterprise modeling: experiences
    and recommendations. In: Krogstie, J., Opdahl, A., Sindre, G. (eds.) CAiSE 2007.
    LNCS, vol. 4495, pp. 546–560. Springer, Heidelberg (2007). https://doi.org/10.
    1007/978-3-540-72988-4_38
26. Van Dyne, L., Pierce, J.L.: Psychological ownership and feelings of possession: three
    field studies predicting employee attitudes and organizational citizenship behavior.
    J. Organ. Behav. Int. J. Ind. Occup. Organ. Psychol. Behav. **25**(4), 439–459 (2004)
27. Veisi, H., Jackson-Smith, D., Arrueta, L.: Alignment of stakeholder and scientist
    understandings and expectations in a participatory modeling project. Environ. Sci.
    Policy **134**, 57–66 (2022)

28. Vernadat, F.B.: Enterprise modelling and integration. In: Kosanke, K., Jochem, R., Nell, J.G., Bas, A.O. (eds.) Enterprise Inter- and Intra-Organizational Integration. ITIFIP, vol. 108, pp. 25–33. Springer, Boston, MA (2003). https://doi.org/10.1007/978-0-387-35621-1_4

29. Wohlin, C., Runeson, P., Höst, M., Ohlsson, M.C., Regnell, B., Wesslén, A.: Experimentation in Software Engineering. Springer, Heidelberg (2012). https://doi.org/10.1007/978-3-642-29044-2

30. Yin, R.K.: Case Study Research: Design and Methods, vol. 5. Sage, Thousand Oaks (2009)

Designing an Ontology for Human Rights Violations Documentation Through Practitioner Input and Information Infrastructure Theory

Jöran Lindeberg$^{(\boxtimes)}$ and Martin Henkel

Department of Computer and System Sciences, Stockholm University,
Stockholm, Sweden
{joran,martinh}@dsv.su.se

Abstract. Human rights groups of varying sizes collect information about human rights violations. Managing this information in a structured way is a challenging task, particularly since many human rights groups have limited budgets. This paper presents the initial work with requirements elicitation leading to the design of OntoRights - a domain ontology for human rights violations documentation that aims at helping human rights organisations to structure their documentation. To ensure that the ontology was grounded in practice, two interconnected surveys of manuals and practitioners were conducted. Moreover, the design used information infrastructure theory to increase the ontology's potential uptake. The resulting ontology extends the legal core ontology UFO-L and is represented in OntoUML. As a demonstration, it was instantiated twice: in a fictitious and in a real case.

Keywords: Ontology-driven conceptual modeling · Human rights · Requirements elicitations · Information infrastructures · Unified Foundational Ontology (UFO) · OntoUML · OntoRights

1 Introduction

Around the world, human rights groups of varying sizes collect information about human rights violations to bring justice to the victims and prevent future aggression. The collected information is stored in repositories of very different types: from paper notebooks to advanced databases. This practice is referred to as human rights violations documentation. While some cases only contain a single piece of information, others constitute a complex puzzle of people, sources, timelines, legal analysis, and connections with other cases.

Managing this information is a challenging task, particularly since many human rights groups work on a shoestring budget [22] and in high-pressure environments [30]. At some point, many of the groups must make the leap from

ⓒ IFIP International Federation for Information Processing 2022
Published by Springer Nature Switzerland AG 2022
B. S. Barn and K. Sandkuhl (Eds.): PoEM 2022, LNBIP 456, pp. 232–247, 2022.
https://doi.org/10.1007/978-3-031-21488-2_15

text documents and spreadsheets to a structured database. Others already have a database but want to improve it. While the costs of these technologies are falling [22], developing database models according to each organisation's needs remains a challenge.

Depending on their area of interest and other factors, different organisations need different data models [5]. Human rights violations occur in a complex social reality and human rights groups are heterogeneous. Some organisations might be very interested in the properties of the people involved (such as gender or ethnicity), others are monitoring violations by a certain actor (such as "police watch" initiatives). Some are collecting evidence that must be strong enough for a criminal court case. Others need to analyse organisational structures to show a chain of command. However, human rights groups also share a common system defined by international human rights law and use variants of the same principles for human rights violations documentation.

One approach for improved data modelling skills in human rights groups has been capacity-building initiatives [4]. A complementary solution is to focus on the creation of *ontologies* for this domain. Ontologies provide an abstract and shared data model, above the implementation of a concrete data system [12]. An ontology contains much embedded knowledge and patterns that can support a group's design of a data model.

However, after an extensive web search, search in academic databases, and communication with human rights professionals, no adequate ontology for human rights violations appears to exist. In this paper, we report on the initial work with the design of OntoRights: a domain ontology for human rights violations documentation. The primary goal of the work was to design OntoRights so that it supports human rights groups that are designing case databases of human rights violations. We base the design on interviews, a document survey, and a survey among practitioners in the field. The design is also grounded in a case study. Moreover, we utilise the information infrastructures (IIs) theory by Hanseth & Lyytinen [15] to guide the design. The full ontology is available online, in this paper we focus on the design process and the outcome in terms of requirements.

The structure of this paper is as follows: Section 2 introduces the domain and previous relevant ontology research. Section 3 introduces the applied overall research framework and design theory. Section 4 is about requirements elicitation. Section 5 presents the OntoRights ontology. Section 6 discusses the process and results, and Sect. 7 concludes.

2 Theoretical Background

2.1 The Human Rights Protection System and Technologies

The human rights system is ruled by international law [29]. A human rights violation is an incident or situation that violates an individual's or group's human rights. Human rights violations can be committed through commission (activity) or omission (passivity). Even if a concrete act is perpetrated without the collusion of state agents, the state could in some cases still be held responsible if it has been unwilling to take measures to avoid the act. In other words, an act in the physical world may have institutional, i.e. legal, implications.

Like other fields, human rights work has adapted to technological development, e.g. by increasingly using computational analysis [30]. However, the journey has been slow. The general lack of resources for human rights practice has caused technologies to seldom be developed specifically for this field.

Today's abundance of social media content, videos and remote sensors is useful for human rights monitoring [30], but also contributes to information overload. Hence, in the words of Guberek and Silva [13, p. 13], "the quantity of data available requires careful organisation and preservation to enable its use in long-term struggles for truth and justice". However, the reviewed literature [22,30,31] conveys the impression that the human rights technology field has given more priority to extracting information than structuring it.

2.2   Previous Relevant Ontology Research

Ontologies can represent different levels of generality. Drawing from Nguyen [27] and Griffo et al. [11], the most important types for the purpose of this paper are, in descending order of generality: foundational ontologies (top-level), core ontologies (mid-level), and domain ontologies. A domain ontology should preferably extend a core or foundational ontology. One reason is reusing thoroughly designed patterns, which facilitates logical coherence [18].

As discussed, no ontology appears to have been designed before for the domain of human rights violations documentation. OntoRights can be compared with, on the one hand, existing legal ontologies, and on the other hand, existing available data models. Legal ontologies such as LKIF Core [18] and UFO-L [10] can express the legal aspects of human rights problems. The underlying legal theory of UFO-L - Robert Alexy's Theory of Constitutional Rights - is better fitted than the more common Positive Theory for human rights law cases, in which conflicting principles must be balanced [10,11]. A domain ontology that extends UFO-L will inherit this strength. However, the domain of human rights violations documentation includes many other important aspects. UFO-L does not cover, for example, organisational structures, places, or information management. Moreover, the design of UFO-L is rather abstract and not optimised for the instantiation of conceptual models for case databases.

Regarding available data models, the prime example is a model designed by the Geneva-based human rights group HURIDOCS, the so-called Events Standard, last revised in 2001 [5]. As the name implies it was designed primarily to represent events and the classical human rights violation question "who did what to whom?". However, it poorly represents other important questions, such as "what are the human rights implications" (the institutional perspective) and "how do we know this?". Also, the Events Standard is closer to a physical model than a conceptual model and is not modularized, which limits its adaptability.

To summarise, there has been work on legal ontologies, and previous work on structuring human rights violations documentation, but there is no ontology that covers all aspects of the needed documentation. While the legal ontologies are too abstract and limited to legal aspects, the Events Standard lacks adaptability and is limited to physical events.

3 Approach to Develop the Proposed Ontology

3.1 Overall Research Framework: Design Science Research

Design Science Research (DSR) [17] as described by Johannesson & Perjons [19] was used to tackle the research goal. DSR is an iterative process consisting of five logically connected phases: explicate problem, define requirements, design and develop artefact, demonstrate artefact, and evaluate artefact. DSR has been used previously in ontology design in the adjacent humanitarian domain [21]. A single DSR project does not necessarily cover all five phases. The main activities reported on in this paper are related to the requirements phase (activity 1-3), the artefact design phase (activity 4) and the demonstration phase (activity 5):

- *Non-functional requirements*: Here we use a case study with interviews, and also information infrastructures theory. The result was seven non-functional requirements on the usage, structure and management of OntoRights.
- *Specific functional requirements*: A document study identified important concepts and relations, which were grouped into seven subdomains.
- *Validation of requirements*: To focus the design, a survey was done among practitioners to rank the priority of the seven subdomains for OntoRights.
- *Ontology design*: The ontology was designed using the Ontology Development 101 method by Noy and Mcguinness [28], and by extending UFO-L. The result was two versions of OntoRights: Full and Simple.
- *Demonstration*: OntoRights was instantiated for one fictional case and one real.

As mentioned, DSR activities are iterative and logical, as opposed to chronological. Designing the questionnaire used for verifying the requirements (step 3) gave additional insights that led to a minor reorganisation of the top themes identified in the document study (step 2). Also, the demonstration activity (step 5) revealed a weakness in OntoRights regarding expressing legal processes, and the design (step 4) was modified accordingly.

3.2 Design Theory: Information Infrastructures

The aim of the OntoRights ontology was that it should be useful for practitioners, to ensure that we employed the socio-technical Information Infrastructures (IIs) design theory by Hanseth & Lyytinen [15]. Hanseth & Lyytinen argue that conventional design theory in general wrongfully assumes a static environment and a designer in control of the design space. This might often be true for less complex types of IT artefacts such as single IT capabilities, applications and even platforms, but not for an II, which the authors define as: "A *shared, open* (and unbounded), *heterogeneous* and *evolving* socio-technical system (which we call *installed base*) consisting of a set of IT capabilities and their user, operations and design communities" [15, p. 4].

The IIs design theory includes what Gregor and Hevner [9, p. 340], refers to as a "kernel theory" in the form of Complex Adaptive Systems (CAS). This fits well with the systemic (as opposed to tool-centric) approach to human rights technology suggested by Guberek and Silva [13].

Hanseth and Lyytinen [15] identify two inherent and conflicting problems of IIs design: the *bootstrap problem* (how to attract a critical mass of users) and the *adaptability problem* (how to prepare the system to grow and thrive). As a solution, the authors propose five design principles that are further broken down into 19 design rules. The next section describes how these principles and data collected using interviews informed the non-functional requirements elicitation of OntoRights.

4   Requirements Elicitation

4.1   Non-functional Requirements Elicitation

A case study was chosen to explicate the problem and define non-functional requirements. This choice may appear contradictory, since an important point of an ontology is being a shared, generic model that represents consensus about a domain [27] and a weakness of case studies is low generalisability [34]. However, even if human rights groups are very heterogeneous, they use variants of the same principles for human rights violations documentation and share a common system defined by international human rights law. Lincoln and Guba [23] argue that transferability (generalizability) depends on the similarity between two contexts, which they call "fittingness". In this sense, the "fittingness" between human rights groups can be expected to be high.

The selected unit of analysis was the human rights group HURIDOCS, for the following reasons: First, HURIDOCS has a probably unique knowledge of human rights violations documentation, since it supports other human rights groups in this particular area. Second, HURIDOCS is not focused on any particular type of human rights issues or region, at least not intentionally. Third, this organisation has access to many other human rights groups in its network. Hence, by working with HURIDOCS the generalizability of the results is arguably relatively high.

The method to explicate the problem and define non-functional requirements was unstructured interviews with HURIDOCS staff. These requirements were then further developed through an informed argument with the support of the IIs design theory.

A general observation is that an ontology, together with its users and related IT solutions, forms an II, and the identified tension between the two II problems had relevance for the proposed OntoRights. The implications of the II *bootstrap problem* are that OntoRights must be useful for, and used by, small human rights groups for developing case databases. However, the II *adaptability problem* requires additionally designing OntoRights so that it can evolve and survive in the long run, and in the future be used also for system integration, machine learning, and semantic web applications. If not, another domain ontology with higher adaptability will probably eventually be designed and replace OntoRights.

With the above in mind, the following requirements were identified:

1. *Usefulness.* According to Design Rule 1 of IIs [15, p. 8], "a small user population needs to be identified and targeted" and "the proposed IT capability has to offer the group immediate and direct benefits". As already stated, human rights groups doing conceptual modelling is the primary target group of the ontology.

2. *Ease of Use.* According to Principle 1 of IIs, "the IT capability to-be-adopted must be simple, cheap and easy to learn" ·[15, pp. 8-9]. Moreover, there is a risk that new technology will make human rights groups redirect too much of their scarce resources from their core mission, a risk that has been coined "technological solutionism" [22, p. 13].

3. *Customizability.* Human rights groups have many different needs depending on their resources and thematic areas. Furthermore, as argued by Hanseth and Lyytinen [15], variety leads to evolution. This requirement also relates back to Requirement 1

4. *Modularity.* Principle 5 of IIs promotes modularity, i.e. OntoRights should not aim to be a complete and controllable system. Human rights violations documentation can be understood as an intersection of other domains, such as events, law, and social networks, including dimensions such as time and location. This is an argument for preferring less-than-perfect alignments with existing ontologies rather than aiming for high completeness of OntoRights as a stand-alone artefact. Mapping to existing ontologies furthermore relates to Principle 2 of IIs (Draw upon existing installed base). Modularity is also a means to an end for Requirement 3 (customizability).

5. *Completeness.* Just as Requirement 4 (modularity), this relates back to Requirement 3 and the necessity to cover heterogeneous needs of human rights groups in a wide domain.

6. *Standards that are widely used.* OntoRights aims to create a bridge between two, so far rather separated, socio-technical systems: human rights violations documentation and ontology design. So far there has been little use of ontologies in human rights work [13, 22, 30, 31]. The challenge will be less if the used standards, e.g. foundational ontology and language, already are familiar to as many as possible of the intended users. Using existing standards is also key for OntoRights to potentially also be used for system integration, which relates to the IIs adaptability problem.

7. *Tools that are collaborative and open source.* According to Principle 3 of IIs, the number of users is in general more important for the value of an IIs than its functionality. New users can also find unexpected ways of using an artefact. This is an argument for using tools that are collaborative and open source. Furthermore, much of the development of human rights technology has been in the open-source sector [13]. Additionally, open-source promotes the above-mentioned "continuous, local innovation" foreseen by Hanseth and Lyytinen [15, p. 16] and can in itself according to van Aardt [1] be considered a viable CAS.

These requirements, such as usefulness, may seem generic. However, to some extent it is in the nature of non-functional requirements to be generic. Furthermore, the above requirements provide a direction for the work - by highlighting the need for OntoRights to have properties that enhance its uptake. This focus on use in real situations may not be the main focus of all ontologies.

4.2 Functional Requirements Elicitation

The functional requirements express what entities, relations and situations the ontology will be able to represent, i.e. competency questions [28]. They were elicited using a qualitative *document survey* with the aim of acquiring a complete picture of concepts used in the domain. The survey was conducted as a document study of authoritative manuals about human rights reporting. The validity of a document is the product of its authenticity, credibility, representativeness, and meaning [26]. An authoritative manual will likely score high on all four dimensions. The sampling was exploratory, purposive and cumulative. The sample started with the several hundred pages long *Manual on Human Rights Monitoring* [29] by the UN Human Rights agency OHCHR. After review, the sample was extended to the 261 pages long HURIDOCS' Events Standard format [5]. Already after reviewing these two samples, the judgement was made that code saturation [16] was reached, and no more samples were added.

After gathering the samples, an analysis was done based on template thematic analysis [3] where extracted text segments were coded as triples, such as "person-employed by-organisation" to create a graph that was also the first step toward an ontology. The result was 560 codes (triples). An interactive Kumu relationship map for visualisations and graph analysis was created.

Next, the triples were collated by assigning themes (tags) to them. The themes were then grouped, which produced a thematic map with 25 themes, which in turn were grouped into higher-level themes forming seven subdomains:

1. Roles and People (7 themes, 73 triples). A possible human rights violation often starts with a concrete event in which a perpetrator commits an action against a victim. In other words: *What happened - Who did what to whom?* This can also include: *where, when, why and how.*
2. Relations Between Events (1 theme, 10 triples). An event can have sub-events, and one event can have more than one super-events. An event can cause other events.
3. Interventions (3 themes, 53 triples). When a right has been abused, international human rights standards stipulate that state authorities have a legal obligation to intervene. It is often unclear when a case is finished, as events keep happening and information keeps coming. *What actions were taken in response - who did what?*
4. Human Rights Protection System (5 themes, 238 triples). The findings should then be compared to applicable human rights standards to answer: *How is this a human rights problem - according to which legal norm?*

5. Monitoring Process (4 themes, 38 triples). A human rights group that follows up on a possible human rights violation is engaging in human rights monitoring. The objective is often dual: to know the facts and to intervene. *What did the human rights group do to investigate and intervene?*
6. Information Management (3 themes, 77 triples). To present a convincing case, human rights groups must keep track of their sources and supporting documentation, and respect the different levels of confidentiality for each piece of information. *How did the human rights group get its information, and how is it allowed to use it?*
7. Organisational Structures, Influence and Risk (2 themes, 70 triples). Effective human rights monitoring requires an understanding of root causes and relations of power. *What are the forces at work that influence a situation?*

4.3 Validation of Requirements

A practitioner survey was used to validate the requirements found in the document survey. The research population was human rights practitioners around the globe with interest in conceptual modelling. The aim was to understand which of the seven subdomains and respective categories identified in the document study should be given priority during the design of OntoRights. The purpose of the sampling was representative, but the approach was pragmatic. HURIDOCS had recently engaged a network of practitioners as a reference group for the production of a Community Resource for database design [4], and most members of this network were offered to participate in the practitioner survey. Clearly, this network only includes a small part of the research population.

The data collection method was a questionnaire in English and Spanish, built with the survey tool of Stockholm University, in which the identified subdomains and some selected expressions from the document survey were reformulated as competency questions (CQs). The questionnaire contained 25 questions grouped according to the previously identified seven subdomains identified in the previous section. It also included background questions about the participants, such as years of experience and geographic focus. The questionnaire asked the participants to: (1) Imagine that their organisation was developing a new database for managing their documented cases of human rights violations; (2) According to perceived importance, do an ordinal categorisation of the identified themes. The questions started with "How important is it that your database can express...";
(3) Perform a ranking of the importance of the subdomains. At the end of the questionnaire, there was a free-text question asking for comments.

In total, 13 participants submitted the form, of which 3 in Spanish. Everyone had experience (all but one at least two years) from working with human rights violations documentation, in particular from managing information from fieldwork in a database. Their joint experience covered all parts of the world that could be selected in the form, with some extra weight on"Northern Africa and the Middle East", and "Latin America and the Caribbean". Common focus areas of the participants included e.g. protection of human rights defenders, persons deprived of liberty, and migrants.

The data from the questionnaire was used to calculate the median and mode for each CQ. The subdomains were ranked according to importance using two methods, with rather concurring results. One method was to calculate an aggregated mean for each subdomain based on the number of received "Very Important" or "Important" for the respective CQs. The other method was based on the ranking done by the participants. Coarse-grained results from the second method can be seen in Table 1. More details are available online [24].

Table 1. Subdomains, and their ranking by practitioners.

Rank	Subdomain	Rank	Subdomain
1	Roles and people	5	Relations between events
2	Information management	6	Interventions
3	Monitoring process	7	Organisational structures, influence, and risk
4	Human rights protection system		

Interestingly, the information management subdomain ranked high (first or second place depending on calculation method). The importance of this domain according to the participants had not been reflected by the number of triples (77) relating to it in the document survey. We consider this an example of the limitations of only using documents such as manuals to discover a domain.

To summarise, the results of the practitioner survey informed which aspects to prioritise in OntoRights during the design and development activity. In other words, the results did not give a reason to modify the subdomains identified in the document survey but did provide a more complete picture regarding their relative importance.

5   The Proposed Ontology

The artefact consists of three parts: Full OntoRights, Simple OntoRights, and Manual for using Simple OntoRights for database design. Full OntoRights extends a foundational and core ontology, which follows non-functional requirement 6 (to build upon relevant standards). Full OntoRights was converted into Simple OntoRights to satisfy non-functional requirement 2 (ease of use).

Ontology design requires choices regarding foundational and core ontology, ontology language and ontology tools. For the construction of OntoRights, UFO [14] was chosen as a foundational ontology, and UFO-L [10] was used as a core ontology. As mentioned, UFO-L builds on Alexy's Theory of Constitutional Rights, which is more suited than Positive Theory for expressing human rights problems. Moreover, UFO has successfully been used to design an ontology in the adjacent humanitarian area [21]. OntoUML [32] was chosen as language, and the OntoUML Visual Paradigm plugin [27] was selected as tool.

5.1 Full OntoRights

Development Process. The ontology engineering methodology draws from Ontology Development 101 [28]. One benefit of the method is its focus on ontology reuse. In addition to UFO and UFO-L, other ontologies such as the E-OPL Enterprise Core Ontology [6] were used for a module about organisations. The design was also informed by other related databases, such as Geonames [8].

As stated previously, a non-functional requirement of the ontology was to have it modularized (requirements 3 and 4). The subdomains identified in previous sections provided the base for partitioning the ontology into modules. However, the modules were slightly changed in comparison to the identified domains, for two reasons. First, the structures of UFO and UFO-L sometimes made it more logical to adjust the partitions to UFO. Second, to achieve high modularisation, sometimes even smaller modules were designed. Note that the modules are fragments of one single ontology.

Description. The complete Full OntoRights, including interactive diagrams, can be accessed online as a published Visual Paradigm project [24]. There are 198 classes in total. Classes that are reused from UFO (20 classes) or the UFO-aligned core ontologies UFO-L (10 classes) and E-OPL (9 classes) are indicated with prefixes. To fully understand the intricacies of OntoRights, the reader is recommended to consult the documentation of UFO [2,33], and OntoUML [32], Griffo's doctoral thesis about UFO-L [10], and E-OPL [6].

In UFO, classes with more than one superclass are common. However, this has largely been avoided in OntoRights to increase its usability for case databases.

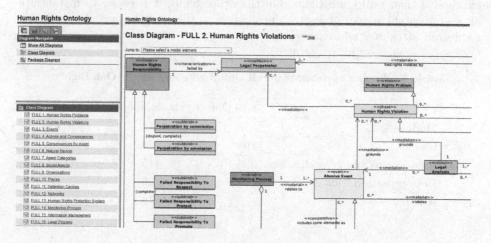

Fig. 1. A module of Full OntoRights published as a website.

5.2   Simple OntoRights

Development Process. The method for converting Full OntoRights into Simple OntoRights can be summarised as follows:

1. Using *single table inheritance* [7] to collapse subclasses into superclasses, and instead use attributes with boolean values or enumerations.
2. Converting the OntoUML stereotypes Mode and Quality into attributes.
3. Adding some direct associations between classes that in Full OntoRights had to be deduced via other classes.
4. Excluding classes whose only purpose was mapping with UFO and UFO-L.
5. Excluding classes to reduce complexity.
6. Changing multiplicities to prioritise flexibility. While the multiplicity of Full OntoRights expresses what exists in the real world, multiplicity in Simple OntoRights is adjusted to what can be expected to exist in a real case database.
7. Removing the distinction between Atomic and Complex classes (concerns Event, Place, Organisation, and Unit). Instead, recursive partOf associations were used.
8. Adding attributes and datatypes.

Description. As shown in Table 2, the number of classes was reduced considerably. Simple OntoRights includes nine ordinary modules and an annex module with data types and enumerations. While Full OntoRights prioritised expressivity and alignment with UFO and UFO-L, Simple OntoRights prioritised ease of use. Consequently, Simple OntoRights is not fully aligned with UFO and is less expressive than Full OntoRights. On the other hand, it is easier to instantiate as a conceptual model of a case database. For this purpose we also included suggested attributes and datatypes.

Table 2. Number of elements in full OntoRights and simple OntoRights.

Element	Full OntoRights	Simple OntoRights
Modules	16	10
Classes	198	34
Associations and generalisations	326	115
Data types and enumerations	0	26
Attributes	0	210

Simple OntoRights is less complex but also less expressive than Full OntoRights. The expressiveness can be compared according to the 25 competency questions (CQs) defined in the practitioner survey. While Full OntoRights can express all CQs but one, Simple OntoRights fails three completely and three partly. However, none of the CQs that Simple OntoRights fails completely had "Very Important" as median or mode. A detailed account is available online [24]. The complete Simple OntoRights, including interactive diagrams, can be accessed online [24]. Like Full OntoRights, Simple OntoRights was designed with OntoUML Visual Paradigm Plugin without any warnings of syntactical issues. To maintain the connection to Full OntoRights (and UFO), the classes in Simple OntoRights are stereotyped as Full OntoRights classes, in addition to their OntoUML stereotypes.

5.3 Demonstration

Simple OntoRights was instantiated twice: for a fictitious case and a real case. The purpose was to practically try out OntoRights' usefulness, ease of use, customizability, modularity, and completeness.

The fictitious case is an organisation that starts with just one module, and then in a total of five iterations adds more modules, either complete or just partly. The instantiation process worked as expected. It was easy to extract the desired components from the ontology to form a reduced but still coherent model. Testing the modularity of OntoRights by iteratively adding additional modules did not pose a problem.

The real case involved one of the human rights groups that had participated in the practitioner survey - Committee for Justice (CfJ) - which monitors cases of detentions and maltreatment in Egypt. It aims to track how different criminal investigations involve different persons, who in turn are sent to different detention centres. The organisation preferred to be public about its participation, and since neither the organisation nor the authors could see any particular risk in this case, the organisation was not anonymized. Even the instantiation designed for CfJ could be published since it was built on information that already was public on the organisation's website [20].

The instantiation can be accessed as a static website [24]. It included six out of nine modules (not counting the Annex module). The main focus was on the Legal Process and Detention Centres modules. When dealing with a real organisation, it became apparent that there is a myriad of potential relations in the human rights violations documentation domain that are unfeasible to include in a general domain ontology. For example, CfJ tracks several different categories of people involved in criminal investigations, which required adding several associations. However, the necessary adaptations of the ontology could be done quickly with no negative effect on the model as a whole - showing the customizability of OntoRights.

CfJ reviewed the proposed instantiation and considered that it would be a useful starting point if the organisation in the future was to do major changes to its database. Regarding the usefulness of OntoRights, the interviewee stated they would definitely both use and recommend it if a case database would have to be designed. A negative aspect, however, is that the model contains so much information that it could be overwhelming for some practitioners - thus pointing towards that the ease of use may conflict with completeness. Regarding completeness, the interviewee considered OntoRights to have very good coverage of the most important areas of human rights violations documentation.

6   Discussion

OntoRights was elicited and designed with a strong focus on usability for practitioners and long-term viability in the wide and heterogeneous domain of human rights violations documentation. The IIs design framework by Hanseth & Lyytinen [15] and its CAS kernel theory offered a theoretically grounded strategy to tackle this reality and manage the inherent contradictions between the "bootstrap problem" and the "adaptability problem". Two important properties of OntoRights relate to IIs theory. The first characteristic is the modularisation of OntoRights, and its integration with other ontologies and important data sources. The second characteristic is that OntoRights consists of two versions. To pave the ground for long-term evolution and survival, Full OntoRights opens possibilities for being used for system integration, AI and semantic web applications. Recall that OntoRights, with its users, forms an II or CAS, and a CAS that does not survive is not useful [25]. For the sake of initial usefulness, Simple OntoRights bends the rules of both UFO and OntoUML, and constitutes a bridge between Full OntoRights and the models of case databases. We believe that future ontology design projects, particularly in wide and heterogeneous domains, also can be informed by IIs design theory, even if it should also be said that not all IIs design principles and rules are applicable to ontology design. We also believe that simplified versions of well-founded ontologies will increase their use and impact.

Considering again the many aspects of the human rights violations domain and the purpose of facilitating conceptual modelling of case databases for human rights groups, eliciting what OntoRights should be able to express became more about identifying priorities than a set specification list. The combined use of a qualitative document survey and a qualitative practitioner survey provided a grounded approach for identifying subdomains, CQs, and their relative importance. Together the surveys formed a funnel that turned written manuals of hundreds of pages into ranked CQs.

7   Conclusion

In this paper we reported on the design of OntoRights: a domain ontology for human rights documentation with the primary purpose of facilitating conceptual modelling of case databases for human rights groups.

Non-functional requirements for the ontology were elicited through a case study strategy and informed argument grounded in IIs design theory. Functional requirements were defined through two interrelated surveys: a document survey and a practitioner survey. Based on the performed demonstration in a real use case we initially conclude that OntoRights fulfils the requirements - with a note that completeness may hinder ease of use.

OntoRights fills a gap between abstract legal core ontologies and existing events-based human rights data models. OntoRights covers more of the many aspects of human rights violations documentation, is modularised for increased customizability, and is published with a relatively easy-to-use standard (OntoUML). Furthermore, OntoRighs extends a foundational (UFO) and core ontology (UFO-L). The latter is based on a legal theory (Alexy's theory) suited for analysing human rights problems. For increased ease of use when designing case databases, OntoRights was designed in two versions: Full OntoRights and Simple OntoRights.

In line with its focus on practical usability, OntoRights needs to be further evaluated, preferably in a fully naturalistic ex post evaluation. Other possible future research could include exploring the subdomains of monitoring and information management but from the perspective of case management.

References

1. van Aardt, A.: Open Source Software development as a Complex Adaptive System: Survival of the fittest? In: Proceedings of the Annual Conference- National Advisory Committee on Computing Qualifications, vol. CONF 17, pp. 455–460. NACCQ, Jan 2004
2. Almeida, J.P.A., Falbo, R.A., Guizzardi, G.: Events as entities in ontology-driven conceptual modeling. In: Laender, A.H.F., Pernici, B., Lim, E.-P., de Oliveira, J.P.M. (eds.) ER 2019. LNCS, vol. 11788, pp. 469–483. Springer, Cham (2019). https://doi.org/10.1007/978-3-030-33223-5_39
3. Brooks, J., McCluskey, S., Turley, E., King, N.: The utility of template analysis in qualitative psychology research. Qual. Res. Psychol. **12**(2), 202–222 (2015)
4. Community Resources (2022). https://huridocs.org/docs/
5. Dueck, J., Guzman, M., Verstappen, B., Dueck, J.: HURIDOCS (Network): HURIDOCS events standard formats: a tool for documenting human rights violations. HURIDOCS, Versoix, Switzerland (2001), oCLC: 51243968
6. Falbo, R.d.A., Ruy, F.B., Guizzardi, G., Barcellos, M.P., Almeida, J.P.A.: Towards an enterprise ontology pattern language. In: Proceedings of the 29th Annual ACM Symposium on Applied Computing, . SAC 2014, pp. 323–330. Association for Computing Machinery, New York, Mar 2014
7. Fowler, M.: Patterns of Enterprise Application Architecture. Addison-Wesley Professional, Boston San Francisco New York Toronto Montreal London Munich Paris Madrid Capetown, 1st edn. (Nov 2002)
8. GeoNames. https://www.geonames.org/
9. Gregor, S., Hevner, A.R.: Positioning and presenting design science research for maximum impact. MIS Q. **37**(2), 337–356 (2013)
10. Griffo, C.: UFO-L: A Core Ontology of Legal Aspects Built on Legal Relations Perspective. PhD Thesis, Federal University of Espírito Santo State (2018)

11. Griffo, C., Almeida, J.P.A., Guizzardi, G.: Legal theories and judicial decision-making: an ontological analysis. In: Formal Ontology in Information Systems, pp. 63–76. IOS Press (2020)
12. Gruber, T.: Ontology. In: Liu, L., Özsu, M.T. (ed.) Encyclopedia of Database Systems, pp. 1–3. Springer, New York (2016). https://doi.org/10.1007/978-1-4614-8265-9_1318
13. Guberek, T., Silva, R.: Human Rights and Technology: Mapping the Landscape to Support Grantmaking. Tech. rep, Ford Foundation (2014)
14. Guizzardi, G., Wagner, G., de Almeida Falbo, R., Guizzardi, R.S.S., Almeida, J.P.A.: Towards ontological foundations for the conceptual modeling of events. In: Ng, W., Storey, V.C., Trujillo, J.C. (eds.) ER 2013. LNCS, vol. 8217, pp. 327–341. Springer, Heidelberg (2013). https://doi.org/10.1007/978-3-642-41924-9_27
15. Hanseth, O., Lyytinen, K.: Design theory for dynamic complexity in information infrastructures: the case of building internet. J. Inf. Technol. **25**(1), 1–19 (2010)
16. Hennink, M.M., Kaiser, B.N., Marconi, V.C.: Code saturation versus meaning saturation: how many interviews are enough? Qualit. Health Res. **27**(4), 591–608 (2017)
17. Hevner, A.R., March, S.T., Park, J., Ram, S.: Design science in information systems research. MIS Quarterly 28(1), 75–105 (2004)
18. Hoekstra, R., Breuker, J., Di Bello, M., Boer, A.: LKIF core: principled ontology development for the legal domain. In: Breuker, J. (ed.) Law, Ontologies and the Semantic Web: Channelling the Legal Information Flood. IOS Press (2009), google-Books-ID: OYhpRvoa1OQC
19. Johannesson, P., Perjons, E.: An Introduction to Design Science. Springer, Cham (2014). https://doi.org/10.1007/978-3-319-10632-8
20. Justice Watch Archive. https://cfjustice.uwazi.io/
21. Khantong, S., Ahmad, M.N.: An ontology for sharing and managing information in disaster response. in flood response usage scenarios. J. Data Semant. Concepts Ideas Build. Knowled. Syst. **9**(1), 39 (2020)
22. Land, M.K., Aronson, J.D.: The Promise and Peril of Human Rights Technology (Introduction). In: New Technologies for Human Rights Law and Practice. Social Science Research Network, Rochester, NY (2018)
23. Lincoln, Y.S., Guba, E.G.: Naturalistic Inquiry. SAGE (Apr 1985), google-Books-ID: 2oA9aWlNeooC
24. Lindeberg, J.: Link List — human-rights-ontology (Sep 2022). https://joranl.github.io/human-rights-ontology/link-list
25. McCarthy, I.: Technology management - A complex adaptive systems approach. Int. J. Technol. Manage. **25**(8), 728–745 (2003)
26. Morgan, H.: Conducting a qualitative document analysis. Qualitat. Report **27**(1), 64–77 (2022)
27. Nguyen, V.: Ontologies and Information Systems: A Literature Survey. Tech. rep., Defence Science and Technology Organisation Edinburgh (Australia) (Jun 2011), section: Technical Reports
28. Noy, N., Mcguinness, D.: Ontology Development 101: A Guide to Creating Your First Ontology (Jan 2001)
29. Manual on Human Rights Monitoring. No. No 7 in Professional Training Series, OHCHR, New York; Geneva (2011)
30. Piracés, E.: The future of human rights technology: a practitioner's view. In: Aronson, J.D., Land, M.K. (eds.) New Technologies for Human Rights Law and Practice, pp. 289–308. Cambridge University Press, Cambridge (2018)

31. Poblet, M., Kolieb, J.: Responding to human rights abuses in the digital era: new tools, old challenges. Stanford J. Int. Law **54**(2) (2018)
32. Suchánek, M.: OntoUML specification - OntoUML specification documentation (2018). https://ontouml.readthedocs.io/en/latest/index.html
33. Unified Foundational Ontology (UFO) (2017). https://dev.nemo.inf.ufes.br/seon/ UFO.html
34. Yin, R.K.: Case Study Research: Design and Methods. SAGE (2009)

Correction to: Generating Low-Code Applications from Enterprise Ontology

Marien R. Krouwel⑩, Martin Op 't Land⑩,
and Henderik A. Proper⑩

Correction to:
Chapter "Generating Low-Code Applications from Enterprise Ontology" in: B. S. Barn and K. Sandkuhl (Eds.):
The Practice of Enterprise Modeling, **LNBIP 456,**
https://doi.org/10.1007/978-3-031-21488-2_2

In an older version of this paper, there was error in the author's Family Name. This has been corrected to "Op 't Land".

The updated original version of this chapter can be found at
https://doi.org/10.1007/978-3-031-21488-2_2

Author Index

Printed in the United States
by Baker & Taylor Publisher Services